O'Neill: Long Day's Journey Into Night

This is the first full production history of *Long Day's Journey Into Night*, by Eugene O'Neill, one of the most influential plays of the twentieth century. It provides a detailed account of the most significant productions throughout the world, on stage, film, and television. Brenda Murphy examines the unique circumstances that led to the posthumous world premiere in Stockholm, in a Swedish translation. Murphy also explores the subsequent first production in English, on Broadway, which established a standard for future directors and actors. The book conveys the unique interpretations of the Tyrone family by such actors as Fredric March, Jason Robards, Laurence Olivier, Ralph Richardson, Katharine Hepburn, Colleen Dewhurst, Ruby Dee, Kevin Spacey, Jack Lemmon, and Alan Bates, among other distinguished theatre artists. An extensive production chronology provides details about nearly 100 productions throughout the world. This illustrated history also includes an extensive bibliography, discography, and videography.

PLAYS IN PRODUCTION

Series editor: Michael Robinson

O'NEILL

Long Day's Journey Into Night

*

BRENDA MURPHY

University of Connecticut

PUBLISHED BY THE PRESS SYNDICATE OF THE UNIVERSITY OF CAMBRIDGE
The Pitt Building, Trumpington Street, Cambridge, United Kingdom

CAMBRIDGE UNIVERSITY PRESS
The Edinburgh Building, Cambridge CB2 2RU, UK
40 West 20th Street, New York, NY 10011–4211, USA
10 Stamford Road, Oakleigh, Melbourne 3166, Australia
Ruiz de Alarcón 13, 28014 Madrid, Spain
Dock House, The Waterfront, Cape Town 8001, South Africa

http://www.cambridge.org

First published 2001

Printed in the United Kingdom at the University Press, Cambridge

Typeset in 10.75/14pt Adobe Garamond   System 3b2   [CE]

A catalogue record for this book is available from the British Library

Library of Congress Cataloging in Publication data
Murphy, Brenda, 1950–
O'Neill : Long day's journey into night / Brenda Murphy.
p.   cm. – (Plays in production)
Includes bibliographical references and index.
ISBN 0 521 66197 8 (hardback) – ISBN 0 521 66575 2 (pbk.)
1. O'Neill, Eugene, 1888–1953. Long day's journey into night.
2. O'Neill, Eugene, 1888–1953 – Dramatic production
3. O'Neill, Eugene, 1888–1953 – Stage history.
I. Title. II. Series.
PS3529.N5 L637   2001
812′.52–dc21   2001025453

ISBN 0 521 66197 8 hardback
ISBN 0 521 66575 2 paperback

For George, the Ideal Critic, and Rich, the Ideal Reader

CONTENTS

ILLUSTRATIONS

[Photos 2, 4, 5, 6, 7, 8, 9, 10, 11, and 12 are from the Billy Rose
Theatre Collection, New York Public Library for the Performing
Arts, Astor, Lenox, and Tilden Foundations and are reproduced by
permission of The New York Public Library.]

GENERAL PREFACE

Volumes in the series Plays in Production take major dramatic texts and examine their transposition, first on to the stage and, secondly, where appropriate, into other media. Each book includes concise but informed studies of individual dramatic texts, focusing on the original theatrical and historical context of a play in relation to its initial performance and reception followed by subsequent major interpretations on stage, both under the impact of changing social, political, and cultural values, and in response to developments in the theatre generally.

Many of the plays will also have been transposed into other media – film, opera, television, ballet – which may well be the form in which they are first encountered by a contemporary audience. Thus, a substantial study of the play-text and the issues it raises for theatrical realisation is supplemented by an assessment of such adaptations as well as the production history, where the emphasis is on the development of a performance tradition for each work, including staging and acting styles, rather than simply the archaeo-logical reconstruction of past performances.

Plays included in the series are all likely to receive regular performance and individual volumes will be of interest to the informed reader as well as to students of theatre history and literature. Each book also contains an annotated production chron-ology as well as numerous photographs from key performances.

Michael Robinson
University of East Anglia

PREFACE

This volume is a critical history of *Long Day's Journey Into Night* in production. It gives as detailed an account as is feasible in the space allotted of *Long Day's Journey* productions throughout the world, on the stage and in the media of film and television, which have contributed significantly to the play's life as an immediate theatrical experience for an audience, and which, in several cases, are themselves significant events in twentieth-century theatre history. The account of the play's composition, its unorthodox pre-production history, and its premiere in English takes up nearly a third of the volume. Because this is the primary production text, the volume offers a detailed account of the artistic process through which director, designers, actors, and others worked in collaboration to fully realize on stage a great play that could no longer benefit from the imagination or craft of its author. In reconstructing this process I have profited gratefully from the wealth of primary material in the Eugene O'Neill Collection at Yale, impeccably catalogued by Miriam Spectre, and the scholarship of those who came before me, particularly Virginia Floyd, Judith Barlow, Edwin J. McDonough, Sheila Hickey Garvey, Edward L. Shaughessy, Travis Bogard, and Jackson Bryer, as well as O'Neill's major biographers, Louis Sheaffer, Arthur and Barbara Gelb, and Stephen Black. Interviews, lectures, memoirs, and letters by the artists have filled out the information that can be gleaned from primary materials such as scripts, notes, and designer's sketches, but always with the caveat that they are subjective sources whose reliability is limited by the subject's personal point of view and ever-less-reliable memory. Where versions conflict, the inconsistencies have been noted.

Subsequent chapters offer necessarily less detailed accounts of productions. The guiding principle in the narrative of later productions has been to focus on the elements of a production that make it particularly significant in *Long Day's Journey*'s stage history. Where possible, scripts, videotapes, recordings, or films of the productions have been examined. The bibliography records the extensive collection of reviews that has been put together and examined in order to reflect the critics' responses to the play and to help construct the narrative of its changing cultural meaning and significance. The production chronology lists nearly one hundred productions that have been significant in *Long Day's Journey*'s stage life. The discography and videography provide information on recorded productions that are available to the reader. The guiding principle in arranging the scholarly apparatus has been the hope that this volume will serve as a starting point for future research into the stage and media life of *Long Day's Journey Into Night*.

ACKNOWLEDGMENTS

First and always, thanks to my husband George Monteiro for his encouragement, moral support, and constructive criticism, and not least for his considerable material help with the research for this book. Thanks also to Victoria Cooper and Michael Robinson for their editorial wisdom and advice, to Heather Masciandaro and Matthew Cella for their research assistance, and to Mary Gallucci and George Monteiro for their expert translations. A number of professional colleagues have contributed in various ways to this book. Sally Thomas Pavetti, Curator of Monte Cristo Cottage, kindly made the scripts of Fredric March and Florence Eldridge available to me and, with Associate Curator Lois MacDonald, gave me the gift of a day in the O'Neills' sitting room while I examined them. David Hays and Ted Mann provided valuable information about the original New York production. Kurt Eisen gave me a crucial video tape. Pat Bozeman provided information from the José Quintero Collection, University of Houston. Ana Antón-Pacheco provided information about the Madrid production. Jeremy McGraw was particularly helpful in obtaining photographs from the New York Public Library, as was Diane Schinnerer from Tao House.

Absolutely crucial to the work on this project were a number of libraries and their staffs: the University of Connecticut Libraries, particularly the Interlibrary Loan Division of Homer Babbidge Library; the Beinecke Rare Book and Manuscript Library, Yale University, and the superb finding list of O'Neill Collection curator Miriam B. Spectre; the New York Public Library for the Performing Arts, particularly the staff of the Billy Rose Theatre Collection; the Charles E. Shain Library of Connecticut College, particularly Special

Collections Curator Laurie Deredita; the Museum of Television and Radio, New York; the Library of Congress, particularly the staff of the Newspaper and Current Periodical Reading Room; the Biblioteca Nacional, Lisbon; the Tao House Board, particularly Diane Schinnerer and Beverly Lane; and the Doe/Moffitt Library and the Bancroft Library, University of California, Berkeley.

I am equally grateful to the University of Connecticut Chancellor's Fellowship for some time to write and to the University of Connecticut Research Foundation for the support that made my research possible.

For permission to publish photographs, I am grateful to Peter Cunningham, the Brooklyn Academy of Music, Max Eisen, and the Billy Rose Theatre Collection, The New York Public Library for the Performing Arts, Astor, Lenox, and Tilden Foundations.

NOTE ON THE TEXT

Note that the abbreviations *LDJIN* and *LDJ* are substituted for *Long Day's Journey Into Night* and *Long Day's Journey*; the abbreviations BEINECKE, NYPL, and SHEAFFER are used in the notes for the major archives; *NYTCR* is used for *New York Theatre Critics' Reviews* and *LTR* is used for the *London Theatre Record*. Full citations may be found in the bibliography.

CHAPTER I

THE NEW YORK PREMIERE

THE LONG ROAD TO BROADWAY

The first record of *Long Day's Journey Into Night* appears in Eugene O'Neill's work diary for 6 June 1939, where he wrote: "Read over notes on various ideas for single plays – decide outlines of two that seem appeal most, and see . . . N[ew]. L[ondon]. family one."[1] The notes for *Long Day's Journey* in O'Neill's work diaries begin on 25 June 1939. He completed a six-page outline for the play nine days later, and then returned to work on *The Iceman Cometh*. In January 1940, he finished "trimming" *Iceman*, and began work on *Long Day's Journey*. After writing the outline, he wrote, "want to do this soon – will have to be written in blood – but will be a great play, if done right."[2] He worked steadily on the play throughout the winter and spring, writing detailed notes throughout February and early March, and beginning the dialogue on 21 March. After finishing a draft of the first act at the end of April, he put the play aside, explaining to friends that he was unable to work because he was depressed and demoralized by the escalating war in Europe. In June he told the critic George Jean Nathan that he had begun work on "Long Day's Journey Into Night":

> not concerned with the present world's crisis, as the title might indicate, but the story of one day, 8 A. M. to midnight, in the life of a family of four – father, mother and two sons – back in 1912, – a day in which things occur which evoke the whole past of the family and reveal every aspect of its interrelationships. A deeply tragic play, but without any violent dramatic action. At the final curtain, there they still are, trapped within each other by the past, each guilty and at the same time

1

innocent, scorning, loving, pitying each other, understanding and yet
not understanding at all, forgiving but still doomed never to be able to
forget.[3]

On 26 June O'Neill reviewed his draft of the first act, and was
surprised to find himself "deeply held" by it. In July, he was back at
work on the play, finishing a complete first draft on 20 September
1940, and a second draft on 16 October. Judith Barlow comments
that, contrary to O'Neill's usual practice, "he made substantial
additions during revision: the first act grew from twenty-two pages to
twenty-eight."[4] Then his wife Carlotta began the long and painstak-
ing process of typing a copy of the script from the playwright's
minuscule handwriting, while O'Neill returned to his work on the
"Tale of Possessors" cycle and other projects. On 19 March 1941,
O'Neill recorded in his work diary that he had finished "going over"
the "typed script – second and I think final draft – like this play
better than any I have ever written – does most with the least – a
quiet play! – and a great one, I believe."[5] After checking dates,
quotes, etc., he pronounced the play finished on 1 April. Carlotta
typed a second version of the script, which she finished in mid-May
1941, and on which O'Neill made minor corrections.

Between 13 January and 8 February 1942, O'Neill's long-time
friend and editor at Random House, Saxe Commins, visited the
O'Neills at Tao House, their home in the hills above Danville,
California, and typed four copies of the final *Long Day's Journey*
script. What happened to the script from this point on is the subject
of considerable disagreement, and was to have a fundamental effect
on the circumstances of the play's production. One copy of the
manuscript remained at Random House until June of 1951, after the
O'Neills had twice separated and been reconciled. Part of the terms
of the second reconciliation included a new will, which O'Neill
made out on 28 May 1951, designating Carlotta as his executrix and
sole heir, and disinheriting his two living children Shane and Oona
(Eugene, Jr. had committed suicide the previous year), and thus
giving Carlotta the sole right to dispose of his literary properties in

1   Eugene O'Neill with Carlotta at Tao House, at about the time he was writing *Long Day's Journey*.

the event of his death. O'Neill's manuscripts on deposit at Random House were immediately sent for, with one exception. O'Neill wrote to Random House President Bennett Cerf on 13 June 1951 to thank him for sending the scripts, adding, "No. I do *not* want *Long Day's Journey Into Night*. That, as you know, is to be published twenty-five years after my death – but never produced as a play."[6] Cerf responded that he would keep the script of *Long Day's Journey* exactly where it was.[7]

In December 1951, on Carlotta's birthday, O'Neill gave her the typescript of *Long Day's Journey*, with the well-known inscription that she published in a volume of his inscriptions to her.[8] He also had a detailed document drawn up, which "irrevocably" gave Carlotta full ownership and command of all his writings, published and unpublished, the author "being desirous of relieving myself of the burden of dealing with, managing or otherwise handling my literary properties to enable effective utilization thereof." Shortly after O'Neill's death on 27 November 1953, Carlotta wrote to Anna Crouse that she had "but one reason to live & that is to carry out Gene's wishes," mentioning the O'Neill Collection at Yale and saying that "the 'twenty-five year box' is the most interesting part of it – all personal except *Long Day's Journey Into Night* – & not to be opened until twenty-five years after Gene's death."[9]

O'Neill's determination to keep *Long Day's Journey* sealed for twenty-five years and the trust he bestowed on Carlotta by giving her a copy of the script were to haunt her efforts to have the play published and produced, efforts which began shortly after his death. In January 1954, Carlotta had O'Neill's agent Jane Rubin acquaint Random House with her plan to remove all of the scripts that remained in their vault. These consisted of the one-act *Hughie* and *Long Day's Journey*. Rubin sent *Hughie* to Carlotta, but noted that she had just learned from Donald Klopfer, a Random House editor, that *Long Day's Journey* was the manuscript under contract to Random House to be published twenty-five years later and so was to remain in the vault.[10] This was not the end for Carlotta, however. She instructed Rubin to withdraw the script from Random House. Her request received a reply from Klopfer that Random House had explicit instructions to keep it in their safe until twenty-five years after O'Neill's death, at which time they were to publish it. Under the circumstances, he concluded, it would be a breach of trust for them to allow the manuscript out of their possession for any purpose whatsoever.[11] Taking another tack, Carlotta recorded in her diary that she gave Bennett Cerf permission to read *Long Day's Journey* on 20 June 1954, with the intention of releasing it for publication. Cerf wrote her a letter in which he said he would relinquish the rights to publication rather than violate the twenty-five year ban. In her diary Carlotta is silent about Cerf's refusal to publish the play, implying that it was her decision: "I can't allow Random House to publish 'Long Day's Journey Into Night' – they haven't the *understanding* or the *feeling* for such a book!", she wrote.[12] She soon began negotiations with Yale University Press, which published the play in February 1956.

O'Neill's wishes may have been set aside in Carlotta's decision to publish and produce the play, but the twenty-five year ban was still the dominant factor in her strategy for publishing it and pursuing an eventual Broadway production. The circumstances leading to *Long Day's Journey*'s world premiere in Stockholm, in Swedish, began with a conversation between Karl Ragnar Gierow, the director of Sweden's Royal Dramatic Theatre (Dramaten), and Dag Hammarskjöld, the Swedish Secretary of the United Nations, in December of 1954. Gierow later recalled that he had heard about the existence of an unproduced play that O'Neill "was unwilling to release" in the spring of 1950. After O'Neill's death, Gierow thought of the play, but was reluctant to approach O'Neill's widow because he was "in some measure familiar with her reputation as a person of a highly volatile disposition, whom one would be wise to avoid."[13] He mentioned to Hammarskjöld, the world's premiere diplomat and a lover of the theatre, that he might pass on the word that Dramaten was eager to undertake production of an O'Neill play should the occasion arise.

This happened in June of 1955, and Gierow wrote to Jane Rubin applying for permission to produce *Long Day's Journey* and noting that Hammarskjöld had given him to understand that the reasons for postponing production in the US might not apply to a production in Sweden. On 14 June, Carlotta wrote to Hammarskjöld, saying that she had intended to write to Gierow to ask if he wanted to do the play without royalty, as a gesture to Sweden and the theatre that produced O'Neill's works so faithfully and so well. She also declared that the play would be produced in neither the United States, nor Canada.[14] Carlotta wrote to Gierow on the 16th, reiterating her intention to have Dramaten produce the play "*sans* royalties" and saying that a short time before Eugene O'Neill died, he had asked her to promise him not to permit *Long Day's Journey* to be produced in the US, but had said that he wanted it produced by Dramaten.[15] Gierow wrote back thanking her for her confidence and her generous offer, but suggested that the royalties be used for an "O'Neill Stipendium" to be awarded to actors, rather than dispensed with. This was the arrangement that was finally agreed upon. Carlotta's explanation for her course of action in publishing the play and allowing it to be produced in Sweden was laid out in a letter she wrote to Gierow in August, claiming that a few weeks before O'Neill died he had dictated a long list of things he had wanted done, and not done. She said that he told her to publish the play if and as she wished, but that it was not to be produced in a US theatre. She went on to say that O'Neil had wanted the Royal Dramatic Theatre to have it as a gesture of gratitude for the excellent productions of his plays and for the Nobel Prize.[16] When the *New York Times* announced the Stockholm premiere, it said that the play was being produced in Stockholm "in keeping with the playwright's deathbed request to his wife that this last of his major dramatic efforts be staged by the Royal Dramatic Theatre of Stockholm, which has produced more of his plays than any other city."[17] Subsequent reviews and articles referred to this "deathbed request," even going so far as to say that O'Neill had "willed" *Long Day's Journey* to Dramaten.

Negotiations for the sale of production rights to *Long Day's Journey* in Europe and North America began shortly after the Swedish premiere, and continued throughout 1956. In May, Carlotta signed an agreement setting out terms for optioning an English-language production of *Long Day's Journey* to Blevins Davis in London, with royalties.[18] In July, she signed a contract with the young Swedish producer Lars Schmidt, granting him the rights to production in the French language. The author's royalty was 6 percent of the gross. Meanwhile, the publication of the play was proceeding in the US. After Random House relinquished the rights, Carlotta gave the American and Canadian publication rights to the Yale University Library. Under the deed of gift, all royalties from the sale of the book were to be paid to Yale for a Eugene O'Neill Memorial Fund, which would be used to maintain the Eugene O'Neill Collection, to purchase books in the field of drama, and to establish Eugene O'Neill scholarships in the Yale School of Drama. Thus Carlotta received no publication royalties for *Long Day's Journey*. To her dismay, however, Eugene O'Neill's twenty-five year ban became well-known upon the book's publication, and Carlotta's renunciation of the profits did not absolve her in the eyes of the press and the public for violating O'Neill's wishes.

The issue of the twenty-five year ban was also a major factor in Carlotta's negotiations throughout 1956, leading toward an American premiere. She had a number of requests for the rights, but the major negotiations for a Broadway production were with the premiere Broadway designer of the 1950s, Jo Mielziner, and two friends who wanted to join with him to produce *Long Day's Journey*, the actors Karl Malden, who had recently acted brilliantly in *A Streetcar Named Desire* and *On the Waterfront*, and Mildred Dunnock, who had originated the roles of Linda Loman in *Death of a Salesman* and Big Mama in *Cat on a Hot Tin Roof*. Mielziner had first discussed *Long Day's Journey* with Carlotta in February of 1955, when she had given him the script to read and had asked him to dinner to discuss it. Writing to thank her, he had replied to her question of who the best director in the American theatre was, naming Elia Kazan, the hottest director on Broadway, who had worked with all three of the would-be producers.[19]

In May of 1956, Mielziner renewed the contact with Carlotta, and she gave a dinner for him and Malden and Dunnock at which she expressed her enthusiastic acceptance of their plan for an American production. Their idea was for Kazan to devote six weeks to rehearsing a first-rate cast, subject to Carlotta's approval, behind closed doors at Actors Studio, and then show the performance to Carlotta for final judgment as to whether it should be produced on Broadway. Mielziner assured her that almost anybody in the American theatre would tell her that Kazan, one of the founders of Actors Studio, was the best director to do this. If Carlotta should choose, they would forgo production and do a staged reading of the play at Yale, the extensive rehearsal period assuring its quality.[20] This arrangement was reported by Sam Zolotow on 11 May in the *New York Times*. Under the heading, "Schools May See Drama by O'Neill," Zolotow reported that "Eugene O'Neill's request to withhold the presentation of his autobiographical drama 'Long Day's Journey Into Night' in this country until 1978 (twenty-five years after his death) is likely to be modified. Such a possibility was acknowledged yesterday by the widow of the dramatist, Carlotta Monterey O'Neill." Should the plan reach fruition, Zolotow reported that Carlotta would impose certain restrictions: "The play will be done only at schools and colleges in the form of concert readings, eliminating scenery. Consequently, Broadway is excluded from the itinerary, a point confirmed by Mrs. O'Neill. The tour would start at Yale, where the playwright's collection is on exhibition."[21] Mildred Dunnock and Arthur Kennedy, who had played Biff in the original production of *Death of a Salesman*, were suggested as possibilities for the cast.

On 3 June, Carlotta gave an interview to theatrical columnist Lewis Funke that suggests she was re-thinking the staged-reading plan. Funke suggested that "the clamor and din for an American production of Eugene O'Neill's autobiographical 'Long Day's Journey Into Night' increases." He drew a picture of a harassed Carlotta, besieged by demands to have the play produced, adding, "aside from a certain disillusionment Mr. O'Neill is supposed to have felt toward Broadway because of its commercial aspects, he also, his widow says, was convinced that 'there was no actress in America who could portray the role of his mother.'"[22] On 17 June, Funke reported on the plans for the staged reading that were then in effect. He noted that Mielziner had disclosed the previous week that the triumvirate had the rights, that "intensive negotiations were in progress to persuade Elia Kazan to stage the venture," and that the author's royalties would be turned over to Yale. Under the heading of "Guesswork," Funke suggested that nothing "could be more intriguing than the rumor last week that if Elia Kazan stages it, it could very well wind up on the New York stage."[23] Carlotta communicated her disturbance by Funke's article to the producers, and Mielziner and Dunnock made haste to calm her. Dunnock wrote, telling her that she understood her being upset and assured her that nothing would ever be urged on her that she did not wish.[24]

On 26 June, Carlotta sent a public statement to Funke in order to "clarify" Eugene O'Neill's position on the production of *Long Day's Journey*. It went as follows:

> Because of the repeated misunderstandings and confusions that have appeared in the press concerning my husband's wishes for the publication or production of 'Long Day's Journey Into Night', most recently in your column of Sunday, June 17th, I have finally been persuaded that I should give you the full background.
>
> When the play was first written, my husband did express the wish and stipulated with his publisher, Random House, for a twenty-five year withholding. This stipulation was made, however, not because my husband was in any way reluctant to have the play produced, but because he had been urged to do so by his son, Eugene, Jr., for his son's own personal reasons.
>
> Sometime after his son's death, which took place in 1950, my husband told me that he could no longer see any reason for withholding production or publication of the play, and we had many discussions before my husband's death looking forward towards its early release.
>
> You can appreciate, I trust, the desire that I have had to keep this portion of family history confidential. I would be grateful, therefore, if you feel that it can remain so. If, however, you feel that it is necessary to use all or any part of this letter to clear the record, you have my permission to do so.[25]

O'Neill had of course reiterated his intention not to have *Long Day's Journey* published until twenty-five years after his death, and never to have it produced, in his June 1951 letter to Bennett Cerf several months after Eugene, Jr.'s death.

On 27 June, Mielziner sent a public statement to the drama editor of the *New York Times* that read:

> Due to conflicting prior commitments involving the key figures in the proposed production of O'Neill's *Long Day's Journey Into Night*, Mrs. Eugene O'Neill and the producers, Jo Mielziner, Mildred Dunnock, and Karl Malden, have decided to postpone any definite plans until a later date when those involved can give their full time to this project.[26]

Funke reported Carlotta's statement on Sunday, 1 July, noting that "ever since the death of Eugene O'Neill in 1953 there have been assorted reports, counter-reports, rumors and denial concerning the playwright's wishes in connection with the publication and/or production of" the play. The column also reported the postponement of the staged-reading plan indefinitely.

Carlotta's story that O'Neill banned the play's production and publication at Eugene, Jr.'s request has been reported by his biographers with varying credulity. Louis Sheaffer quotes an elaboration of the story in the letter to Funke that Carlotta gave him in an interview shortly afterward, in which she said that Eugene, Jr. thought *Long Day's Journey* "'a very wonderful play,' but asked his father to withhold it for twenty-five years because he felt it would not 'be good for my social position at Yale,' and O'Neill assented to his request."[27] Sheaffer, however, adds that the credibility of Carlotta's story is undermined by the fact that O'Neill had reaffirmed his twenty-five year ban when he wrote to Random House in 1951. He also mentions an interview with Eugene, Jr.'s friend Frank Meyer, who said that Eugene had told him about the play and the ban, "and he didn't think it was a good idea; he thought it should be released without delay."[28] Judith Barlow notes O'Neill's letter to George Jean Nathan in January 1941, seven months before Eugene, Jr. had read the play, in which the playwright wrote that "there are good reasons in the play itself why I'm keeping this one very much to myself, as you will appreciate when you read it. It isn't a case of secrecy about a new play merely for this or that practical reason, as with 'The Iceman Cometh.'"[29] Even more telling is O'Neill's letter to Eugene, Jr. on 28 April 1941: "In the past two years I've written two plays I'm really enthusiastic about: *The Iceman Cometh* and *Long Day's Journey Into*

Night. They will rank among the finest things I've ever done, I know. But they – and particularly the second – are emphatically not plays I want produced or published at this crisis-preoccupied time."[30] On 4 September, O'Neill recorded in his work diary: "E[ugene]. reads 'L[ong]. D[ay's]. J[ourney]. I[nto]. N[ight]. – greatly moved, which pleases me a lot."[31] There was no mention of any discussion of the play's hurting Eugene, Jr.'s social position. Saxe Commins reports in his memoir, "Another Journey," that Eugene, Jr. came to see him when he returned to New York from his visit to California in 1941 with high praise for the play. "His praise was extravagant but manifestly genuine," Commins wrote, and "not a word was said between us about his father's insistence that the play be neither produced nor published until twenty-five years after his death." Commins did not know whether Eugene, Jr. knew of the twenty-five-year ban or not at that point, but said that he "talked of the problems of producing and casting as if there were a great urgency in bringing the drama before the public." Speaking as O'Neill's editor, Commins commented that "it is hardly likely, in any case, that the son could have influenced the father who always made his own decisions in the theatre and in his books."[32] Carlotta herself supports this view obliquely in her account of helping O'Neill to tear up and burn the manuscripts of the extant plays in the "Tale of Possessors" cycle. Asked by an interviewer whether she tried to dissuade O'Neill from this wholesale destruction of his work, she replied: "Why, certainly not. I'd not be so presumptuous. No one would get very far trying to persuade him to do anything . . . He wasn't that kind of a man."[33]

That Carlotta was preparing the way for a full-fledged Broadway production with the Eugene, Jr. story is evident from her actions after placing it. Her next move was the most startling one she made, and the most fateful one in the whole saga of the play's production. She decided to give the play to the three young men who had staged the extraordinarily successful revival of *The Iceman Cometh* that had opened on 8 May at the Circle in the Square Theatre – José Quintero, Theodore Mann, and Leigh Connell.

2   José Quintero and Ted Mann

THE PRODUCTION TEAM

Carlotta O'Neill's decision to give *Long Day's Journey* to Quintero, Mann, and Connell was partly owing to the influence of O'Neill's agent, Jane Rubin, who had urged Carlotta as early as February 1955 to consider a request by Quintero and Mann to produce *Beyond the Horizon* Off-Broadway. While she turned down most "downtown" theatre offers automatically, Rubin told Carlotta, she had passed this one on because Quintero was a fine director whose work she had seen and been impressed with.[34] When the Circle in the Square applied for the rights to do *Iceman*, Rubin wrote to Carlotta that Quintero would do a fine job, reminding her that Quintero had given Tennessee Williams' *Summer and Smoke* a new life with his restaging of it, and suggesting that the production might serve as a showcase for selling the film rights.[35] Carlotta wrote in the margin of the letter, "Tell Jane she can go ahead with this but I am against it!"

By her own account, it was the success of the *Iceman* revival that led Carlotta to give the rights to Quintero. "Oddly enough," she said in an interview, "José was the only director or producer in New York who did not ask me could he do the play":

> I finally said to him one day, "José, would you like to put on 'Long Day's Journey'? I ask you because you deserve it for what you did for 'The Iceman Cometh.' You took a play that had been badly produced on Broadway and revived it – though in New York revivals are poison – and you made a success of it. Now I trust you. I know you, your subtlety, the way you know what O'Neill says, and nobody else I know of in this business does."[36]

Carlotta said, "I thought the man was going to faint. He stumbled out and said, 'I'm a wreck.'"

Quintero told the story of the incident many times, and wrote about it more than once.[37] In a long essay for the *New York Times Magazine* in 1988, Quintero said that his "relationship with Carlotta Monterey O'Neill was marked by a tantalizing sense of unreality . . . because she was dominant, our friendship mirrored her personality and took on a Gothic sheen, as fantasy and reality fused harmoniously."[38] In 1974, he told Mel Gussow: "'People take sides about Carlotta . . . I happened to have liked her enormously. I found her a fascinating, dramatic, bright, glamorous woman – capable of absolutely surrendering herself to be molded and remolded."[39] At the same time, Quintero has recorded in dramatic detail psychotic episodes when Carlotta addressed a stuffed monkey as if it were the dead O'Neill and begged him to stop haunting her, and has suggested that her obsessive guilt arose from violating the twenty-five year ban on *Long Day's Journey*, her explanation for which was not credible to Quintero.

Quintero reported that, shortly after the deal with Mielziner, Dunnock, and Malden had been terminated, he was summoned to Carlotta's apartment with a mysterious phone call. There Carlotta offered him the rights to do *Long Day's Journey* on Broadway, provided that he would not cut the play. He was so overcome with the prospect that he became sick to his stomach and left the apartment in a hurry, phoning his Circle in the Square partners Ted Mann and Leigh Connell immediately to tell them the story.[40] They, of course, were delighted and immediately set about finding backers for the show, which was not difficult.

Long Day's Journey was capitalized at $80,000, with 200 shares being sold for $400 each. The contract, which was signed on 11 July 1956, called for payment to Carlotta of an advance royalty of $1,000 toward the author's royalty of 5 percent of the first $5,000 of the gross weekly box office receipts, plus 7.5 percent of the next $2,000 of such receipts, plus 10 percent of all such receipts in excess of $7,000. The terms were the same for the two weeks of "tryout" performances in Boston, beginning on 15 October, and in New Haven, beginning on 29 October, except that the author's royalty could not exceed $750 per week for tryouts. The terms were also the same for the touring company, with the exception that the author's royalty would be paid only up to the point where it would produce an operating loss for any given week, beyond a minimum of $250.[41]

This clause was evoked during the early weeks of the tour, for the touring production did not become profitable until it scored a hit in Chicago. Because of its demanding roles and its running length of three hours and forty-five minutes, only six performances of *Long Day's Journey* were given each week, instead of the usual eight. Nevertheless, the show, which opened in New York on 7 November 1956, had recouped its investment by 18 February 1957. The profit for the fiscal year ending 31 July 1957 was reported as nearly $140,000. At the Helen Hayes Theatre in New York, weekly receipts for sold-out weeks totaled a little over $30,000, of which the theatre collected about $8,500 in rent. The production's weekly expenses were about $13,800, leaving a profit of $7,500 to $8,000 per week. The author's royalties came to about $2,700 per week. *Long Day's Journey* ran for 390 performances, 65 weeks, in New York, and from December 1957 until May 1958 on the road. From the production side, the show was generously capitalized. The total production cost came to $57,493.82. This included about $13,000 for scenery and $5,000 for costumes. José Quintero's director's fee was $3,500 in addition to a 2 percent royalty, rising to 3 percent after expenses were recouped. David Hays, then a young designer who had worked extensively with Quintero at the Circle in the Square, including the design for *The Iceman Cometh*, received a flat designer's fee of $2,000.

Casting

The business terms having been settled, the producers set to work immediately at casting the show. Quintero said that there had been no question about who they wanted for the roles of James and Mary Tyrone: "Fredric March and Florence Eldridge leaped to mind as the virtuoso players needed for the father and mother of the doom-haunted Tyrone family. They were, thank Heaven, available and eager to play the roles."[42] Florence Eldridge told an interviewer that she and her husband had agreed earlier to do the play with a "young producer" who could not secure the rights. "A while later, José Quintero came to us about it," Eldridge related. "He had got the rights, doubtless because of his success in reviving 'The Iceman Cometh.' As both of us already knew the play he wanted to do, it took only about five minutes' talk with him to settle everything."[43] The director was equally sure of who he wanted to play the part of Jamie Tyrone – the explosive young actor who was playing Hickey in his production of *Iceman* at the Circle in the Square: "The part of the older brother was immediately given to Jason Robards, Jr., in my opinion the most brilliant young actor in America."[44] The part of Edmund Tyrone, however, took the producers on a long search. Quintero estimated the number of actors interviewed as low as 150 and as high as 500, but there is no doubt there were a lot of them. He wrote in 1957: "We saw five hundred youngsters, each of whom was sure the part was written for him. Finally a young man named Bradford Dillman came into my office, and after two readings I got into a cab with him and took him to see Mrs. O'Neill. She talked to him for five minutes – and the part was his."[45] Carlotta had reserved the right to approve the actor who was to play Edmund because she wanted to make sure there was a resemblance to Eugene O'Neill. She gave an interview to Boston critic Elinor Hughes, who reported on the day of the Boston premiere: "Of Dillman, who plays Eugene O'Neill (called Edmund) as a boy, Mrs. O'Neill said: 'I said something to amuse him, so that he smiled, and his smile was like Gene's. I made him angry for a moment and his scowl was like my husband's.' "[46]

José Quintero

Quintero, who often made the point that he had never been trained as a director and had never had a single class in directing despite his year at the Goodman Theatre School in Chicago, was anything but orthodox as a director. His approach resembled that of the Method director in that it focused on the emotional authenticity of the performance, but it was far more intuitive and personal than that of the followers of Stanislavsky. He did not prepare for rehearsals by blocking the scenes or by making detailed notes on the characters, their backgrounds, and their dynamics. His preparation had more to do with the creation of an emotional affinity with O'Neill and an understanding of the artistic foundation of the play than with the specifics of performance. He reported, for example, going to New London to see the O'Neill house, Monte Cristo Cottage: "He found the house on the outskirts of the town hard by the Thames River. It was a pale green, two-story, spooky edifice embellished with turrets, cupolas, verandas and a widow's walk . . . Mr. Quintero listened moodily to the sound of foghorns and boat bells floating up from the harbor, made a note for sound effects, photographed the exterior of the house, peered through some of the windows, and came away feeling enriched."[47]

Quintero's direction proceeded from a deep affinity he felt with the playwright, almost as if he were an alter ego. He said that he shared with O'Neill "his anticlericalism; his mystical attitudes toward religion; his Dionysian inclinations" and "the guilt that all men of the Western world, particularly those raised Catholic, have over the fact that their mothers had to have sex to have them." In fact, he said, "'O'Neill's life so paralleled my own life and feelings that it was as if he had had a hand in my upbringing. When I read him, there is nothing strange about him. It is all so painfully familiar. His mother was raised in a convent, so was mine. His father was an actor, mine a politician who behaved exactly as his father did. Outside the house, my father was absolutely charming and everyone said, 'Viva Mr. Quintero.' But at home, if you wanted 25 cents to go to the movies, you had to give all the reasons why you were good enough to deserve it."[48]

While he was intensely involved with O'Neill, Quintero made it clear that it was the artist who interested him, not the autobiographical character:

3   Monte Cristo Cottage and its view of Long Island Sound

> I am so tired of hearing that *Long Day's Journey Into Night* is an autobiographical play. For Christ's sakes, what great work of art is not? . . . *Long Day's Journey Into Night* is a masterpiece to me. A work of art. A play. That it takes place in Waterford [*sic*], Connecticut, where he actually spent his summers, is of no more importance to me than a photograph. What interests, fascinates me is that Edmund lived in a prudishly elegant town in a big house that had the innocent, vacant look of respectability, with a green lawn, scarred by a road which prevented it from gliding down to the beach, a short run to his sea.   (Q 216–17)[49]

Resisting the idea of O'Neill as a realist, he wrote in his memoir that he felt in his plays "a sense of existing in two entirely different kinds of realities: the commonplace, photographic reality and the interior reality of fantasy. I think the struggle of these two realities – where the impossible can happen among the commonplace; where the figures become regal, monumental and totally equipped for tragedy – gives that unbelievable tension to his works. O'Neill just happens to have double vision, that's all" (Q 223).

Quintero's conception of *Long Day's Journey* proceeded from the conviction that it was high tragedy, and as such to be treated with reverence and a quietness approaching ritual. Like James Tyrone referring Edmund to his Shakespeare, he told an interviewer that "the theme of the new play is to be found in a speech from Shakespeare's 'Julius Caesar.' That speech reads: 'The fault, dear Brutus, is not in our stars but in ourselves, that we are underlings.' "[50] His directing technique proceeded from a perception that O'Neill's dramaturgical architectonics were intricately built on his thematic development: "People say O'Neill's plays are repetitious, but he wrote like a composer, building theme on theme, and variation on theme."[51] In *Long Day's Journey*, it was the motif of the fog that gave Quintero the key to his physicalization of O'Neill's tragic vision, both visually and aurally.

Quintero's memoir *If You Don't Dance They Beat You* is itself a performance, a dramatization of his memories to lead the reader to an understanding of his subjective vision of the past. It is also a good indication of how he worked with actors to help them understand their characters' feelings in a given scene. He wrote frankly that, although his detailed account of the rehearsals of *Long Day's Journey* is framed as dialogue: "I did not keep a diary. I knew I would always remember what was truly important, that is why sometimes I will insert in one day, one meeting, what actually took many days and many meetings to find the right key for the right door. Of course, everyone who was involved in the production, particularly the actors and designers, have their own private version" (Q 217). Thus his description of events is to be taken more as a dramatization of his later understanding of them than as a transcription or record of what literally occurred. In his memoir, Quintero has himself saying that the foghorn must be "a combination of something lonely and unreal. Something that would guide Mary through the fog in her journey backward and yet be real enough to jail the three of them right in this room" (Q 257). Stage manager Elliot Martin confirmed Quintero's indication of the centrality of the fog to his concept of the play, noting that "the only sense of rhythm that José used was in the foghorn. He said that he wanted to use that rhythm as the heartbeat of the play. He said that to me, he didn't say that to the actors . . . I didn't have a sense that José was directing with pauses, with a sense of loud/slow/fast, in there at all. José doesn't do that" (M 57).[52] The counterweight of the foghorn was the silence, which Quintero employed essentially in this play, despite its length. As he told an interviewer just before the New York opening: "I like silences; they are as eloquent as words. A character without silences tends to be too secure, too mechanical. I never try to keep audiences awake with bang-bang staging."[53]

Quintero's technique for working with actors was founded on a respect for their art and a genuine affection for actors as a group. He told Gilbert Millstein in 1960:

> You have to understand . . . that they are not just actors. You must peer
> into what you think are the ways to make them act; what works for one

does not work for another . . . It is my obligation to seek out the actor, rather than to demand that he disrobe himself at once to produce the emotion the play requires. The director has to be a lover, and, for those weeks of rehearsal, wary and concerned about the actor as though he or she were the loved one. Because what, after all, you are after – the genius in actors – is, as in all of us, a frightened child afraid to expose itself.[54]

Quintero told Millstein: "I have had to be strong as a director, but I have been fortunate that I've always operated on the idea that the dignity of man is more important to preserve than just to get a moment the director has secured as if the actor were an animal. If I cannot reach an actor in the manner prescribed for me, that matches my idea of man, then I find someone else I can reach in that way."[55]

The Set

The choice of a set designer for the production was never a question for the three young producers. David Hays had designed all of the recent plays at the Circle in the Square. Quintero considered him "the greatest and most resourceful designer" he had worked with (Q 157). In the mid-1980s Hays was asked by Edwin J. McDonough how Quintero discusses a set with his designers, and what kinds of suggestions he makes. Hays replied:

> He doesn't. I read the play and come up with a thought and then we discuss it. We can talk about the script a little, as we did in those days, and maybe there's an impression or something vague, vague but stimulating, and then we go at it and take it apart . . . He might mention some staging considerations, but by and large, you have a lot of leeway with José. (M 25–26)

In his book *Light on the Subject*, Hays used Quintero's talk about *Long Day's Journey* as an example of the kind of communication that goes on between director and designer: "José Quintero asked for the kind of light that he saw or felt in shrouded Victorian rooms. In the buzzing stillness of summer afternoons the light seemed to him to hover, not touching walls, floor, or ceiling. Can we light a stage this way? No, but the image is provocative and nourishing."[56] In his memoir, Quintero dramatizes his thoughts about the set for *Long Day's Journey* as a series of interpretive conversations with Hays, which register his ideas although they cannot be taken as a record of what actually was said in 1956. To Hays, Quintero tried to convey the sense that:

> the title itself implies immediately a moving thing. I'm well aware that it's the characters in the play that make the journey, but the journey must be accompanied and intensified by the various speeds and moves that the sun experiences as it makes its long voyage across the sky, because we're going to have to personalize the sun, tear into his chest a multicolored palette in the shape of a heart, one which corresponds to the palette of the human heart and mind.   (Q 219)

The challenge for the designer, as Quintero saw it, was "to bring nature into the set": "You have to give me windows where I can see clearly its joyful rising, its angry noon and its majestic downfall. Which room, do you think, of all the rooms in the house, is the room where a family spends most of its time in the summertime?" Another important motif for Quintero was the family's desire to keep the truth about it hidden: "we have during the course of the play so many things to hide, things that cannot be exposed, things which in no way will mar the innocent respectability of the face of the house choked by the manicured collar of its green lawn" (Q 219). The single set must also serve as the environment for the constant pendulum swing of mood changes. Quintero suggested that Hays consider "What room in a house has the genius to distort laughter into tears, purity into decay, joy into terror?" (Q 219).

More practically, Quintero told Hays to use as little furniture as he could, "for I'd like to have enough space to be able to isolate each one of them whenever the script calls for it." One piece of furniture that he thought essential was a rocking chair, which was woven deeply into the characterization that he and Florence Eldridge developed for Mary:

A rocker is a woman, it's a mother, rocking back and forth until you have fallen peacefully and completely asleep against her belly, your little arm gently resting on her breast. How deeply Florence will have to suffer in that rocking chair. They will turn it into a witness box and lock her in it every once in a while. They will watch her, first out of the corner of their eyes, and then the trial will begin.   (Q 220)

Also very important to Quintero was the center table around which the characters are often gathered in battle and reconciliation. Quintero insisted that "the center table has to be oval . . . a wound clean, a scar-clear embrace . . . Don't you ever think of oval as complete embrace?" (Q 221). In his view, the Tyrones argue with such desperation because they cannot complete the embrace. In the 1980s, Hays recalled that:

José had the proper reverence for O'Neill's stage directions without being particularly slavish to them. For example, O'Neill called for a central table and José felt with justice that would give you a funny kind of ping-pong match. If the table's right in the middle, you're either looking to the right or to the left. We worked very hard on the kind of room in which the table would have the feeling of being centered in the room, but that the room was seen at a very slight angle, so the table was actually off to the left.   (M 52)

For Hays, the crucial design element was the three large windows, bordered with geometrical colored glass, that took up most of the back wall. He said:

That was how the set got off the ground, a phrase designers use, by really having such an expanse of window which could show the four different times of day. I used little bits of colored glass because they dressed up the windows enough so that I didn't need curtains and yet they were perfectly bare. They were built for the house, but it didn't look as if anyone had taken care of them one way or another. The light shooting through these squares of glass made the first act very cheerful, the overhead light of noon didn't come through the glass but you saw the light outside through the glass which was a different look. In the fog, there was a bluish feeling throughout and you weren't aware of the

4   Bradford Dillman, Jason Robards, Florence Eldridge, and Fredric March, as Edmund tells the Shaughnessy story. David Hays's windows form the background. The Monte Cristo pillar can be seen through the far right window.

> details of the window. In the last act there was the ugliness that stained glass has from the inside when there is no light outside. That's the act when you want it to seem most inhospitable.   (M 53)

Hays has said that his design bore no relation to Monte Cristo Cottage, or to O'Neill's drawing of the set, which is now well known.[57] Although Hays was later to live at Monte Cristo Cottage for two years, at the time of the production, he has said:

> I never saw the house. People were invited up there and a photograph was published in the *Times* of Leigh, Ted and José. I wasn't invited that day. It seemed curious, because I was the one person dealing with the physical structure, but I wasn't invited. I went up to New London to see the types of houses up there and someone showed me photographs of

the actual house, but when I drove up there, no one from the management pointed out to me which house it was. I didn't particularly care.
The only thing from the house that came out in the set was a little bit of
porch detail, a very small bit of it, quatrefoil, which was outside the
windows anyway and was seen by no one but a few people and
me.   (M 50–51)

Hays said that his set rendering was "recreated exactly from the stage
directions. I drew my own sketch from [O'Neill's] description" (M
51). The final product was, in José Quintero's words, "one of the
most beautiful sets I have even [*sic*] seen. It was such a magnificently
deceptive trap. [Hays] had trapped the play. He had trapped me, and
he was going to trap the actors. When Florence tipped the tiny little
rocking chair [in the model] with her finger, she already knew that
this was going to be her chair" (Q 222).

David Hays's design was a single set, and essentially a single room,
with lines that suggest a kind of amphitheatre, focusing on the center
table under the chandelier where the family does battle. The set was
blue-grey, the walls covered with a diamond-patterned wallpaper in
the colors of blue, grey, and mauve. At the far stage right of the set
was a step leading to the doorway to the parlor, through which could
be seen a maroon plush sofa and chairs, and drapes with a green,
brown, and pinkish floral print on a white background. Stage left of
the doorway on the wall of the main room were two framed pictures,
and a plaque reading "God Bless Our Home." At the center of the
back wall were the three double-framed windows, all without
curtains. They had blue Roman shades, which were up throughout
the play. As noted by Hays, the windows had rectangular decorative
panes with pieces of stained glass in green, blue, yellow, mauve, and
amber framing a clear square in the middle. The porch railing and
part of the outside wall of the house could be seen through the
windows. There were red plush window seats in front of the windows
at left and right, and a low, two-shelf bookcase holding the leather-
bound sets of books that O'Neill describes in the stage directions,
and that clearly belong to James, Sr. There was a step down from the

window-seat area to the main room. Slightly left of center stage was the famous chandelier with its four bulbs and an electrical wire plugged into one of them. Below it was a grey wicker table surrounded by, from stage right, a wicker rocker with a grey and pink floral cushion, a wooden chair with a high back, a smaller wicker chair, and an easy chair with a dark wooden frame and a deep red plush carpet back and cushion, all set on a round area rug. At stage right, between the doorway and the window, was a wicker chaise longue with a cushion and a small, round wicker table next to it.[58]

Quintero has described the effects he wanted the lighting to achieve in the production – emphasizing two central motifs. The most sustained element was of course the fog. He dramatizes his desire as a conversation with lighting designer Tharon Musser. "Wouldn't it be wonderful to see or feel that fog pressing against the windows? Even intruding into the room through a tiny crack in the window sill?" (Q 221). The second lighting element was the literal journey into night that takes place during the sixteen hours the play encompasses. Quintero wrote that he had asked Musser to consider the darkness as beginning in the middle of the third act, during Mary's modified monologue:

> Right when she begins talking about her wedding dress. It should be early evening by then. A soft summer evening. That sliver of time that belongs to the remembrance of love, the time for gentle hellos and gentler departures . . . Then it grows darker. The foghorn cries out that it's time to begin again from where they left off and go on through the endless darkness of the night . . . It must have a feeling of a never-ending tunnel that goes deeper and deeper for forever . . . All nights pressed together makes our night.   (Q 220–21)

As Act 4 began, Quintero's idea was that "we will have to jail Edmund and his father under a tiny pool of warm light that comes from the electrical bulb from the old, dingy chandelier above the table. We have to obliterate all of the familiar objects, sofa, chairs, pictures, posters, vases. In short, deny them access to any props which would remind them of the preconceived relationship of father and son. They are two fighters in a tiny arena. With the dark and the fog pressing in; nailed by the distorted footsteps of the mother, wife, coming from upstairs" (Q 221).

In his book, David Hays provides some anecdotes that show the detail with which he and Musser approached the design. The formal back parlor, which was not entered by the actors in the production, was present to the audience as a glimpse of drapes and maroon plush furniture. Thinking about how to convey to the audience that it was an unlighted room, dark even in the daytime, "the part of the lighting design signifying darkness, mustiness," rather than simply an un-lighted space, "as if the designer had forgotten it," they decided to "open the drapes a half inch, and let a streak of sunlight cut through the dusty air. This contrast dramatized a room closed off from sunlight. The first impression carried the message through the rest of the play."[59] This impression also contributed to a dramatic moment in the production, when Mary came downstairs, and, before she came into the living room where the men were seated, snapped on a light in the back parlor. The audience gasped at the unexpected brightness, which of course signified the merciless light that was being cast on Mary's character at this point in the play.

Even the brief comments on the set that emerged in the newspaper reviews show that the production team hit their mark with the set design and the lighting. Wolcott Gibbs of *The New Yorker* called it "a living room hideous even by suburban 1912 standards . . . a fitting graveyard for all mortal hopes."[60]

THE ACTORS PREPARE

Fredric March

The most imposing figure in the original New York production of *Long Day's Journey* was Fredric March. In 1956, March was 59 years old, and had achieved the rare status of being both a distinguished and respected stage actor and a Hollywood movie star with two Oscars. He had met his wife, Florence Eldridge, while playing summer stock in Denver. At the time of their marriage, she was far better known than he, but his film career being more successful than hers, he became the star. The two of them had toured in Theatre Guild productions, and acted together on Broadway when they could. Veterans that they were, "the Marches," as they were known, knew what they were up against in the roles of the elder Tyrones, and they prepared for the production exhaustively and meticulously.

Two scripts that the Marches used in the production are now in the possession of the Eugene O'Neill Foundation, Monte Cristo Cottage.[61] Fredric March's script is particularly heavily annotated. It gives a good sense of his preparation for the role as well as his characterization of James Tyrone. March's conception of James was clearly based on James O'Neill, and he did substantial historical research to help him understand Eugene O'Neill's characterization of his father. His script contains two interesting sets of handwritten notes, one a page of quotations from newspaper reviews describing James O'Neill, and the other his notes on the character. Among the descriptions of O'Neill that he copied are

> handsome face
> luminous eyes
> fine presence
> magnetic personality
> keen artistic perceptions
> splendid intelligence
> strength & *power*[62]

James's Irishness was a key to the character for March. Quintero remembered in the early 1970s that March had asked at the first reading of the play whether the director thought James should have a brogue:

> As I hadn't thought about it, I answered, "I don't know."
> "Neither do I," you said, "but we mustn't forget that he was pure

potato-famine Irish, and regardless of how he tried to disguise it, he wouldn't really forget anything, not even his brogue. There's something there that needs to be explored. It may sound strange to you, but I have a feeling that hidden in this brogue business is one of the keys to my character. Leave it to O'Neill to do something like that. He really intends for me to take a long day's journey into night backwards. To go back to the beginning." And, by God, you were right![63]

March eventually used the brogue as a means of physicalizing James's regression to his roots, as he traveled back in his mind to the childhood poverty that he finally describes so wrenchingly to Edmund, a journey not unlike that of Brutus Jones in *The Emperor Jones*. As Quintero described it:

> You began the play impeccably dressed, speaking in pure, perfect stage-English. Secure, rich and seemingly happy. Then slowly, every day a little more, I saw you, I felt you, peel away all façade until we got to the pit of James Tyrone's character. And the pit had greatness in it. The frightened, potato-famine Irish immigrant had genius in him . . . So, it was only in that last act, when all façade had been peeled off, that you used the sad, remembered song of an Irish brogue.[64]

The dialogue was clearly the lynchpin of March's realization of James. He approached the character through the dialogue, carefully marking the beats in every line, as well as directions about volume and pitch, and notes to himself of the mood or subtext to be conveyed in a scene. An example gives a sense of how he attacked the script. When the boys enter in the first scene, after they have been laughing together in the dining room, and Mary asks them what the joke was, O'Neill's text reads:

> TYRONE
> *With a painful effort to be a good sport.*
> Yes, let us in on it, lads. I told your mother I knew damned well it would be one on me, but never mind that, I'm used to it.   (22)

As annotated by March, the script appears as follows:

TYRONE
With a painful effort to be a good sport. ✔ !!!

"Good   Yes,/ let us *in* on it, lads. [I told your mother I knew
Sport"   *damned* well it would be one on *me*, but never mind *that,/*
  !!   I'm used to it.]

March also paid careful attention to the stage directions. He circled and underlined O'Neill's directions when they concerned James, and he also wrote marginal notes to himself, such as "slight strain bet. them" (15); "chuckle relief" (17) "lifts [Mary] up in air" (17); "Big fight all out of nothing" (21); "Big and *Angry!*" (26); "He now *knows*" (67); "'she' *betrayed* me!" (78); "very *hard* to say" (85) "Frown!" (126); "Proud!!" (147); "*sweetly*" (151); "to Self & Broken" (152).

The other prong of March's attack on the character was the use of props and business. March was no Method actor. Rather, much like Laurence Olivier, he got to the character's insides by means of externals, by feeling at home with a prop, a costume, or a gesture. He wore a facsimile of the boots of the period from the first day of rehearsal and a gold fob and big-faced gold watch, hidden in the vest pocket. Quintero noted that he would use the watch "to hide in, pretending to look at the time, but really pitifully trying not to see what you didn't want to see."[65] March had written "prop" in big letters in his script, and circled O'Neill's stage direction, "*He fumbles with his watch*" (91). From the first run-through of Act 4, March was dressed in a faded red dressing gown that helped him to feel his way to James.

March's stage business was centered on three major props, all of them indicated by O'Neill – the cigar in Act 1 and the playing cards and whiskey in Act 4. The cigar came out when James said to Jamie, "You're a fine lunkhead!" (29). Thereafter, March carefully indicated in the script when James was to smoke. He circled "*playing solitaire*" in the stage directions at the beginning of Act 4, and wrote at the top of the page, "Casino starts p. 137." He noted when he should pick up the pack of cards and when he should put it down. As O'Neill obviously intended, the cards gave March and Bradford Dillman something to do during the long modified monologues of Edmund and James. They followed O'Neill's directions for the playing of the cards, with a few additions, such as James's toying with the cards when he warned Edmund, "Don't start your damned atheist morbidness again!" March paid careful attention to the treatment of drinking in Act 4, and the effect it had on his character. He wrote "✓ STINKO (meaning)" next to the stage direction indicating that he and Edmund first take a drink (130), and "THICK mouthed" next to the line, "You have a poet in you but it's a damned morbid one!" (131), and "DRUNK" next to the third stage direction to pour a drink in Act 4 (146). He wrote "SOBER" next to the improbable direction as Mary enters at the end of Act 4, "*He gives up helplessly, shrinking into himself, even his defensive drunkenness taken from him, leaving him sick and sober*" (172).

Quintero's overall conception of James's character saw his tragedy as the central theme of the play. He dramatized his analysis of James in his memoir as a conversation with Bradford Dillman:

> His miserliness to you all can hardly compare to his miserliness to himself. For a few thousand dollars he cheated himself of the chance to touch the hand of God; to take his place in the brightest constellation in the pure heaven of art. He cheated himself more than he could ever cheat any one of you. The fear of poverty that crawled in through the marrow of his bones and ran like a trembling nerve through every vein of his body left him with no choice.   (Q 263)

This tragic conception was the spine of March's characterization, but his performance was no lofty abstraction of the play's tragic theme. It was part of his technique to pay careful attention to the psychology of James, and to externalize the traits that he thought important. The Museum of Television and Radio owns a copy of a 1958 *Ed Sullivan Show* which preserves in black-and-white most of Act 2, scene 2 (79–95) as it was filmed live for television. March's use of the cigar to dramatize James's acting of self-confidence is clearly in evidence here. To concretize his closeness with money, March pulled out his roll of bills when he gave Edmund $10.00, and snapped a rubber band off it, turning slightly away from Edmund's gaze as he selected the bill. After he put the roll back in his pocket, he gave it a careful pat to make sure it was there.

In March's script is a sheet of handwritten notes that suggests the kinds of perception that informed his performance. As is evident from his work with the brogue, March saw James O'Neill's Irishness as important to Tyrone's character: "For all his bluster (& he *should* bluster in a fine, *Irish* way) he is something of a gentleman – he is self-made, surely – but so is Gene Tunney & so is Jim Cagney." Although March "took the actor home"[66] in his characterization of James, it was his identity as father, head of the family, that was for March the core of his self-conception in the play: "Despite all . . . he is still PAPA. He is *responsible* for 'the family' – the food – the car – the house, etc.," he wrote. In his relationship with Mary:

> He is so *RIGHT* (by his *thinking*) ("Never let a woman ruin your life" – J. F. B.) A very beautiful little girl came back stage (among *many* others) & he happened to know *her father* she amused him & captivated him (she was *very* beautiful) *&* Catholic
>
> since she in a sense, sought *him* out – why shouldn't she *travel* with him & sleep in lousy hotel rooms & have Babies whenever the Hell *he pleased* (He, by God pays for everything, & always the one who P.A.Y.S. is the imp. one.)[67]

Quintero said that he had "never seen anybody work so intensively and relentlessly on a part" as did March on James Tyrone.[68] The result was a complex and integrated interpretation, and a deeply moving performance. Brooks Atkinson wrote that March gave "a performance that will stand as a milestone in the acting of an O'Neill play": "Petty, mean, bullying, impulsive and sharp-tongued, he also has magnificence – a man of strong passions, deep loyalties and basic humility. This is a character portrait of grandeur."[69]

5   Florence Eldridge and Fredric March in the final scene

Florence Eldridge

Florence Eldridge was a more experienced stage actor even than March when she began her work on *Long Day's Journey*. Eldridge's approach to acting was similar to her husband's, and they knew each other so well and had worked together so often that they began with a wordless understanding about their approaches to the roles and several common techniques. Her acting script is less copiously annotated than March's, but the annotations are of the same character. As it was for March, dialogue was clearly the entry point for her creation of the role. In the script, the dialogue is marked for emphasis and for pauses, and movement is indicated even more specifically than it is in March's, particularly in the first scene. She also occasionally indicated Mary's motivation or frame of mind. She wrote, for example, "he knows about me" next to Edmund's line, "you certainly look grand, Mama"; "*he* knows about me" next to

Jamie's line, "I heard him, too"; and "guilt into hostility" next to her line, "Your father wasn't finding fault with you" (21). She wrote "Final retreat from reality" next to her speech, "Doctor Hardy! I wouldn't believe a thing he said, if he swore on a stack of Bibles! I know what doctors are. They're all alike" (27). As Edmund tries to talk to Mary about her addiction, warning her to "take care of yourself. That's all that counts," Eldridge noted that she should "leave him," crossing to the center, and then on to the window, "to get away from the discussion – ricochet!" (43). As Mary enters in Act 2, Eldridge warned herself, "Don't let them notice your eyes" (58). In the scene with James in Act 2, scene 2, she wrote "she would like to say she's sorry and vindicate herself" next to the line, "Don't go yet, dear. I don't want to be alone" (82) and, "I love you I'm sorry" next to the line, "There is something I wanted to say" (82).

In the *Ed Sullivan* clip of Act 2, scene 2, it is evident that much of Eldridge's characterization of Mary was vocal. She exaggerates the beats of emphasis in the speeches slightly to give the sense that Mary is "performing" almost everything she says. While her voice is cultured, almost melodious, it becomes irritating because of the undercurrent of self-righteous victimhood that Eldridge plays. In her speech about the death of Eugene, for example, she plays the passive–aggressive subtext, emphasizing Mary's blaming of James by saying that she is to blame. There is a rhetorical element to her speech that suggests it is a practiced one, and she knows just which words to emphasize in order to press James's buttons. Fredric March sits looking out front and reacting with grieved resignation as he listens to the speech:

> It was *my* fault. I should have in*sis*ted on staying with Eu*gene* and *not* have let you persuade me to *join* you, just because I *loved* you. *Above* all, I shouldn't have let you *insist* I have another baby to take Eugene's place, because you thought that would *make* me forget his *death*. I *knew* from experience by then that *chil*dren should have *homes* to be born in, if they are to be *good* children, and *women* need homes, if they are to be good *mothers*. (88)

While she brought out the nagging, maddening side of Mary's speeches very effectively, Eldridge did not play her on one note. In the context of this delivery, her angry shouting of the line, "the past is the present" (87) and of her self-accusation at the end of Act 2, "You're lying to yourself again. You wanted to get rid of them" (95) is a shock to the audience and a potent reminder that she is losing control of herself.

Like March, Eldridge looked at the character psychologically, and she approached Mary through an understanding of the experience that informed the character at the time of the play. The unavoidable key to the character from this point of view was understanding what it was like to be addicted to morphine, and Eldridge approached this issue head on. As she explained in 1979:

> In an attempt to understand the character's drug addiction, I went, through the kindness of a doctor friend, to observe addicts in Bellevue Hospital and noticed their garrulousness and high-pitched voices when they were in need of drugs and the somnolence and peacefulness that followed drug-taking. I tried to fit the knowledge gained from my visit to Bellevue into the pattern of the script in the scenes that preceded Mary Tyrone's going upstairs to find relief and her returns, but there was something that did not fit.
>
> I then went to Dr. Marie Nyswander, an authority on drug addiction, and gave her the play to read. Her conclusion was that if O'Neill had accurately observed his mother's behavior, there was pathology involved as well as addiction, so I made the choice to play what was written. Interestingly, when the curtain came down each night and we "set up our psychiatrists' couches" to receive the traumatized and those whose mothers had been addicts – or alcoholics – or schizophrenics – we discovered *all* had identified.[70]

In 1957, while playing the role, she told Helen Ormsbee that "the doctor's opinion was that addicts are seldom made by being given narcotics to deaden pain." Rather, "there is generally some psychological weakness that makes it easy to take refuge in the drug. The clews to Mrs. Tyrone's weakness are in the lines of the play. As a child she had been indulged by her parents and shielded, and by the time of the drama she is a woman who has never quite grown up – not at all the person to cope with her extremely difficult husband and sons."[71]

The other central issues were aspects of Mary's character that become thematic in the play. The arthritic hands that she uses as an explanation for taking "painkilling" drugs are also a symbol of the ugliness of her present reality in opposition to the beauty of her past dream of being a concert pianist. The New London house is to her an ugly environment and a constant reminder of the failure of her dream of an ideal home. In approaching the arthritic hands, Eldridge asked herself, "were they that badly crippled? Were they an excuse?," deciding finally "not to emphasize Mary Tyrone's crippled hands as I felt that her emotional and spiritual deformity was more important."[72] She told Ormsbee that "the pain of arthritis in her hands is the excuse she uses to get her shots." Of the home, she wrote that:

> another clue came when we went to New London to see the O'Neill house that is the scene of the play and the cause of Mary Tyrone's lamentation for a decent home. I was surprised to find it full of attractive possibilities and charmingly situated looking out on the sound. I decided then that Mary Tyrone was a victim, not only of her life but also of her own inadequacies, and must be played as an immature person.[73]

One piece of background research was suggested by José Quintero, who told Mel Gussow, "I think Mary Tyrone in 'Long Day's Journey Into Night' has much of Carlotta. The actual mother of O'Neill was too small a character to become that character on stage. Where did his mother begin and Carlotta end?"[74] Eldridge has written that "José Quintero was particularly anxious for me to meet Carlotta O'Neill as he felt that O'Neill had woven a bit of her into the character of his mother." Talking to Carlotta over a lunch arranged by Quintero, Eldridge said that she could find "echoes of Mary Tyrone's speeches in Carlotta's love-hate anecdotes. She would start to reminisce so sweetly and suddenly repressed resentment would burst through into bitter complaints or self-pity just as Mary Tyrone does repeatedly when she is reviewing the past with James Tyrone."[75] Eldridge's use of this perception in her acting is evident in the description of her performance by a New Haven critic: "Florence Eldridge, as the near-demented wife carries a massive part impeccably and concisely projects the alternating aspects of drugged dream and waspish candor that illuminate her life and her family's."[76]

Jason Robards, Jr.

Fredric March and Florence Eldridge were described by critics as having reached the peak of their careers with *Long Day's Journey*. But it was Jason Robards, Jr., as he was still known in 1956, who was the big sensation. When he was given the role of Jamie Tyrone, Robards was playing Hickey, to great popular and critical acclaim, in the Circle in the Square's production of *The Iceman Cometh*. Robards, like his silent-film-star father, studied at the American Academy of Dramatic Art. In the 1950s, he spoke rather contemptuously of the Method actors who were then very much the fashion on Broadway and in Hollywood. In 1958, he described acting as "a craft, with techniques to learn, work to be done," saying that "too many actors nowadays concentrate too much on self-analysis without paying enough attention to the play or the actors working with them."[77] He first worked with José Quintero in 1953, when he landed a role in the Circle in the Square's production of *American Gothic*, and immediately recognized a kindred spirit. "With José," he said once, "it's just you and him talking."[78]

Although he was not a Method actor, Robards, like Quintero, went back to his own experience to help him understand the character of Jamie. He said that he was "closely attuned to the spirit of O'Neill and particularly to the character of the despairing Jamie." Like Jamie, he was the son of an embittered, once-famous matinee idol. Robards also pronounced Jamie to be "the kind of drunk I understand. He uses drinking to be more drunk than he actually is –

he's a two-purpose drunk – the kind who, when he really wants to say something, says it and then covers up as a drunk. He switches back and forth. That's the way I used to drink."[79]

While he eschewed what he considered the self-indulgent introspection of the Method, Robards' technique was far from the Marches' careful construction of their roles. His approach to his role has been described by Elliot Martin as "very organic": he "just lets it hang out and happen to him. He doesn't need, at least in his work with José, long speeches. He just needs a little thing. They use a short-cut language between the two of them" (M 57). Robards was to act in many productions directed by Quintero, including *Hughie, A Touch of the Poet*, and, most memorably, *A Moon for the Misbegotten*, as well as *Iceman*, and *Journey*. Theirs was very much a collaborative process. Quintero told Barbara Gelb, "Jason and I understood each other, inside, right away" when they worked together for the first time at Circle in the Square. "There was an open corridor between us, with no obstructions. There was never a feeling that I had to be careful, you know, not to say that. It has always been like that, also with Colleen [Dewhurst] and Gerry Page. They don't have to hear what I say, they sense what I feel. That's my kind of actor and I'm their kind of director." Confirming this, Robards told Gelb, "I don't remember José actually telling me anything . . . he's *acting* with us."[80]

Robards' performance as Jamie made him a star. As Henry Hewes noted, March's performance as James made it "possible for Jason Robards, Jr. to explode and steal the show."[81] What Robards achieved in Jamie's fourth-act modified monologue, with Quintero's help, was a technical tour de force, and an expression of primal emotion seldom seen on Broadway. Walter Kerr provided a powerful description of Robards' performance and its effect on the opening-night audience in New York:

> As the venom poured forth Mr. Robards told us very clearly that he was fiercely devoted to the boy he was whipping, that he knew in his secret heart he had tried to destroy him in order to reduce him to his own ape-

like level, that he was now passionately torn between vindictive triumph and violent self-loathing.

As the actor drove his fury to a crescendo, gasped out the last harrowing and faltering syllables like a wildly sputtering candle and collapsed beside a table in stunned exhaustion, the house broke loose. The sound out front was suddenly as shattering as the sound on stage had been . . . the passionate "bravos" that swept down from the back of the house did not interrupt or destroy the action on stage; they joined it . . . It was quite as though a great arm had suddenly swept about the auditorium gathering author, players, and spectators into a single shared experience.[82]

Robards told an interviewer that he did not bring the play to a standstill again after opening night: "Not because I can't. I've been asked not to, because the next speech is Freddie's (Fredric March, star of the play). It's easy to do – if you're an actor who knows his craft." Much later, Robards revealed that an interesting dynamic was going on between himself and March during these performances: "He'd say to me, 'You're dying out there kid. Take it easy.' Every time I took it easy, he'd come out and blow me right off the stage. That made me really love him. He was a sly old bastard."[83] Unfortunately, the 1958 *Ed Sullivan Show* clip contains little of Robards' performance as Jamie, although he was to recreate the role for the 1962 film directed by Sidney Lumet.

Bradford Dillman and Katherine Ross

The 26-year-old Bradford Dillman was by far the least experienced and the most nervous of the four principal actors in *Long Day's Journey*. The son of a wealthy San Francisco stock broker, he had acted in college productions at Yale and in summer stock, and had had a season at the Off-Broadway Theatre de Lys. His only Broadway credit when he was chosen by Quintero and approved by Carlotta to play Edmund was as a young soldier in *Third Person* the previous year. He had been enrolled at Actors Studio for a year (in the same class as Marilyn Monroe) when he was cast as Edmund. Quintero has described Dillman's relationship with Robards as a kind of mentorship, very close to that of the Tyrone brothers: "To watch and hear this interplay between them was miraculous. Slowly, without inventing it or forcing it, I began to regard them as brothers. Their play, without their being aware of it, was leading them, as it were, out of the forest of their totally different worlds into a common clearing, where the embrace and battle of brotherhood was to be waged" (Q 211). The rehearsal process for them was to build on this fundamental connection between the two actors. Unfortunately, there is no video record of Dillman's performance. He had been replaced by Albert Morgenstern when CBS filmed the excerpt for *Ed Sullivan*.

Katherine Ross, who was cast as the maid Cathleen, was, like Robards, a Circle in the Square actor who had done extensive work in live television. To Quintero, she was a familiar and proven actor who could be relied upon to turn in an authentic performance in this small but important role.

THE REHEARSAL PROCESS

The first reading of *Long Day's Journey* by the cast took place at the Marches' country home in Connecticut. The cast immediately felt like an ensemble. According to Florence Eldridge, that was about the extent of the preparation until the formal rehearsals began in September.[84] They did, however, work very hard on their roles. According to stage manager Elliot Martin, both Eldridge and March arrived for the first day of formal rehearsals with their carefully annotated scripts, "letter-perfect, knowing their parts completely. A four-hour play, both of them . . . Jason didn't know word one and neither did Brad" (M 54).

When the company met at the Helen Hayes Theatre for the first day of the four-week rehearsal period, Quintero gave the director's customary opening speech to rally the troup. The speech was recalled by Frank Hamilton, who understudied both sons in the touring company, and Elliot Martin. Both remembered that Quintero used his own relationship with his family as a basis for elucidating the relationships of the Tyrones. Hamilton told Edwin J. McDonough:

> I remember references to the Catholicism with its whole "don't" system. It's a part of the Tyrone family and of José's . . . Edmund wants to create, but the family says no, even though the old man was an actor. He is told that he cannot create, he is not well. There is a crushing of Edmund in the play. Jamie is oppressed as well . . . If there is a leitmotif in the play, however, the word is love, a kind of yearning to be close to people. There's a lot of hatred in *Long Day's Journey*, but if they really hated each other so much they would not stay in New London. It is love that holds them together. The boys have a terrible need to love. José understands that.   (M 55)

Martin remembered Quintero saying that "the play dealt with guilt and that he wanted to see this though their eyes":

> He said, "This is a play about eyes. If there's a sound upstairs, everyone's eyes must register it." . . . With almost all of José's earlier productions, his direction was all related to his own family. In his preamble for *Long Day's Journey*, he did identify the guilt of the father with his own father's guilt and the treatment of his own mother . . . He said, "this is so much out of my background, the way they dealt, they would shoot knives at one another in their speech."   (M 54–55)

In his memoir, Quintero wrote a chapter that dramatizes his memory of the rehearsals and his conversations with the actors. It is a doubly revealing account of his direction, for not only does it show what he thought were the significant communications in this process, but it demonstrates his method of communication. Quintero was a histrionic man, and performance was his major means of communication, whether he was writing or directing. Rather than give specific directions to the actors, he tended to indicate the point he wanted them to reach through physical demonstration, and then gently urge them on while they found their way there in their own acting terms.

Barbara Gelb has described his behavior in rehearsals for *A Touch of the Poet*:

> Quintero in action prowls the stage and the dim aisles of the empty auditorium like a lithe and restive ocelot. He is choreographer, dancer, conductor, vocalist, therapist, diplomat, spiritualist, seer and actor . . . He raises an arm, index finger pointing skyward, marking a pause in dialogue. He smashes his fist onto a prop table, not so much to show the actor how to perform a bit of stage business, but because he is feeling the role. He had been silently mouthing the actor's lines in this particular scene and the emotions here dictate a violent physical comment. Quintero does not necessarily expect the actor to copy his gesture, but is merely communicating how the character feels. He hums along when the actors break into song, nods his head and stamps his feet when they perform a little jig, beams when they joke and laugh, twists his features into a grimace of despair during a speech of anguish, reaches up with both arms as a scene draws to a close, in a gesture resembling a benediction, calls softly, "curtain." He is a complete performance.[85]

Story-telling was another aspect of Quintero's communicative performance. He tended to elucidate the meaning of a particular scene or interaction in the play by means of an anecdote from his own experience, allowing the actors to infer its significance by analogy rather than to dissect an emotional truth through rational analysis. Two examples of this technique that Quintero dramatizes in his memoir are his telling Fredric March an anecdote about the humiliating process of getting his father to give him fifteen cents so he could see March in *Anthony Adverse* when he was a child (Q 230–32) and his comparison of Mary Tyrone's experience with that of his mother (Q 241–42).

In making his actors into an integrated ensemble, Quintero had a difficult task that would have been daunting for a less flexible director. He had to find ways of reaching a Method-trained actor in Dillman, a Method opponent in Robards, and two veterans who approached their roles linguistically and "from the outside in," in the

Marches. Elliot Martin recalled that Quintero gave more specific direction to Florence Eldridge than he did to the men, getting up on stage and acting out her role down to details of gestures and sitting (M 57). In his memoir, Quintero records his disagreement with Eldridge's preparation for the role of a drug addict:

> "Florence, darling, you don't have to go and see how drug addicts act or what their outward behavior is. You are an actress, not a doctor. Drugs make you forget, take you far away to a tolerable world. Why? This is where all of our energies and talent and sweat are going to go. It's going to be harder for you, Florence, to live a day of Mary's life than it was for her to live all the days of her life"   (Q 217).

For her he discussed the rocking chair as a "witness box" into which she is locked while the men watch her, "first out of the corner of their eyes, and then the trial will begin." (Q 220)

A good example of the substance of his communication with March is his dramatization of his discussion of March's handling of the wedding dress in the final scene: "She drops her wedding dress. James, get up and bring to your hands all the deep and now and forever love you have for her and pick up the empty gown and hold your gone-away bride close to your chest, and ever so gently, so careful not to harm it. She's free of you, now at this moment, never married you, never gave birth to you, Jamie, and certainly never to you, Edmund. For there was only one marriage. The one performed in the miracle of the Immaculate Conception" (Q 264). March's cradling of the wedding dress was one of the unforgettable images of the production.

THE TRYOUT PERIOD

The first production of *Long Day's Journey Into Night* in English took place on 15 October 1956, at the Wilbur Theatre in Boston. According to stage manager Elliot Martin,

> Freddie didn't know a line, not a line. It was terrible. I had two assistants

> on the show and I put them both right behind the porch. They lay there for the whole show with flashlights and a script because Freddie didn't know line one. Our arrangement was that Freddie was to cough if he was going to go up. Everyone thought that this was going to be a disaster. Florence knew her part, she was perfect, so smooth. The notices came out the next morning. "Fredric March is brilliant in this play. Unfortunately he was suffering from a severe head cold and was coughing all the way through the show." Florence was letter-perfect but didn't get good notices at all. She was also very good on the night after we opened in New York. She was just not a good opener.   (M 60)

Martin's memory is a bit exaggerated. The Boston notices were full of praise for both March and Eldridge, and none that I have seen mention a head cold. It was Eldridge who missed two performances in Boston due to laryngitis. And Eldridge's Boston reviews were, if anything, better than her opening night reviews in New York. The Boston *Traveler* reported that "the husband-and-wife team of Fredric March and Florence Eldridge could not be surpassed as the elder Tyrones, Miss Eldridge's being remarkable in its subtle changes."[86] *Variety* reported that "Miss Eldridge gives a tremendous performance, handling the role of the narcotic crazed wife, who lapses from moments of sanity to unreality, with superb skill."[87] In the *Herald*, Elinor Hughes wrote that "Florence Eldridge is at her peak in the pitiful role of Mary Tyrone, who retreats from gentle affectionate humor to total blank refusal of actuality in a dream of the happy past."[88]

The Boston opening was a triumph. Cyrus Durgin wrote in the *Globe* that the "American premiere" was "one of the splendid dramatic accomplishments of the decade," noting that the cheering at the final curtain was "something almost unheard of in a Boston theatre in this reviewer's time."[89] The one dissenting voice was that of Elliot Norton, who objected to the play's four-hour length, declaring outright that the play was "unnecessarily long. It should be cut to eliminate wearisome repetitions."[90] Elinor Hughes recognized that "what seems, on superficial examination, like a tendency to repetition, is quite often revealed as frugal development of a theme: it is the same only with a difference." Less arrogantly than Norton, she suggested that while *Long Day's Journey* "does move slowly, I'm not going to say that it should be cut, for to cut a text so closely written would be like taking a piece out of a tapestry."[91] Florence Eldridge later remembered that, after the Boston opening, "all the smart theatre people came up to see the play" and they "insisted that it must be cut as it was too repetitious. Fortunately, Carlotta O'Neill stood firm. Not one word could be touched." Eldridge wrote that all the artists involved in the production understood that the play could not be cut: "The more one worked on the play, the more one realized that it was a symphony. Each character had a theme and the 'repetitions' were the variations on the themes. That was the power of the play – the ceaseless pounding of the themes. Had it been cut, it would have unravelled."[92] Although the running time was cut by fifteen minutes between Boston and New York, no substantial cuts were made in O'Neill's dialogue.

After the two-week Boston run, *Long Day's Journey* was received just as warmly in New Haven, opening on 29 October for a week's run before it opened in New York. In the poll conducted by the *New Haven Register* on the plays and actors that previewed in New Haven in the 1956–57 season, *Long Day's Journey* was the unanimous choice for best play, and Fredric March was voted best actor, followed by Florence Eldridge.

NEW YORK

When *Long Day's Journey* opened in New York on 7 November 1956, it was to a great deal of expectation on the part of audience and critics, and it did not disappoint them. The opening night reviews were ecstatic. The *Daily News* reported that the play "exploded like a dazzling skyrocket over the humdrum of Broadway theatricals."[93] The *New York Times* declared that, with the production of *Long*

Day's Journey, "the American theatre acquires size and stature."[94]
Newsweek commented that "both theatre and audience alike magnificently met the demands of one of the great tragedies of the American
theatre."[95] Most of the reviews echoed the *Journal American* in its
approbation of all the actors:

> There are only five people in the cast and they are all superb. As the
> mother, Florence Eldridge gives the most commanding and incisive
> performance of her career, and she is matched by a brilliant and
> exhaustive contribution from Fredric March, as the husband. Both
> roles are enormously demanding . . . Equal stature must be accorded
> Jason Robards, Jr., who, as the older son, has one of the greatest scenes
> of drunken introspection in theatre history. Bradford Dillman, as the
> other boy, is tortured, sensitive and always brilliant.[96]

The *World-Telegram* complained that Jason Robards was "unable to
hint at the relieving strain of humor which certainly ought to be
there"[97] and the *Post* suggested that "there is a bit more to the part"
of Mary than Florence Eldridge "quite captures,"[98] but these were
small demurs in the overwhelming flood of praise.

Some of the critics saw beyond the great performances to the
power of the theatrical experience, a tragic catharsis rare in the
contemporary theatre. Walter Kerr described the play as an "endlessly
savage examination of conscience . . . deliberately, masochistically
harrowing in the ferocity of its revelation." Nevertheless, he wrote,
"the agony that O'Neill felt whenever he contemplated his own
beginnings is not passed onto his audience. It is in some curious and
even exalting manner exorcized, washed away, leaving in its place an
undefined dignity, an agreed-upon peace, a powerful sense of exhila-
rated completion."[99] John Chapman said that "A theatregoer cannot
fail to come out of the Helen Hayes Theatre without sensing within
him an incredible surge of uplift. And he cannot leave the playhouse
before cheering four of the great performances of our time."[100]

While the actors received nearly equal praise on opening night,
subsequent considerations of the production produced some reservations about Florence Eldridge's performance. Walter Kerr, who had

found Jason Robards so overwhelming, wrote in his Sunday follow-up piece: "I am not going to say that Florence Eldridge's careful, canny portrait of O'Neill's destroyed mother is on a level with the major male performances. The grinding depths of the third act – a plunge into the relief of nothingness – are not quite reached; the momentum of the play falters briefly."[101] *Variety* reported in February that "Miss Eldredge's [*sic*] interpretation has grown into a sort of sub-paragraph, with a question-mark in the broad debate which has raged this winter on the play itself. The actress most of all the five players has been the victim of the celebrated Manhattan parlor game of re-casting hits . . . It is the 'fey' tone of her mental drift that may lack 'familiarity' for her audiences . . . It may be added that when the parlor game of re-casting goes on round the town these days, people quickly run out of names they think could do it better."[102]

The production was an overwhelming success, running for 390 performances. It won a posthumous Pulitzer Prize for O'Neill, his fourth, as well as the Drama Critics Circle Award, the Outer Circle Award, and Tony Awards for both the play and Fredric March. March and Florence Eldridge won *Variety*'s poll of the New York first-string critics as best actor and actress of the season.

ON THE ROAD

In February 1957, a startling decision on the part of the management was announced. *Long Day's Journey* had been invited by the State Department and ANTA (The American National Theatre and Academy) to represent the United States at the International Drama Festival in Paris, and the producers had decided to close the show for a month in order to bring the entire production to France. In the context of the Cold War, the State Department was happy to pay the $20,000 cost of production. As Elliot Norton noted, "it is important that there be an American play at Paris, for there will certainly be more than one from the Soviet countries."[103] The show closed in

New York on 29 June, allowing time for the cast to fly to Paris and prepare for the opening on 2 July, the first of five sold-out performances at the 2,500-seat Théâtre Sarah Bernhardt. Because there was no time to transport the scenery from New York, David Hays arrived in Paris two weeks earlier to put together the sets that had been constructed from his drawings and blueprints by Chevreux et Pellegry, under the direction of Roger Harth. Hays ran into a few difficulties, such as finding period wicker furniture in Paris, and he had to substitute an innocuous landscape for the plaque reading "God Bless Our Home." He finally gave up trying to find an American screen-door spring for the door to the porch, and had one hand-made for the production.

The play opened during an unusually severe heat wave in Paris, and the un-air-conditioned theatre was stifling. Sitting though the production, which, with lengthy intermissions, ran from 8:00 p.m. until 1:00 a.m. proved to be something of an endurance contest. The *New York Times* reported that "during the lengthy last act some of the audience headed for the doors," but "those who stayed cheered and applauded the New York cast."[104] The *Herald Tribune* said that "there was a five-minute ovation, marking the most enthusiastic reception ever accorded an American play in France."[105] Understandably under the circumstances, the first thing the French critics noted about the play was its length: "Le long voyage dans la nuit dure quatre heures" began the review in *Le Figaro*.[106] Overall, however, the French reviewers were uncharacteristically enthusiastic and respectful of this American play and production. *Variety* summed up the triumph of the French engagement: "Despite record-breaking heat, lack of air-conditioning and the fact that four-hour dramas are unknown in Paris, 'Long Day's Journey Into Night' was a spectacular success here last week."[107] Following the Paris engagement, the cast took a vacation, returning to Broadway on 25 August. *Long Day's Journey* ran another eight months, closing on 27 March 1958.

The National Company for *Long Day's Journey* opened in Cleveland on 13 December 1957, thirteen months after its premiere, and while the show was still running in New York. The timing of the national tour was the subject of some controversy among the Broadway pundits. *Variety* reported that "various other managements have argued that a second company, if sent out at all, should have been formed within a reasonable period after the opening of the original Broadway edition, when the publicity about the posthumous O'Neill tragedy was at a peak." The conventional wisdom was that, having missed that moment, the producers should have waited until the New York production closed, and used the scenery, lighting, and props from New York, and ideally the stars, for the road company. Instead, as the New York production showed signs of nearing the end of its run, a new physical production was built at an estimated cost of nearly $30,000.[108] As it happened, with disastrous engagements in Cleveland and Detroit, the tour nearly closed within a month.

The National Company lost $5,400 during its week in Cleveland and $9,000 during its two weeks in Detroit. Ted Mann announced a closing date of 1 February after the company lost nearly $3,000 during its first week in Chicago, but a campaign on the part of the critics forestalled the closing, and saved the tour. Claudia Cassidy, whose well-known championing of *The Glass Menagerie* had saved that production in Chicago and arguably launched the career of Tennessee Williams, led the fight to save *Long Day's Journey*. With the opening line of her review in the *Tribune*, she chided Chicago for its neglect of this great work. "One of the great plays of a lifetime came to the Erlanger last night," she wrote, "and there were empty seats in the house . . . if we let it die here we have only ourselves to blame that the town is turning into a theatrical desert." While she did not find the production flawless, she told her fellow Chicagoans, "if you asked me which town has the superior cast, New York or Chicago, I couldn't tell you."[109] Other critics wrote in similar terms of the opportunity the production presented to Chicago, and gradually the box office began to show the effect. The production ended up with a profit of nearly $20,000 for the four-week Chicago run. With the touring schedule reinstated, the production moved on to Pittsburgh, St. Louis, Philadelphia, Washington, Baltimore, Denver, San Francisco, and Los Angeles. While it was not nearly as successful as the New York production, the road company showed a profit of about $34,000 overall during its total operation from 13 December 1957 to 31 May 1958.

The set for the touring company was a faithful reproduction of Hays's set for the New York production, and Quintero directed the new cast of Fay Bainter, Anew McMaster, Roy Poole, Chet Leaming, and Liz Thackston. The company did not have the recognizable names that sometimes generate audiences for road companies. Bainter had won an Oscar for her performance in *Jezebel*, but otherwise was not well known to the American public. Her co-star, Anew McMaster, was an Irish actor well known in England and Ireland, but making his American debut in *Long Day's Journey*. The other three had acted only in Off-Broadway and regional theatre. With the occasional exception of Poole, however, they received almost as much enthusiastic praise from the regional critics as the New York cast did. Richard Coe wrote in the *Washington Post* that "Miss Bainter and her Irish co-star satisfied me far more than I was that memorable Gotham evening of over a year ago."[110] Cassidy praised Bainter's playing in "the addict's sly pretending, and in the pitiful withdrawal into a withered wraith" and McMaster's progression as James: "a shell of a withering actor at the start, with a touch of ham – a mighty actor as the shell cracks and the man shows."[111] Another critic praised Bainter's "wondrously mobile face and expressive eyes – capable of smoky dullness or psychotic brilliance as the situation demands."[112] The critics were divided over Poole, whose performance was variously described as "altogether impressive and skillful"[113] and as "seldom more than caricature."[114] The screenwriter Dudley Nichols, a long-time friend of the O'Neills, wrote to Carlotta when the production reached Los Angeles that Poole was a little too terrifying as Jamie and Liz Thackston was a dull and wooden Cathleen. Nevertheless, he thought Fay Bainter even better than Florence Eldridge, and dubbed the production a "great night" overall.[115]

CHAPTER 2

PRODUCTIONS IN ENGLISH

GREAT BRITAIN AND IRELAND

Edinburgh; London, 1958

As noted in the previous chapter, in May of 1956, Carlotta O'Neill had optioned *Long Day's Journey* to Blevins Davis for a production in London and, should she consider the production successful, other venues in Europe. For various reasons, Davis' production never materialized. The European premiere of the play in English took place instead at the Edinburgh Festival on 8 September 1958, produced by New Watergate Presentations and H. M. Tennent in association with the original Broadway producers, Leigh Connell, Theodore Mann, and José Quintero. The original plan for the production was to bring Fredric March and Florence Eldridge to Edinburgh, and subsequently to London, to repeat their roles. Again directed by José Quintero, the production was expected to be much like the Broadway version. This plan was publicized in New York in early February and announced by the Festival on 19 March 1958.[1]

A week later, however, the *New York Times* carried two items regarding the production. One reported that the Marches had dropped their plans to do the British production, noting: "We feel this is a play that has to do with four people, each of whose contribution is equally important. We are most anxious to know who the two sons would be. The producers feel this is no concern of ours."[2] Ted Mann told the reporter that the Marches had withdrawn from the production because of unspecified "contractual differ-

ences." On the same day, it was announced in the *Journal American*
that Shirley Booth, who had told Carlotta through her agent Audrey
Wood that she wanted to play Mary as early as June of 1956, had
been signed to star in the British production.[3] In June it was reported
that Celia Johnson would play Mary. When the play opened in
Edinburgh, however, it was Gwen Ffrangcon-Davies who played
Mary, with Anthony Quayle as James, Ian Bannen as Jamie, and Alan
Bates as Edmund.

The casting proved to be crucial, along with the decision to cut
approximately one quarter of the dialogue for the British production.
Apparently the producers agreed with Carlotta's often-repeated
opinion that the British and the French would never sit still for a
four-hour play as "serious" as her husband's, and so did most critics.
In the words of a representative British critic, "a quarter of the text
has been jettisoned for the English production, and a good thing,
too. What survives is ample material."[4] As for the casting, it was
generally agreed that Anthony Quayle was "not quite happily cast as
the husband," giving "no impression that the character is a successful
and popular actor with a florid style."[5] Kenneth Tynan voiced the
unspoken comparison to March: "Anthony Quayle falls short of
Fredric March. Mr. March, with his corrugated face and burning
eyes, looked as weighty as if he were made of iron. Mr. Quayle,
though he conveys every syllable of the part's meaning, never seems
to be heavier than tin."[6]

Both Ian Bannen and Alan Bates, on the other hand, improved in
their parts as the production went on. Bates had trouble sustaining
his concentration at first, and more than one critic complained about
his accent, which was "more related to the English Midlands than to
America."[7] After the production moved to London, they were
described as "first rate as the brothers, and Mr. Bannen is especially
successful in conveying the fine shades of the wastrel's mingled
hatred and envy of his brother."[8] As has been the case with many a
production, this one faltered on the character of the maid. As one
Scots critic put it: "The comic, drunken, Irish skivvy of Miss Etain

O'Dell's performance had no place in this play at all, and it is the director, Mr. José Quintero, who is to blame for it."[9]

The star, and the saving grace, of the show was clearly Gwen Ffrangcon-Davies, who emerged in this part as a great actor. In Edinburgh, Ffrangcon-Davies' performance was recognized as "a beautifully exact study of the woman who moves capriciously in and out of reality, fearful that her odd behaviour may attract notice until she has safely passed out of reality altogether."[10] When the production reached London, her performance was recognized as a triumph of naturalistic acting and she was being called "magnificent" by more than one critic. It was the carefully martialled details of her performance that registered: "her little laughs, her neurotic gestures, and the way she held her twisted rheumatic hands as if she were manacled."[11] And it was the subtlety of her performance that most impressed:

> At the start, we see her, nervous and on edge, about to return to the drug addiction for which she has had a cure. When she succumbs she becomes less nervous, just slightly more voluble. A most subtle transition.
>
> The self-deceptive innocence with which she keeps saying: "I don't know what you are talking about," when accused of returning to the drug, is more than a lie. Miss Ffrangcon-Davies makes it seem a negation of all honesty, the final murder of truth.[12]

She seemed "to age and grow more childlike as this poor, prattling, self-pitying wreck of a beautiful woman fidgets in every nerve in her constant craving for morphine."[13]

The New York production had been most emphatically James's play. With the strength of Ffrangcon-Davies and the comparative weakness of Quayle, the Edinburgh/London one showed English-speaking audiences how it could be Mary's. This had also been the case with Inga Tidblad in Sweden, Grete Mosheim in Germany, and Isabela Corona in Mexico, and it was shortly to be true of Gaby Morlay in France, Ria Mooney in Ireland, and Dalila Rocha in Portugal. One of the fundamental truths about *Long Day's Journey* that emerges from production is that its dynamics of conflict, and thus its thematic import, is by no means fixed. There is truly no protagonist in this play "of old sorrow," but four characters interacting in a form that is like a piece of classical music with a number of intricately interwoven motifs. When a director chooses to emphasize one character, particularly by cutting the dialogue, or when one powerful performance is given among three that are merely adequate, the play becomes "about" something. This is to hear one motif, as it were, louder and perhaps more often than the others. It affects all of the motifs and their interaction with each other, so that, in this play where each of the Tyrones offers his (or her) own apologia for the past, the audience's understanding of the whole is quite different from performance to performance. In 1958, critics and audiences were just beginning to find this out. In the nearly fifty years of the play's stage life, it has become one of the excitements of each new production.

London, 1971

According to Laurence Olivier, the major motivating force for the 1971 revival of *Long Day's Journey* by the National Theatre was money. The National Theatre, of which he was the director, was at a very low ebb financially and he was urged by Kenneth Tynan to produce the play with himself in the part of James Tyrone. In Olivier's words: "At the time, if we were to be frugal, it seemed the ideal play to put on. One set, and five in the cast. So the great god Money, and Ken, won."[14] Olivier had been, as he put it, "wary of the role" after seeing Fredric March play it: "It wasn't that March put me off, though it was a giant performance to follow; it was that I didn't really want to play the part of an actor."[15] What concerned him was that "if you play an actor, you have to be a bit florid, a bit theatrical, and even with all that, the audience may not be quite sure if it's you, or the part you are playing." In order to establish his actorly authority, and of course to make a useful literary allusion, he had twelve lines from *The Tempest* inserted for James, "enough to assert my role as an actor, enough to create that stillness you need in the theatre."[16] Olivier has also made it clear that he wanted to distinguish himself from March in his conception of James's character. March, he felt, "took the actor home," suggesting that James's essence was performance, even with his family, while Olivier tried to create a more domestic, perhaps more human, James Tyrone.[17]

In the *Sunday Times*, Harold Hobson sounded the prevailing note when he wrote that Olivier's performance was "beyond criticism and beyond praise; and it finds a depth and a poignancy in O'Neill's play which a mere reading of the text, however intelligent, does not reveal."[18] The acclaim was certainly earned, but the power of the production was also owing to an intelligent and nuanced job of direction by Michael Blakemore and a very strong ensemble cast, which Olivier was much too intelligent an actor to upstage. Unlike Quintero twenty-three years earlier, Blakemore gave a full four hours to the play, and this time no one seems to have found it long or tedious. Even *Punch* was moved to ask, "how could this story of the doomed Tyrones be shorter? And why should we want it shorter?"[19] The crucial factor in Blakemore's direction was his ability to orchestrate the ever-building tension in the play, to bring out its musical architectonics as O'Neill had intended. As *Variety* put it: "the cumulative intensity is what Blakemore has sensed and defined in the production."[20] Irving Wardle offered an explanation of the relationship between the production's tension and the text:

> Mr. Blakemore's hand is apparent in his sense of the play's structure: the underlining of poisonous little details that ache under the surface of the dialogue, and the presentation of character and situation from sharply contrasted angles. Above all, he and his company think in the huge dramatic paragraphs with which O'Neill's text passes again and again over the same material like a spirograph pencil, adding to and enriching a picture whose outline is plain from the start.[21]

The precision of Blakemore's direction, and his reading of the text, was evident in "small but unforgettable moments"[22] of detailed staging, blocking, and gesture. The only substantial criticism was that there was too much of this: "too much physical movement, as if an Equity ruling had decreed that every chair and sofa must be sat on at least once in the first hour."[23] Michael Annals' realistic set, closely modeled on Monte Cristo Cottage, with its dark wood-paneled walls, its wicker furniture, and its round table with a Victorian fringed plush cover, was praised for its inconspicuous creation of the perfect milieu for the production. *Variety* said it was "atmospherically just right,"[24] although Hugh Leonard thought that Robert Bryan carried the atmosphere a bit too far in the lighting, so that the fourth act was underlit for an audience that was tired.[25]

Blakemore was clearly the perfect director for Olivier in this role. Working in Olivier's characteristic manner, together they created the external details for James Tyrone that allowed him to imagine the inner being that gave integrity to the performance. One critic described "the dejection that settles on Olivier from the beginning – his body hunched in a baggy suit, his mouth cracked into a small mean line so as to create a receding chin."[26] Clive Barnes noted that Olivier's being "a heroic actor rather than a realistic one – his gestures are larger than life, his technical command is stressed rather than concealed . . . works admirably . . . for Tyrone is himself an actor and the histrionic tricks that Olivier uses are perfectly in character for him."[27] Olivier's performance followed the arc of Blakemore's production, ever-so-slowly building in intensity up to the explosive last act, a process that Hugh Leonard described in detail:

> He began quietly, almost anonymously: a bull-like figure in a shabby suit, omitting O'Neill's hundreds of exclamation marks as he growled at his sons with the absent-mindedness born of a multitude of family squabbles. Within twenty minutes he had ceased to be Olivier, and was James Tyrone, creating a foundation from which – keeping pace with Mr. Blakemore's production – he might unleash the thunderbolts of the last act. I was, I own, ready for the famous howls, but I did not expect to be so moved; not only by the pyrotechnics, but by the stubborn despair of his "I'm not complaining, Mary." At one point, Olivier quoted from

The Tempest, and both he and we wondered whether it was James Tyrone or Olivier who was playing Shakespeare at that instant.[28]

There were the characteristic Olivier tricks in the performance, particularly the acrobatics of his descent from the table, that were mentioned in nearly every review, and that were a source of glee for the 64-year-old actor. But as Irving Wardle noted, what was most evident in this performance was "its breadth: all the components are there all the time – the tightwad, the old pro, the distracted husband, the ragged Irish boy – and there not only in the sense that O'Neill is presenting the character, but that Olivier is exploiting them for the character's advantage."[29] Helen Dawson concurred: "what is remarkable about his Tyrone is its totality: the bullish selfishness; the flashes of Irish flair; the moments of tenderness; and then despair, setting hard across his shoulders . . . It's a performance of immaculate detail, and the magnificent drunken spree in the last act . . . is delivered with breathtaking range, his whole body echoing the strain of the confession."[30]

Perhaps surprisingly, this production was by no means seen as a star turn for Olivier, but as a fine instance of ensemble playing, and there was praise for all the actors, including Jo Maxwell-Muller, whose portrayal of the maid was "perfectly in accord with the drama."[31] For many, "in the company of Olivier, the big surprise is Constance Cummings, who undergoes the transformation from the gentle maternal presence of the opening to the spectral morphine addict of the last act with an authority and spiritual intensity that thoroughly earns the part its central position."[32] Dawson agreed that Cummings' performance was "the revelation of the evening":

> Avoiding histrionics, the performance is most delicately paced. She begins the day very gently, a natural radiance almost within grasping distance, allowing her panic to show itself only in small ways, and then slowly bares the darkness beneath as she drums her crippled fingers on the table, chokes off the intimacy she needs, smiles vacantly as she rambles back into the comforting fog of the past, until she has retreated

beyond all help. The final image of a mad, girlish ghost is surely as haunting as O'Neill intended.[33]

As for the sons, Ronald Pickup was praised for avoiding the pitfall of self-pity and for his "restrained, but dramatic reaction"[34] as Edmund listens to the modified monologues of James and Jamie in Act 4, one of the crucial qualities in the performance of any actor who plays Edmund. Barnes praised his quality of "fiery listlessness (strange mixture of despair and passion)" and Denis Quilley's "boozily affable Jamie, with eroded good looks and a convivial charm that seems to exude an inner insecurity."[35] The believable rapport that Pickup and Quilley established between Edmund and Jamie also helped to make Quilley's confession particularly devastating. Filmed for ITV in 1973, a version that is discussed in Chapter Four, and shown in both Britain and North America, this production became a benchmark for future productions, and critics have mentioned Olivier's as the definitive portrayal of James Tyrone nearly as often as they have March's.

The most common adjective that was used to describe the several major productions that were mounted in Britain toward the end of the twentieth century was "suburban." The 1984 production by the young Ludovica Villar-Hauser at the Arts Theatre in London, with Trevor Martin and Darlene Johnson, was careful and respectful, noted for its creation of "a convincing family feeling amidst the bristling, snarling and occasional savaging of the eternally interlocked foursome."[36] Of the production at the Royal Exchange, Manchester the following year, directed by Braham Murray, one critic confessed tellingly: "I was simply not engaged in this rather seedily suburban and excessively verbose family and their sordid problems."[37] In 1996, a kindlier, gentler *Long Day's Journey* was presented by Theatre Royal Plymouth under the "revisionist" direction of Laurence Boswell. Here, where the theme of "understanding for all the four haunted Tyrones" was stressed, Richard Johnson played James as a father whose "relationship with each of the others" showed "both inherent tension and a wisdom which allows him continually to refrain – at exactly the right moment – from causing further hurt."[38]

The most important production of this period was a revival in May 1991 at the National's Lyttelton Theatre directed by Howard Davies, with Timothy West and Prunella Scales, described as an earthy couple "slugging it out suburbanly in John Gunter's mist-laden summerhouse, beneath an attic of tangled furniture."[39] Another critic remarked that "the Wests remain as a husband-and-wife couple resolutely low-key, rather as if 'Macbeth' were to star the Macduffs."[40] The most interesting aspect of this interpretation was the resultant emergence of the sons as the focal point in the production. One critic remarked that they filled "the parental void with raw performances of superlative theatricality."[41] *Variety* noted that "the two failure sons emerge even more dramatically as the most pitiable wrecks in a family of victims." This production, by no means an unqualified success, did demonstrate the significance of the sons in the play's architectonics, and showed that a tipping of the balance in one way or another makes an important difference in our understanding of it.

Dublin, 1959

The first production of *Long Day's Journey* in Ireland took place on 28 April 1959 at the Queen's Theatre, under the auspices of Ireland's de facto national theatre, the Abbey. The four-and-a-half-hour production began at 6:30 p.m. so that, with two twelve-minute intervals, it would finish at 11:00 p.m., in time for its audiences to take some well-earned sustenance at a nearby pub. It was a doubly significant event for the Abbey, a reassertion of its serious purpose at a time when its repertory was dominated by "peasant comedies" of rural Irish life and a chance to assert the Irishness of Eugene O'Neill's vision. According to Vincent Dowling, who played Edmund, this production and its revival in 1962 "had a profound effect on those in it . . . many of the Abbey company, the media, the academics, other artists, and a significant public. A significant number of us changed utterly. Not only did Frank Dermody's direction and production set a new standard for Ireland of the time, the oneness felt with Eugene O'Neill, an international theatrical giant, re-awakened Abbey artists and audience to their participation in world theatre."[42] One critic explained the Irish interpretation of the play: "O'Neill's characters differ from their Nordic and Slav counterparts in that they have the double vision – they live in a world of fantasy, but they know that they live in it, and can analyse their reasons for doing so . . . Their sons are imprisoned in the fantastic bondage of the imagination bequeathed by their parents."[43]

The production was an overwhelming success. Despite its length, the audience attended to the play "with an intense interest." And "when the final curtain fell there was let loose an enthusiasm the Abbey has not experienced in recent years."[44] The focal point of the production, done in the starkly naturalistic style for which the Abbey is famous, was the performance of Ria Mooney as Mary. Her performance showed that the mother country of both the O'Neills and the Tyrones understood well the centrality of the mother to this Irish-American family. Mooney played Mary's drifting away from the men effectively at two levels. Within the realistic aesthetic of the production, she gave "a magnificent performance, vividly tracing the retreat from reality to a dream-world, and the final climax of suffering."[45] As an enactment of the Irish double vision, she gave a "flawless representation of the tortured mentality of the addict, the unassailable dignity of the dreamer, which seems exactly what O'Neill was seeking for in the part."[46]

After the productions in 1959 and 1962, *Long Day's Journey* became a standard play in the Irish repertoire. It was produced in Belfast, Northern Ireland in 1965 and again at the Abbey in 1967, following a tour of the cities and towns in the West and North of Ireland. In 1985, Ireland's most distinguished actress, Siobhan McKenna, appeared as Mary in a production at the Abbey directed by Patrick Laffan. It was revived in 1998 at Dublin's Gate Theatre, with Donald Moffat as James and Rosaleen Linehan as Mary. While each of these productions was recognized as a powerful interpretation, Dermody's production remained the standard to be met in Ireland.

AUSTRALIA

Adelaide; Melbourne, 1973

The most significant Australian productions of *Long Day's Journey* have originated in Adelaide. In 1959, the Elizabethan Theatre Trust presented the Australian premiere at the University Theatre there, later transferring the production to Sydney. Dinah Shearing was a memorable Mary and veteran Frank Waters played James in the production directed by Robin Lovejoy. The most significant production, however, was the South Australia Theatre Company's 1973 production directed by Rodney Fisher, which originated in Adelaide and transferred to Melbourne for three weeks beginning on 14 November.

In 1973, the Australian critics were by no means ready to accord O'Neill's last play the status of a classic. Gerald Mayhead referred to *Long Day's Journey* as a "wildly self-indulgent, libellously warped biography of his family," and suggested that the whole final act should be cut because, "while offering the mother a worthwhile scene, [it] is, every line of it, secondary, and would not be missed."[47] In the opinion of most critics, however, the production's powerful acting and effective staging made up for the play's length and repetitions. So effective was her portrayal of Mary, Patricia Kennedy was in danger of "taking over the stage while the men revolve around her," according to one critic, if it were not for Rodney Fisher's direction, which maintained "a careful balance, shifting emphasis from one to the other and bringing out their relations in counterpoint."[48] Kennedy's was deemed the best female performance on the

Melbourne stage that year. As one critic said: "The other family parts are marathon talking roles, but hers is the one that takes the meaning from them and transmits it in terms of suffering . . . O'Neill, through Patricia Kennedy, is a powerful claimant for the mind."[49] The response to the other actors was not universally positive. While Neil Fitzpatrick was praised for creating "with painfully observed detail, the decadence of the elder son," Brian James was criticized for underplaying James, and allowing "a husband's compassion to undermine his role's theatrical magnificence."[50]

Largely because of Patricia Kennedy's performance, the 1973 *Long Day's Journey* is generally considered one of the landmark productions in the Australian theatre. It has since become part of the repertoire, with notable productions in 1979 by the Sydney Theatre Company, with Patricia Conolly, who had played Cathleen in the premiere, as Mary, and in 1982 by the Playbox Theatre Company in Melbourne. In the Northside Theatre Company's 1987 production in Sydney, Ron Haddrick won a Sydney Critics' Circle Award for his portrayal of James and Dinah Shearing, who had played Mary in the Australian premiere in 1959, repeated the role opposite him.

NORTH AMERICA

Montreal, 1959

The Canadian premiere of *Long Day's Journey* was the enthusiastic project of Rupert Caplan, a well-known stage and radio producer, as well as the director of all the English-language plays at Montreal's Le Théâtre du Nouveau-Monde. Caplan had known O'Neill during the Provincetown Players days, and had directed a number of his plays for stage and radio. Determined to get the Canadian rights, Caplan went directly to the source. He had won the goodwill of Carlotta O'Neill with the tape of an impressive CBC radio tribute he had done following Eugene's death in 1953. Besides being a personal triumph for Caplan, the Montreal production, which opened at the Orpheum Theatre under the auspices of Le Théâtre du Nouveau-Monde on 9 March 1959, was recognized as "the most important single event in Montreal theatrical history."[51] The reason was partly the much advertized fact that this was "the first, and so far, only production of the play on this continent outside New York."[52] Another important factor was that Caplan's securing the rights was seen as a "victory in the long slow process of separating Canadian stage rights from American rights."[53] This major production of what was already being recognized as O'Neill's greatest play was an important step in Canada's artistic emancipation from the US and a source of great pride, not only to the artistic community, but to Canadians in general.

In keeping with Carlotta's wishes, Caplan originally planned a four-hour production of a "full, uncut" version.[54] "There will be no cuts in this autobiographical work," he said. "My version will be faithful to the text. I visualize it as a string quartet."[55] Caplan tended to stress tragedy rather than realism in his approach to the play: "I am not directing it as a dramatized documentary – but as a significant, lasting work, which will take its place as a monument to the memory of America's greatest playwright," he said. "The play is a sort of catharsis, an outpouring of O'Neill's inner self, and explains the man and his work."[56] Caplan also made it clear that he hoped to bring out the "subtle, humorous elements that give it wholeness" in his production.[57] In the end, the script was cut, with the playing time coming in at three-and-a-half-hours, but Caplan succeeded in conveying his interpretation.

The cast included Mildred Dunnock, who finally had the chance to play Mary three years after her original negotiations for the Broadway rights had broken down, Ian Keith as James, and three Canadians in the supporting roles: Michael Kane as Jamie, Roland Hewgill as Edmund, and Eileen Clifford as Cathleen. Dunnock's performance placed Mary at the center of the play, and emphasized the tragedy of her experience. At least one critic asserted proudly that her playing of the final scene surpassed that of Florence Eldridge.[58] According to him, the extraordinary intensity of her eyes and the simplicity of her pathos moved the audience to tears when she contemplated the past. The audience watched as "little by little the vital substance of her being was played out and she gave way to the implacable play of the blind forces" that overwhelmed her.[59] Keith was an able James Tyrone, and Michael Kane was praised for the power of his confessional scene. Roland Hewgill gave a particularly strong performance as Edmund. Robert Prévost's set was a suitable psychic landscape for the tragedy enacted within it, "without hospitality, mean, moldy, ruined."[60] As Caplan had hoped, the production was truly a landmark, and an important moment in the coming-of-age of the Canadian theatre.

Promenade Theatre, New York, 1971

The production that premiered at the Off-Broadway Promenade Theatre on 22 April 1971 was the first revival of *Long Day's Journey* in New York since the original production in 1956. It was inevitable that this production be compared with the first, which, after fifteen years, was still a vivid memory for audiences and critics who had seen it. This was only the third New York production for the play's young director Arvin Brown, the artistic director of the Long Wharf Theatre in New Haven where he had staged *Long Day's Journey* in 1966. Aware of the inevitability of comparison, Brown and his cast were somewhat aggressive in presenting the differences between their interpretation of the play and that of Quintero and company. Brown said in an interview that, although James is usually seen as "the aggressor" in the play, his interpretation would present Mary as the aggressor and James as the victim, the one trying to "keep things together" in the family. He also said that he saw the play as a "love story," one that is "painful, difficult, neurotic, not detached or cool." Brown acknowledged that he expected this approach to be controversial, because it was not as "pretty" or as "comfortable" as the audience wanted it to be.[61] Geraldine Fitzgerald credited Brown with giving her the courage to essay a new conception of Mary's character.[62]

Brown called this a "relatively harsh" portrait of Mary: "She does feel anger, hate, and she does lash out."[63] Brown saw the play as growing out of neurosis. Explaining the character with reference to Eugene O'Neill's mother Ella, he said that Mary was not a controlled or cold person, but one who imposed "the façade of aloofness – the 'perfect lady' – over a basically emotional nature. In the play we see it breaking down."[64] Fitzgerald went further along this line. She said that she had had a great deal of difficulty in finding an "active verb" on which to base Mary's character, moving from "escape" to "protection" to "mothering," or playing at mothering, like Wendy in *Peter Pan*. What she finally found in the character was that Mary was not trying to escape *from* something so much as going *toward* something – a place where her son could not be in danger – in other words, a reality of her own creating. Fitzgerald saw Mary's drug use as working in the service of her psychosis. She said that Mary tries at first to save Edmund by keeping him out of the hands of Dr. Hardy, but when she fails, she takes "too many drugs" to try to kill herself and "get out of the world forever," to go back into the past, to "unbear" her son so that he will never be born and become sick.[65] Although her character is driven, in a sense, by her feeling for Edmund, Fitzgerald insisted that Mary is not "maternal" in the normal sense:

> She is forever complaining about the home that her husband didn't provide, but traditionally – *certainly* in her day, in 1912 – it was up to the mother to be the homemaker. Mary is not a victim; she's spoiled, sharp-tongued, she has refused to mature, has turned her husband into her father, and that's been a *large* part of their problem. At the same time, she's tough – hard. She has a sly gallows humor.[66]

This is a long way from the fragile bewilderment of Florence Eldridge. Arvin Brown said that he had cast Fitzgerald in part because of her qualities of strength, forcefulness, and earthiness.[67] These qualities defined her Mary.

As Eldridge had, Fitzgerald consulted doctors about the effects of morphine on addicts, and found an approach that she could use:

> Mary gets what's called the "cat reaction" to the drug. She gets more and more excited, not depressed, and I use that. And I thought about how easily she gives herself the needle, another key to her toughness. She says to her husband, quite boldly, "You can come upstairs and watch me, if you like! In other words, I face what I am, I can handle it . . . I'm all right, Jack, don't you know?"[68]

Fitzgerald spoke of Mary's speech at the end of the play, as "a song of joy. I am released! And I'm not without some hope . . . Mary's no loser, she only has the look of one."[69] Fitzgerald emphasized that Ella O'Neill had indeed freed herself from drug addiction eventually.

This approach to Mary necessarily altered the approach to James as well. Brown said that he had cast Robert Ryan partly because of his qualities of warmth, gentleness, and innocence. He spoke of him as a "soft man" and a "just man."[70] In fact the difference between Robert Ryan's approach to James and Fredric March's was even greater than that between Eldridge's and Fitzgerald's. In 1971, Ryan was a Hollywood star of the strong, silent type, known for his rugged good looks and his portrayals of cowboys and villains. His style of acting was understated, his voice flat and Midwestern. As an actor, his style could not have been further from that of the melodramatic matinee idol James O'Neill. What is more, unlike Fredric March, he chose not to "bring the actor home." He approached James as an Irish-American husband and father rather than as a matinee idol. He told an interviewer that James "was trying to be a good father" and that "he wasn't a chaser – and that's unusual in this profession where men are constantly being thrown together with attractive women – but he was aware that he had failed his family in many ways and he felt guilt because of it."[71]

Ryan's approach to James was controversial, with several critics complaining that the quiet-spoken and gentle figure he created was not believable as the old-time actor. T. E. Kalem said that, because Ryan "never quite suggests the commanding matinee-idol presence

6   Robert Ryan and Geraldine Fitzgerald

that Fredric March brought to the role," the production shifted the emphasis of the play from James to Mary, and "the change somewhat distorts O'Neill's intent."[72] Martin Gottfried thought Ryan had been "disastrously cast" in the role.[73]

Clive Barnes and Walter Kerr rose to Ryan's defense, praising his understated, realistic James. Kerr wrote that, in the final act, "as Robert Ryan digs his heels into the floor to resist the fury that is coming from his tubercular youngest son . . . the spleen of the play and the rotted affection of the play leap together to make a blaze like the points of an arc lamp fusing":

> He hears, he understands, he keeps what temper he can, he sets his teeth. He surrenders nothing, not even his stubborn, fatuous certainty that Shakespeare was an Irish Catholic . . . He silences the boy by the steel in his eyes and the sores on his soul he is perfectly ready to expose. His very candor is kindness; he disembowels himself to show that he was made of good stuff . . . In his cups, he has a grip on his psyche that no one can dislodge. He is character locked into itself, aware, obtuse, knowing and unalterable. The portrait, in its all-of-a-piece complexity, is beautifully composed, and Mr. Ryan explores the mea culpa in which no forgiveness is asked with admirable, leather-tough control.[74]

Fortunately, a video record of the production exists, albeit in rather primitive black-and-white form, at the New York Public Library for the Performing Arts. I think it validates Kerr's assessment. Ryan's James is the right match for Fitzgerald's down-to-earth, pragmatic Mary, and his performance realizes Arvin Brown's approach to the production.

Brown, who felt that "the greatness of the play is the photographic ability, both inner and outer, with which O'Neill was able to capture the reality of the family," played two subtexts based on the family. On the one hand, he tried at an "organic level" to bring out the "cathartic blood-letting" – violence, destruction of others, and self-destruction – that he thought an undercurrent of even the happiest family. On the other, he felt that there is something "relatively pleasant" in the everyday life of the Tyrones that keeps the "boys" returning as adults and keeps them together as a family.[75] He also chose to "emphasize whatever humor there is in the play. There is very little, and most of it is ironic humor, but it does add some levity which is sorely needed,"[76] he told an interviewer. His approach led to a light and humorous first act, in which the Tyrones interacted warmly as a family, with only an occasional hint of the dark depths below the surface.

The reaction to Brown's overall direction was mixed. Both the director and the designers, Elmon Webb and Virginia Dancy, were hampered by the small stage at the Promenade. The decision to build a rather elaborate set, with a staircase upstage, restricted the playing space even further, so that the action had to take place downstage, on a narrow, horizontal plane. The movement – and Brown kept the actors, particularly Geraldine Fitzgerald, in motion – was necessarily from side to side in the room, which gave the effect of actors constantly playing out front to the audience, rather than within the scene. Brown also had trouble finding the arc of the play. As Clurman wrote, it was missing "a grand design wrought of deep inner characterizations and understanding of the play's basic mood – its tragic essence."[77] There was praise, however, for Brown's "quiet-ness," which "lets the play speak in its clarity and relentless crescendo of power."[78]

In general, this first New York production after the premiere succeeded at its announced goal of realizing a new interpretation of the play and its lead characters. Quieter, less histrionic, and more intensely psychological than Quintero's production, Brown's invited the audience to see the Tyrones as a not-so-exceptionally dysfunc-tional American family. Fitzgerald's Mary was a smart, pragmatic woman who was immature and narcissistic, but also complex and likeable. She knows she is addicted and pursues her avenue of relief despite her husband and sons. Ryan's James was played against the tempting rhetorical display of O'Neill's lines as a repressed and dignified man, defensive and perplexed by his failures in the face of so much success, and trying to keep his family together. Although the production offered nothing that was fundamentally new in its approach to Jamie and Edmund, Stacy Keach and James Naughton were almost universally praised for their acting. Naughton, in his first New York appearance, was particularly praised for his fine delivery of the poetry in the fourth act, although, like Bradford Dillman's, his delivery of Edmund's difficult modified monologue came off as somewhat artificial. The designers were not able to rise imaginatively above the limitations of their cramped Off-Broadway stage, but Brown had the good sense to depend mainly on the skills of these four fine actors to realize O'Neill's work.

Washington, D. C.; Brooklyn, 1975

During the 1960s and early 70s, a number of regional productions of *Long Day's Journey* were mounted, often essayed as proof that a theatre was capable of a first-rate production of O'Neill's difficult masterpiece. In 1963, Nina Vance produced it as the inaugural offering in a major fund-raising season at the Alley Theater in Houston, the goal of which was to build a new state-of-the-art theatre. Her strategy worked. "If there are any doubts about the right of the Alley Theater to think of expansion, the current production of 'Long Day's Journey Into Night' should help to dispel them," said the *New York Times*.[79] In 1971, Helen Hayes played Mary in a "guest appearance" at the new Hartke Theater in Washington, D. C. In the same year, Teresa Wright played a "wraithlike and lost"[80] Mary opposite Robert Pastene at the newly emerging Hartford Stage. Washington's Arena Theatre had a particular desire to create a successful production, staging the play in 1962 with Michael Higgins and Dorothea Hammond and in October of 1975 with James Broderick and Leora Dane. The latter was well respected and highly praised, nearly upstaging the Kennedy Center's Bicentennial production, which took place in December.

The Kennedy Center production had the added hook of Jason Robards playing James Tyrone, nineteen years after he had originated the role of Jamie. The production, which moved on to the Brooklyn Academy of Music from the Kennedy Center, was also Robards' debut as a director, and the double assignment proved to be too much for him. In a pre-opening interview, he told Mel Gussow, "I've had a terrible time getting into the old man because I'm 'the one,' the director. I have to get into all the characters' problems. I have to split myself."[81] His approach to directing was modeled on José Quintero's "air of informality and intimacy . . . There's no big hammering authority around here . . . We share a lot. No one says, 'You do this or that.' "[82] Unfortunately Robards did not have Quintero's gift for integrating four different schools of acting into one production. As one critic put it, "the trouble with the revival is that the four stars, having distinct and impressive acting styles of their own, have not been sufficiently acclimated to the Tyrone household."[83]

After re-examining the script, Robards said, he had decided that it was neither James nor Mary nor Jamie at the core of the drama, but Edmund. "It's about the growth of Edmund – of O'Neill – of his finally cutting the cord away from his mother," he said. "Edmund listens and grows. A tremendous change occurs in him."[84] Michael Moriarty's performance had elements of this interpretation in it. As Watt described it:

> For most of the evening, Michael Moriarty . . . gives the odd impression of playing an adolescent. The thin, clear, high Moriarty voice, underemphasizing his lines, makes of Edmund a greater stranger than O'Neill intended any of these lonely people to be to one another. He gets his laughs this way, but it's not until the game of casino with his father that the character grows up, and then Moriarty rises to the occasion brilliantly. But only to relapse as the magnificent scene begins to taper off, the performance becoming mannered once more.[85]

Most of the critics simply complained that Moriarty seemed remote, isolated, languid, and that his speech was mannered.

As for Robards, he had not completely found his way to James when the show opened. His characteristic high-energy performance was simply not there. One critic complained that he played James as

if he were in a game of statues: "(one move and you're out)" and that
he had reverted to the "staccato vocal mannerisms that marred the
middle of his career," so that "his final soliloquy seems so long he
may be reciting it still."[86] Zoe Caldwell, like Geraldine Fitzgerald,
created a slightly revisionist Mary, which dredged up some of the
darker elements that had been missing in earlier performances. Edith
Oliver called it a "brave and utterly unsparing performance":

> Miss Caldwell is not the fragile-looking Mary we have become used to;
> she looks sturdy and healthy, and her white hair is thick. All the sickness
> and bitterness are inside, and the acid seeps out in the same sweet tones
> as endearments; her very pronunciation of the recurring words "dear"
> and "home," all but takes the skin off her husband and sons . . . yet she
> retains enough vestiges of sanity and charm to justify her family's love
> for her.[87]

In short, there was a great deal of substance in the performances, but
the problem was integration. As Michael Feingold put it, Robards
and his co-workers "make a row of interesting actors, not a family
inextricably bound to one another."[88]

One of the exacerbating factors of the production was Ben
Edwards' set. His minimally furnished living room was pulled deeply
in behind the proscenium arch. Side panels cut down the proscenium
opening to make the set look even boxier and created a wide stage
apron that became "a dark gulf between the actors and an already
distant audience."[89] As Feingold noted, "of all plays that need to be
shared closely with the onlookers this is surely the unwisest on which
to try such distancing effects,"[90] an opinion that certainly held for
this production, at least. With Robards' rather static direction
keeping the actors within the exaggerated box set, the audience's
natural point of view was distant and judgmental. When the
production was moved to the Brooklyn Academy of Music, it was
originally planned for the intimate Playhouse Theatre, which might
have made a difference. The set was so large, however, that it had to
be moved to the huge Opera House at the Academy, which had the
same distancing effect as the Kennedy Center staging. Overall,

7   Michael Moriarty, Zoe Caldwell, and Jason Robards.

probably because of directorial inexperience, what could have been an interesting reinterpretation of the play for the mid-1970s simply failed to come off.

As the twentieth century progressed, Mary and James Tyrone became established as roles that climaxed a distinguished acting career. Regional theatres have had little trouble finding well-known actors who wanted to play the parts, sometimes for validation of their claims to be serious actors and not just stars. A good example of this was the 1977 production at the Ahmanson Theatre in Los Angeles with Charlton Heston and Deborah Kerr, directed by Peter Wood. While Kerr turned in a credible performance, Heston was clearly not up to the role, and his rather wooden acting was panned by the critics. In 1980, the Stratford Shakespeare Festival in Ontario produced a version with Jessica Tandy and William Hutt as Mary and James, Graeme Campbell and Brent Carver as the sons. Director Robin Phillips, who had just resigned as the Stratford's artistic director, was perhaps particularly distracted by the Stratford's chronic managerial feuding at that point. In any case, the performances showed that his direction was not as controlled as it might have been. Brent Carver overdid his drunken lurching, and Jessica Tandy, playing a little too much of the Blanche Dubois in Mary, exaggerated her frailty in the early scenes and pushed the production "dangerously close to melodrama."[91] It was a lost opportunity. With this very talented cast, it could have been a much better production.

Another proof of the play's classic status in 1980 was its use in the Wooster Group's *Point Judith*, the "Epilogue" to its Rhode Island trilogy, which is based on the life of actor and writer Spalding Gray. The Wooster Group works collaboratively to develop multi-media theatre pieces that make use of cultural sources whose texts and images are quoted, reworked, layered, and juxtaposed against each other. Directed by Elizabeth LeCompte, *Point Judith* is an exploration of contemporary notions of masculinity. *Long Day's Journey* forms the text for Part II, *Stew's Party Piece*, which features snatches of recorded dialogue coming over a loudspeaker while the performers huddle in a strange little house, sometimes miming, sometimes shouting their lines through megaphones. Spalding Gray called it "a household prop ballet to Berlioz' 'Roman Carnival.'"[92] As Tyrone, Gray played three levels of reality, sometimes observing the action, sometimes directing it, and sometimes participating in it. Mary Tyrone was played by Willem Dafoe in drag, and she was shadowed by 12-year-old Matthew Hansell playing "Boy in Blue Dress," who represented a youthful Mary. Ron Vawter played Jamie, and Edmund was played by the 12-year-old Michael Rivkin. David Savran suggests the import of the piece in commenting that "although none of the characters is liberated in the course of *Long Day's Journey* including O'Neill's surrogate, Edmund, the play is clearly intended to attest to the playwright's deliverance. As the Wooster Group deconstructs the play, it examines the quality of that deliverance by questioning its definition of sex roles."[93]

Richard Allen Center, New York, 1981

One of the most important productions of this period was directed by Geraldine Fitzgerald under the auspices of The Richard Allen Center, a producing organization for African-American performing artists founded in 1968 by Hazel J. Bryant. The production was originally staged at the Theatre at St. Peter's Church on 3 March 1981, but was moved to the Public Theatre two weeks later, where it had a run of 87 performances. The powerful cast included Gloria Foster, Earle Hyman, Al Freeman, Jr., Peter Francis-James, and Samantha McKoy. This all African-American casting of the great Irish-American play was inevitably controversial in 1981, and an effort was made to explain the artists' treatment of ethnicity for the public. In an interview, Earle Hyman denied that ethnicity played any role in the production:

> The fact that the cast is black is other people's problem, not mine. Let's face it. The play has a universal theme. It's a picture of the human condition: we love each other, yet we hurt each other. We say we're sorry and then go on hurting each other forever and ever . . . With any three-dimensional part, the Irishness or blackness is only on the surface. The rest is internal. Otherwise, you have an ethnic play, which this is not.[94]

For Hyman, the fact that he and O'Neill were both Libras was more significant than their ethnic differences, and he noted that the affinities he felt with O'Neill were crucial: "his love for his work, a touch of mysticism, the extraordinary closeness of his family, a bit of self-destructiveness."[95]

Although hyper-aware of the actors' ethnicity, most audiences and critics granted the artists their *donnée*, as Henry James would say, and evaluated the production on its own terms. In the *New York Times*, Mel Gussow wrote that "the actors do not try to overlay an interpretation. They approach the material from a position of non-ethnicity, ignoring their own racial background just as they overlook the family's Irishness. The characters are not specifically the O'Neills of New London but the archetypal Tyrones of the play, a tragic community of warring temperaments."[96] Embracing the theory of universality, Clive Barnes wrote that "the color of Tyrone's family that fateful Connecticut day in August, 1912, is no more the issue of the play than were the unashamed English accents of two of the most celebrated interpreters of Tyrone – Ralph Richardson and Laurence Olivier."[97]

Not everyone accepted this approach, however. At one extreme was John Simon who flatly stated that the production turned *Long Day's Journey* into a "mirthless farce" because "Black actors do not begin to convey the bio- and autobiographical elements that are not unimportant to O'Neill's play, and their blackness runs counter to much of what is explicitly stated even in this trimmed version." The racism in his description of Hyman's acting was not even below the surface: "Hyman slithers, slouches, sashays about, and spouts his lines in untenable tempos and in gushes of chaotic sound uncivilized by consonants."[98] A more thoughtful consideration of the issue of ethnicity in the play was offered by Christopher Sharp, who thought that the up-tempo first act did not go well, and suggested that its problems "might be related to the transition to the problems of a black family. In traditional productions of this show we are reminded that O'Neill's family was not only in the acting profession, they were also Irish-American, with an ethnic instinct for what makes good drama." The significance of this ethnicity to the play, he suggested, was that "we can assume that even at the height of their tears, their histrionics and their cries of torment they were taking some pleasure in the great theatre they created. In this revival of O'Neill's autobiographical play, a lot of that pleasure is omitted, and tormented lines are accompanied by tormented thoughts."[99] While the issues surrounding questions of ethnicity were by no means resolved, the clear and outspoken stance taken by the artists and the effectiveness of the production contributed to the current freedom to cast actors in roles regardless of ethnicity.

8   Gloria Foster and Samantha McKoy

Fitzgerald's direction was controversial for other reasons than ethnicity. Her version of the play ran for just two hours and forty-five minutes, one of the shortest on record. This was partly due to the breezy tempo she maintained in the first act, but there was also a significant amount of cutting. On the whole, the success of Fitzgerald's lively version, with its fast-talking Tyrones and its stressing of the first-act humor, showed that her new interpretation of the play was a viable one, and it prepared the way for other departures from the José Quintero interpretation such as Jonathan Miller's more radical speeding-up a few years later.

Gloria Foster's interpretation of Mary was the third controversial element of this production. In casting an actress whose previous roles included Clytemnestra, Medea, Volumnia, and Mother Courage, Fitzgerald was envisioning a Mary who belonged in the company of strong, classical heroines rather than a frail, wraithlike victim. Foster's Mary was not a lost, bewildered soul, but a strong woman who undergoes a tragic fall from grace. For the most part, audiences and critics showed admiration for this classically conceived characterization, but others found it wrong for the play, particularly in the context of Fitzgerald's otherwise rather homely and warm conception of the Tyrone family. According to Gussow:

> Gloria Foster, who is imposing in classical tragedy, lacks the fragility of Mary Tyrone. We do not believe that she is retreating to anesthetize herself with drugs. When she glances out of the window and comments, "How thick the fog is," she makes a simple statement sound as if it were a weather report delivered by Lady Macbeth. Hearing her misreading, we remember the full wistfulness of the line as delivered by her illustrious predecessors in the role, including Miss Fitzgerald in the 1971 Off Broadway production.[100]

Of the men, Al Freeman, Jr. received the highest accolades, one critic saying that he "practically tears the stage apart with his galumphingly irresponsible Jamie, in the most memorably energetic performance I've seen for quite a while."[101] Another suggested that his was one of the "best drunk acts that has been seen in the theatre in a long time. We finally learn there is some charm to this character, and yet he hasn't found a way to reveal this charm without drinking."[102] Earle Hyman played James Tyrone as a dignified and cultivated gentleman, gentle and vulnerable, a suitable consort for Foster's Mary, but not forceful enough to suit some conceptions of the role.

The Richard Allen Center's production paved the way for other ethnic theatre groups, notably the National Asian American Theatre Company (NATCO), to produce the play without having to make an issue of ethnicity. In 1997, NATCO, which "presents western classics without forced Asian cultural association,"[103] produced *Long Day's Journey* at The Mint Space in New York, directed by Stephen Stout, with Ernest Abuba as James, Mia Katigbak as Mary, Paul Nakauchi as Jamie, Andrew Pang as Edmund, and Jody Lin as Cathleen. Unlike Fitzgerald, who simply erased the ethnic references from the dialogue, Stout did not delete or de-emphasize the Tyrones' Irishness, and even had Abuba and Lin speak with a brogue. The only ethnic reference that was cut was James's remark that Jamie has the "map of Ireland" on his face, one that would foreground the ethnic difference between character and actor. The audience had no trouble accepting this version of the Tyrone family and took its Irishness for granted.

Broadhurst, New York, 1986

Jonathan Miller was already a controversial figure in the theatre when he took on the directing assignment for *Long Day's Journey*, best known in the US for the six plays he directed for the BBC Shakespeare series and his television series on the history of medicine, *The Body in Question*. In 1986 he had not directed a straight play in the theatre for a number of years, preferring to concentrate on opera. Miller said he had had the idea of directing Jack Lemmon in the play for some time. "I wanted to liven it up a little . . . I thought that someone like Lemmon, who is an unlikely choice in many ways, someone with his pathos and power and tremendous energy, would rescue it from Arlington National Cemetery. It's not all that solemn. It's also funny."[104]

Miller's interpretation stressed the play's realism rather than its tragedy. "The play is about actual life," he said. "By actual I mean not the life of the actual Tyrones but something recognizable, a family speaking fast and bitterly on top of one another, with that volatile iridescence that ordinary conversation has, instead of being a series of set pieces."[105] Miller realized this concept in his controversial approach to the play's dialogue, which he had spoken quickly and overlapped, as if it were real conversation, cutting the production's length from the usual four hours to two hours and forty minutes. It has generally been assumed that a substantial amount of the dialogue was cut in this process, but Miller insisted that only two pages had been cut, mostly from Edmund's recitation of Baudelaire. With his considerable recent experience in opera, Miller directed the dialogue as music rather than as poetry. As he explained:

> One of the most distinctive features of conversation is the fact that there is not a regular, orderly alternation of speaking. It is a layering of talk. Without a reliable notation playwrights have no means of controlling the play, and so it gets pulled out and lengthened. In music there is a very accurate notation to effect simultaneity. A playwright forced to use the traditional notation, finds himself writing in sequence. The actors then take the lay-out on the page as being a representation of what the author intended. We experimented with these conversational modes and found the play automatically assuming this overlapping character.[106]

He said that he rehearsed the dialogue musically, "like a Beethoven quartet." He even invited conductor Zubin Mehta to listen to the dialogue, receiving the reassuring response that it was "like a piece of music – solos, duets and trios."[107] In establishing the dialogue as "a series of competing discourses, rather than as an alternating set of recitations of great verse," he felt that the production had "restored the play to the naturalistic masterpiece that it is."[108]

So complex was the timing that it was decided to do a series of previews at Duke University, performances that were closed to critics so the cast would be completely comfortable when the play opened for its official out-of-town tryout in Washington, D. C. Peter Gallagher, who played Edmund, remembered that the technique "was a little too much at Duke when we first were trying it out. We were so proud of ourselves in doing it that at times – it was not a question of overlapping anymore but of responding when the time was right." He echoed Miller, however, in his contention that "the repetition in the script was so enormous that no information is lost. We found that the information was not that precious. In fact we found it more truthful in a way, for us, just for us, that they weren't listening to each other. Everyone was a little too afraid. What held everyone together was the love, not the bitterness and the hatred."[109]

The response to the production tended to depend on how familiar the auditor was with the play. Several critics who seemed to be seeing it for the first time found it frustrating to have to choose one character to listen to, and to be missing a number of the lines. More significant was the objection that the play's meaning was being obscured, as when Mary's crucial "None of us can help the things life has done to us" speech was delivered as just another part of her "continuous, disregarded gabble."[110] On the other hand, Jack Kroll's point of view is representative of the old hands who were familiar with the play and its tradition of production. "Miller's daring and difficult idea, executed by a fine cast, blows the museum dust away and taps into the energy of the play," he wrote. "Never before has the bickering, savaging Tyrone family seemed so much like one flesh, one nervous system. They don't make speeches, but feint, collide and ricochet like the veteran antagonists they are. Their love and hatred for each other seem to explode in the same instant."[111]

Miller's determination to keep the play within the realistic realm also extended to the characters. Calling on his knowledge as a physician, he advised Peter Gallagher on the realistic portrayal of tuberculosis and developed a pathology for James as well, coaching Jack Lemmon on the indication of a pain in his stomach that foreshadowed James O'Neill's fatal cancer.[112] His advice to Bethel Leslie on portraying Mary's drug addiction was in keeping with their overall development of the character. "People expect an addict to be spacey," he said, "but actually Mary's drifting in and out of reality is terrifyingly real to her."[113] There was no "saintliness" in her character, he said: "She's a flinty lower-middle-class Midwestern Irish Catholic girl . . . I've seen hundreds of them; it's the lace curtain."[114]

It was inevitable that Jack Lemmon portray James as a "regular guy," since nothing in his style or his gifts as an actor would suggest an interpretation in the grand manner. Aware of his "Everyman reputation," Lemmon said that "it may be difficult to get people to accept me as Tyrone. I think a lot of people don't. But I was surprised that a few people early on said, 'Gee, that's the first time I liked the old man.'"[115] Lemmon regarded Tyrone as "a decent man with some indecent traits, a faded dandy aware of his self-delusions, a man as much victim as victimizer."[116] Characteristically, his performance

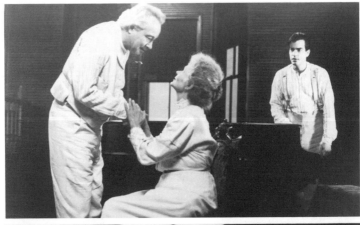

9   Above, Jack Lemmon, Bethel Leslie, and Peter Gallagher. Below, Leslie and Lemmon.

was carefully built on details of business and gesture. A defining piece of business for the character was his combing his hair at strategic times, pointing up his somewhat pathetic vanity as well as his need to put on the best face even before his family. His was a life-size, rather than a larger-than-life Tyrone, and his performance was often compared to Dustin Hoffman's as Willy Loman two years earlier. Both the strengths and the weaknesses of his approach were reflected in the reviews. Jack Tinker wrote pithily that "Mr. Lemmon brings to the miserly patriarch, complete with all the small actorly vanities of a former matinee idol, that special tragi-comic chemistry of frailty and arrogance at which he so excels."[117] Clive Barnes, who considered this a "landmark production" of *Long Day's Journey*, wrote:

> Last, and always, there is Lemmon wandering, eyeless in Gaza, through the play as James Tyrone – lost, betrayed by his past, a loving man who finds himself killing everything he loves.
>
> The miasmic pain of Lemmon, the walk, the eyes, the voice! Especially that voice, from its jocular nervous opening to the night's final long cry – that tortured gurgle from the throat is the most terrible noise to echo in our playhouses since Olivier's 40-year-old primal cry of guilt in Sophocles' *Oedipus Rex*.[118]

On the other hand, Frank Rich complained that "this star still can't quite bring himself to let an audience hate him, however transitorily."[119] Other critics, like Richard Hornby, were irritated by the inescapable Lemmon manner: "Lemmon filled the performance with all the naturalistic mannerisms that he has come to use on the screen, the twitches and graces and added noises, especially that quick little 'ho-ho-ho' that has become his irritating trademark."[120] Peter Gallagher and Kevin Spacey, playing Jamie in his first major role on Broadway, were praised for their naturalness and for the intimacy and explosiveness they achieved in their Act 4 confrontation.

Tony Straiges' design deliberately copied the furnishings of Monte Cristo Cottage, the unmatched wicker furniture serving his purpose of reflecting the family's "tenuous hold on stability."[121] Emphasizing the isolation of the family and the general undercutting of the grand style that permeated the production, Staiges surrounded the realistic living room with four tall, black areas of wall that loomed constantly over the characters, giving the effect, as Peter Gallagher said, of "being disconnected. I have the feeling that if I get too close to one of those things I'll get sucked into the void. It's tenuous. It's not at all solid."[122] The lighting was harsh and sterile, emphasizing the stark realism of Miller's interpretation.

Despite very favorable reviews overall, the production ran for only two of its planned six months in New York, closing on 29 June. *Variety* noted that this made four consecutive Broadway flops for revivals of Eugene O'Neill dramas.[123] After a short hiatus, the production opened in London on 4 August for a planned two-month run, and then went to Tel Aviv for a 12-performance run. It was filmed for television the following year, a production that is discussed in Chapter Four.

New Haven; New York, 1988

The chance to reverse O'Neill's reputation as box-office poison came two years after the Miller production, during the centennial year of the playwright's birth, with the last two actors to score a Broadway hit in one of his plays, Colleen Dewhurst and Jason Robards, whose *Moon for the Misbegotten* had run for 313 performances in the 1973–74 Season. Robards returned for his second crack at James Tyrone after the unsuccessful 1975 production, and José Quintero returned to direct *Long Day's Journey* for a third time with two of the actors with whom he had worked most closely for thirty years. The production began at Yale Repertory Theatre. In celebration of the centennial, *Long Day's Journey* directed by Quintero, and *Ah, Wilderness!* directed by Arvin Brown, were played in repertory, with Robards and Dewhurst playing the parents in both plays. The productions were brought to New York as part of the First New York International Festival of the Arts, with *Journey* opening on 14 June 1988. The repertory production invited audiences to see the two plays as O'Neill's complementary light and dark representations of the family, the one he yearned for and the one he had. To emphasize the contrast, the same set was used for both productions in New York, Ben Edwards' dark living room, based on Monte Cristo Cottage. For *Long Day's Journey*, it was sparsely furnished with the inevitable wicker and chintz, looking seedy and gloomy. For *Ah, Wilderness!* a more homey atmosphere was created with plants, table shawls, and bric-à-brac.

José Quintero had not approved of the revisionist Jonathan Miller production, and he reestablished what one critic called the "grand agony"[124] of his original direction by recreating its ritual rhythm with this three-and-a-half-hour version. Clive Barnes noted that this was Quintero's third production of the play, and "on each occasion, he seems to have refined the acting, made the play sparser, colder yet more passionate, and heightened its darkening shadows. He now perfectly judges not just the play's momentum, but its moment, that time in the space of feeling of which O'Neill says – echoing – 'the past is the present, it is the future too.'"[125] Nevertheless, Quintero did not neglect the humor in the text, and, particularly in the first act, he achieved a lighter touch than had been evident in the earlier productions, making for a less ponderous, more down-to-earth interpretation of the Tyrones. One critic even referred to the humor as having a "sit-com quality."[126]

Jason Robards was criticized for overdoing the humor in New Haven.[127] By the time the play opened in New York, however, Robards' performance was fully developed, and although a few complained that his gestures and acting tricks were becoming too familiar in O'Neill's plays, most agreed with Douglas Watt that he had finally "grown into the role of the older Tyrone. He has outdone himself with the most rending and majestic account of the much-played part we are ever likely to see."[128]

Quintero's direction was clearly conceptualized around Mary in this production, particularly her relationship with Edmund, who was played by Colleen Dewhurst's own son, Campbell Scott. It was a ready-made opportunity for the Quintero directing techniques, and Dewhurst played the subtle undercurrents of Mary as they had never been played before. Frank Rich called her Mary "extraordinary, almost shockingly unsentimentalized . . . she's a killer, forever twisting the knife in old familial wounds."[129] Another critic called her "poisonous."[130] This was no Lady Macbeth, however. Dewhurst's Mary was a particularly Irish-American mother, combining a rather remote judgmental dignity with a "seductive girlishness."[131]

10   Colleen Dewhurst and Jason Robards

With lines such as Mary's "you didn't *mean* to humiliate me" in response to James's gift of a second-hand Packard at the core of her relationship with her husband, this performance developed the implications of Kenneth Tynan's remark that Mary was on the surface a pathetic victim, but at heart an "emotional vampire."[132] Dewhurst's Mary exhibited a practiced, passive–aggressive emotional manipulation of the men in the family, playing one son against the other and constantly manipulating James's guilt. The real achievement of the performance, however, was in finding the tragic dimension of the "poisonous" Mary. This was most evident when she was left alone in the house, left to contemplate loneliness without the distraction of her men. As Frank Rich put it, "the panic and longing on her pained face seem so lacking in focus that we see the internal chaos that drives her to drugs."[133] This was a pitiless, brutally honest interpretation of Mary, and probably the closest to the character in O'Neill's text that has yet been realized on the stage.

Campbell Scott was completely in sync with Dewhurst, her "born victim," as Rich put it. After "absorbing each shock into his burdened soul until he just can't take it anymore," his "belated, angry lashings out at his mother, brother and father drive the last act."[134] Scott's Edmund seemed the more dominant in the last act because Jamey Sheridan did not achieve the soul-rending emotion during Jamie's confession that actors like Robards and Spacey had in the role. In making Edmund an active agent rather than the passive observer he often becomes, Quintero and Scott changed the dynamics of the last act, focusing it more on the explosive encounter between Edmund and his father than on the confrontation between the brothers. He succeeded in making the production not only a new interpretation of the play but "a genuine tour de force."[135]

Despite the overwhelmingly strong reviews, the production was not a success, closing after just forty-seven performances. *Variety*'s story was entitled "Public Says No, No O'Neill Again; Fifth Straight B. O. Flop on B'way."[136] Although this production proved a *succès d'estime* rather than a box-office success, O'Neill was proving during his centennial year that he was not box-office poison outside New York. An imaginative staging in a circular playing space brought an intriguing physical dimension to *Long Day's Journey* at the Denver Center Theatre.[137] A production directed by Tom Haas at the Indiana Repertory Theater was conceived with passionate enthusiasm, although not too effectively executed.[138] In Syracuse, the production of *Long Day's Journey* by Syracuse Stage was greeted as "a production that will be difficult to surpass this or any season."[139] And Brooklyn audiences were overwhelmingly enthusiastic about the Ingmar Bergman production when it was brought there from Stockholm.

Stratford, Ontario, 1994

Fourteen years after he had played James Tyrone opposite Jessica Tandy in 1980, and thirty-five years after he had played him at the Bristol Old Vic, William Hutt returned to the role at the age of 74 for the Stratford Shakespeare Festival. This time he was playing opposite Martha Henry, whom many critics consider Canada's finest actress, on the occasion of her return to Stratford after a long absence. Directed by Diana Leblanc, with Peter Donaldson playing Jamie and Tom McCamus as Edmund, the production became the benchmark interpretation of *Long Day's Journey* in Canada, and "one of the most remarkable dramatic events in recent memory," according to the *Toronto Star*.[140]

All of the strengths of the artists seemed to come together in this production, which was very much in sync with the culture of the 1990s, with its non-judgmental moral relativism and its preoccupation with the politics of victimhood. David Richards described Leblanc's interpretation of the play: "Yes, the Tyrones are cursed creatures, responsible for the misery that slowly descends over them like a shroud. But they're also not responsible. Each character is somehow both guilty and innocent, victimizer and victim at the same time. Ms. Leblanc refuses to make hard, categorical judgments. Or rather, she manages to find the extenuating circumstances for everybody's failings and to forgive them all for the cruelties they inflict on one another."[141] More than one critic referred to the Tyrones in this production as a "dysfunctional family." Leblanc's was no easy talk-show take on the Tyrone family, however. As Richards noted, hers was a fresh interpretation that brought out "the bewilderment in the anger, the helplessness in the pain, the compassion in the vitriol. Rather than just showing us how the Tyrones are pulling away from one another, she wants to investigate all the humble ways they still come together, or try." As a result, "the warmth of her vision immeasurably humanizes a drama generally mined for its monumental passions."[142]

The Stratford Shakespeare Festival's Tom Patterson Theatre served this vision well. A small, intimate theatre with a runway thrust stage, it placed the audience in intimate contact with the family and enhanced an acting style that eschewed the "grand theatre" aspects of the Tyrones, emphasizing their interaction as human beings. Astrid Janson's staging was a kind of abstract quotation of the traditional *Long Day's Journey* set. It included the usual shabby wicker furniture with its worn, chintz-covered pillows made more gloomy by Louise Guinand's rather dark, moody lighting. In an expressionistic departure from the usually quotidian realism of the design concept, Janson suspended two large sheets of cloth overhead, on which images of lush summer foliage were projected at the beginning of the play, suggesting the determinedly hopeful mood with which the family starts its day. As the day went on, the darkness and the Tyrones' self-created doom engulfed them, the hopeful images were erased, and at the end the hangings became "ghosts keeping watch over a haunted house."[143]

William Hutt used his age in playing the part. At 74, he was believably weary, worn down by his difficult family. Rather than the grand actor, his James was a well-meaning and even accommodating paterfamilias, whose arrogance and anger emerged with the aggravation of old hurts and hits at his vanity, despite his best efforts to control them. One critic suggested that Hutt played Tyrone's "residual vanity," along with an Irish charm and a careful watchfulness of Mary's mood swings: "Instead of magnifying the character into some sort of demi-god, Hutt allowed his weaknesses to show, and yet these disclosures had a paradoxical force. Hutt's Tyrone revealed enormous potential cracked by a loss of vocation and a loss of faith in himself and his family."[144]

Hutt's understated playing of James made it possible for Martha Henry to shine as Mary. In the words of one critic, she "simply grabbed the play by the scruff of its literary neck and forced attention on herself, no mean feat when up against the knowing craft of Hutt."[145] Her performance was called "an object lesson for aspiring actors in how to change mood without collapsing credibility."[146] Her Mary was more of the ethereal, otherworldly school of a Florence Eldridge or a Jessica Tandy than the realistic tradition of Geraldine Fitzgerald and Colleen Dewhurst, but she also managed to bring out the negative qualities in the character that were so arresting in Dewhurst's performance. As one critic put it: "In many ways, Mary is a thankless role, since the woman is so relentlessly manipulative and theatrical: her presence grates, like fingers down a blackboard. But Henry, while portraying all of this, also catches Mary's indomitable will to survive in any way or shape she can."[147] Her performance was carefully built on details, particularly gestures, that developed the variations of the character: "Mary's sardonic humour, her arcs of gloom, desolation, and irony, her alternations of apology and attack and her skipping joy of morbid evasions were all charted in detail."[148] Henry's performance was detailed almost to a fault, with the physical business perhaps inhibiting the edge that comes from spontaneity. When the successful 1994 production was revived for the 1995 Festival, Keith Garebian complained that Henry's performance had become too much an exercise in technique:

> She overdid the fussing with her hair, the broken little runs, the barefooted distractedness, the swirls, dips and skips, the claw-like semaphores – resembling at times more an aging Ophelia than

O'Neill's ravaged, self-pitying victim. Even her voice was mannered in its repetitive mockery, raillery and shy charm . . . there was too much technical calculation behind every gesture and vocal inflection, and some of the stylized hand movements were held in a frozen tableau. Mary Tyrone looked like the real actor in this family, but only as someone seeking moments to put her soul on histrionic display.[149]

Most critics recognized the technical tour de force of Henry's performance, and did not consider the technique excessive. The production was the basis for the 1999 film discussed in Chapter Four.

While the two landmark performances by Hutt and Henry tended to overshadow the performances of Peter Donaldson as Jamie and Tom McCamus as Edmund, the cast performed as an ensemble, and the young men played up to their standard. McCamus and Donaldson were particularly well-balanced, so that the Act 4 confrontation did not become a star turn for Jamie, as sometimes happens. In keeping with the overall interpretation of the production, he was more a disillusioned, vengeful victim of his mother's and his own addiction than a tortured, self-hating destroyer of his loved and hated rival brother. McCamus found the wit in Edmund that undermines the morbidity and cynicism and helps him to accept his father in the end.

O'Neill's popularity in the repertoire underwent something of a revival in the last decade of the twentieth century, particularly in an American regional theatre that was rediscovering the classics of American playwriting. *Long Day's Journey* had several significant revivals in the 1990s, with varying approaches and varying success. In Britain there was the 1996 revival by the Theatre Royal Plymouth at the Young Vic, directed by Laurence Boswell, with Richard Johnson as a low-key James and Penelope Wilton as Mary, "a triumph of nervous self-awareness."[150] In the same year in the US, an equally affecting portrayal of Mary was created by Claire Bloom in the American Repertory Theatre's production directed by Ron Daniels, in which Bill Camp made a particularly powerful Jamie. A production that began with a successful run at Houston's Alley Theatre in March 1998 was directed by Michael Wilson, with Ellen Burstyn as Mary and David Selby as James. This production was essentially revived at Hartford Stage, where Wilson had become artistic director, the following year. With Andrew McCarthy as Jamie and Rick Stear as Edmund, the production at Hartford essentially remained a star turn for Burstyn. In the same year, Laird Williamson directed the play for the American Conservatory Theater in San Francisco in a production that was grounded in Williamson's awareness that O'Neill was reading Eastern philosophy at the time of *Long Day's Journey*'s composition.[151] Although none of these productions was an overwhelming success in itself, the fact of their existence testified to a new interest in O'Neill on the part of a generation that had grown up with a suspicion of dead, white, male playwrights. The fact that young directors were eager to take on *Long Day's Journey* and even, as in the case of Diana Leblanc, to create new and revealing interpretations, is a good sign that its stage life will continue to grow and develop in the twenty-first century.

CHAPTER 3

PRODUCTIONS IN TRANSLATION

SWEDEN

Lång dags färd mot natt, Stockholm, 1956

Sweden takes a position of primary importance among the countries where *Long Day's Journey* was produced in translation, for several reasons. Because it was Sweden's Kungliga Dramatiska Teatern (Royal Dramatic Theatre or Dramaten) that Carlotta O'Neill allowed to do the first production of the play, in a translation by Sven Barthel, it was in Sweden that the world formed its first conception of *Long Day's Journey*. And it was partly because Dramaten, since 1923, had produced nine of O'Neill's plays, a number exceeded only by the Provincetown Players and New York's Theatre Guild, that Carlotta had been so eager to give the play to its director Karl Ragnar Gierow. In 1956, when O'Neill's reputation in most of the world, including the US, was at a low point, he was still treated with both respect and interest in Sweden, where he was recognized as a winner of the Nobel Prize as well as a self-described heir to Ibsen and Strindberg. After the triumphantly successful world premiere of *Long Day's Journey* in translation, which took place on 10 February 1956, Carlotta O'Neill also gave to Dramaten the premieres of *A Touch of the Poet*, *Hughie*, and finally *More Stately Mansions*. The story of the posthumous productions of Eugene O'Neill, therefore, is very much bound up with the Royal Dramatic Theatre of Stockholm.

Karl Ragnar Gierow's negotiations with Carlotta O'Neill for securing the rights to *Long Day's Journey* are detailed in Chapter One. During the process, Gierow flew to New York several times, and the two developed a mutual admiration and friendship. Although Carlotta did not go to Stockholm to see the play, she continued to be closely involved throughout the course of the production, and she and Gierow exchanged numerous letters, which are now in the archives of Dramaten and at Yale's Beinecke Library. Dramaten made good use of the fact that its production was the world premiere in its publicity, and it made sure to mention in its press releases Carlotta's statement that O'Neill had told her "on his deathbed" that he wanted Dramaten to do the play, even going so far as to say that O'Neill had "willed" the play to the theatre.[1] Although Carlotta's choice may not actually have been Eugene's, it proved to serve him well.

Gierow at first planned to have *Long Day's Journey* directed by Olaf Molander, who had directed *A Moon for the Misbegotten*, *The Iceman Cometh*, and *Mourning Becomes Electra*, but Molander proved too heavily committed to take on the new play, and Gierow chose Bengt Ekerot to replace him. Ekerot, who had recently directed a summer touring production of *Moon*, was, like José Quintero, a young director just making his way. Thirty-six years old in 1956, he was a graduate of Dramaten's famed School of Drama who had made his first impact on the Swedish theatre as an actor dubbed "the young intellectual" for his intense, soul-searching performances. In an article for a theatre magazine, Ekerot described *Long Day's Journey* as "a remarkable example of modern tragedy . . . it is tremendously urgent and is so, of course, right through the whole autobiographical structure, because it gives human beings insight into themselves and the life they are to live."[2] He saw the play as "the end of an epoch, the end of the Ibsen–Chekhov line," because he did not see how "one can proceed further within this style. It seems consummated with O'Neill's play."[3] Ekerot's direction was in keeping with this notion of the play as an endpoint in the development of realistic, humanistic, modern tragedy. It was psychologically based, steeped in naturalistic detail, and in every way possible, invisible to the spectator. As one reviewer wrote, "one did not think of a directing force behind the

11   This photo demonstrates the naturalistic detail of the Dramaten production. From left, Jarl Kulle, Inga Tidblad, Lars Hanson, and Ulf Palme.

drama . . . everything appeared as emerging from an inner compulsion in each actor."[4]

In an interview, Ekerot identified the single set as "at once its greatest challenge and ultimate success," adding that the play seemed almost to have been written for the Swedish audience which, in the land of the midnight sun, "appreciates better than most the transition from daylight to darkness" and which is prepared by its theatrical tradition to appreciate "a long interplay of human emotions on human personalities in which the dominant mood is one of pity and compassion."[5] Carlotta praised the set when designer Georg Magnusson sent her a picture of it, particularly its pictorial composition.[6] Magnusson followed the stage directions closely, producing the expectedly dreary turn-of-the-century, middle-class parlor with its center table covered with a heavy cloth, its bookcases, and its overhead chandelier. If anything, the atmosphere was heavier and more somber than that of the New York production, for Magnusson used dark, wooden furniture instead of the wicker that Hays used.

With its implication of stultifying bourgeois propriety rather than transitory summer life, the overall effect was even more intense and claustrophobic than that of the New York production.

In his review, Stephen Whicher wrote of "an awareness of life as a mysterious shaping force, a vague dark enemy" in *Long Day's Journey*, which "rises quietly and naturally from the human situation and gives it tragic stature." In Dramaten's production, he recognized the foghorn as the chief device for conveying this effect, noting:

> Perhaps this "sick whale in the back yard" – which the Swedes, not having our Moby Dick reflexes, translated "sick elephant" – seems over-obvious in the reading. As handled by "*Dramaten*," however, that living yet inhuman voice in the background of the last two dark acts, punctuating and commenting on the action and calling us back, as it does the characters, to the thought of the fog and sea around us, has sometimes almost intolerable power.[7]

The rhythm of the production, whose bass was the foghorn, was carefully managed by Ekerot. Despite the production's four-and-a-half-hour playing time, there were few calls for cuts among the critics. The taut underlying pattern of O'Neill's construction was clearly recognized and approved. As one critic put it, the rhythm was characterized by "the violent short flush of emotion, the quick repentance, then like a swell, the eager consolation, the retreat, or the fumbling, more or less falsifying and revealing explanation."[8] Henry Hewes made the interesting observation that the sense of rhythm might have been enhanced by the play's translation into Swedish: "The lilting rhythm of the Swedish language gives the play a move-ment and a music that it sometimes lacks in English. Each of the arguments thus acquires the rhythm of a point in a tennis match, and indeed expletive sounds have been inserted at appropriate times in order to keep the ball in play."[9] In the words of one Swedish critic: "Everything in the dialogue is so architectonically calculated that even the few words and poetic quotations that Bengt Ekerot has cut out were missed."[10] In short, the organic unity that Ekerot perceived in the play underlay the whole production.

When Dramaten's production came to New York and Seattle as part of a cultural exchange program for the Seattle World's Fair in 1962, several American critics who had seen Quintero's production were surprised to find Mary Tyrone at the center of the play. Walter Kerr commented that, while the Quintero production had been "an essentially masculine occasion," the Swedish production "offered us something else: a play about a woman," finding it a "curious, fascinating, even most persuasive shift of focus."[11] Writing in the *Christian Science Monitor*, however, Melvin Maddocks questioned this view, suggesting that it might be more reflective of Swedish culture than of O'Neill's play: "This might almost be called the Strindbergian interpretation of O'Neill: compulsively insisting with all the Swedish playwright's demonic power that, where there is a vortex of destruction and self-destruction, a woman must be near the center."[12] This focus on Mary was perhaps exaggerated in the production these American critics saw in 1962 because the original James, Lars Hanson, had been replaced for the tour by Georg Rydeberg, who did not even quite have his lines down. The balance between Mary and the men has become a perennial issue for new productions of the play, however, its resolution often depending on who the "star" is, or who emerges as the most powerful performer, in a particular cast. In the repertory company of the Royal Dramatic Theatre, there were no stars – or there were not supposed to be. The decision to place Mary at the center of the play was a conceptual one that was borne out by the powerful acting of Inga Tidblad.

Tidblad was widely praised for the gradual descent into a drug-induced psychosis that she portrayed in Mary. As Henry Hewes put it: "We see this old lady retrogress into a child as she drifts away from the shabby existence around her into a drug-inspired peace."[13] This was done through a wealth of naturalistic detail, as suggested by Walter Kerr:

> Miss Tidblad scrapes the palm of one hand, in spastic rhythm, against the wrist of the other; she digs at the nap of a tablecloth, as though some secret could be wrenched from it; she fingers her beads as though

> one last bead, somewhere, could save her from shipwreck, and then
> spreads her arthritic talons across her eyes.[14]

Hewes noted that, "when she craves narcotics her hands move uncontrollably about the arms of her chair like frantic animals trying vainly to escape a trap."[15]

It was clearly not by default that Mary Tyrone occupied the central focus of the Swedish production. Lars Hanson was recognized as the greatest actor on the Swedish stage when he undertook the role of James. In O'Neill's plays, he had already played Orin Mannon and Phil Hogan, and was to go on to play Cornelius Melody. Like Tidblad's his approach to acting was naturalistic: "What he wanted was veracity and he also knew how to reach it, by background research, thorough analysis of the part in relation to the whole play, building his characters, with sharp observation of human behavior, on details and nuances in the dialogue."[16] In other words, his approach to the part was very much like Fredric March's. His James began as an "ordinary man," quiet and understated, but as the play progressed, and his inhibitions broke down under the effect of the alcohol, he became histrionic, pompous, and full of himself. One critic said that he managed "exquisitely" to bring out "the Irish ebullitions of temper between reckless bragging and compassion, between anger and sentimentality, between magnanimity and greedy meanness."[17] Finally, in Act 4, as another Swedish critic described it:

> His warm wisdom, and deeply egoistic, masculine dramatic character is broken with exquisite effectiveness against his almost instantaneously demonstrated, bragging Irish cunning and stinginess; then it emerges again to dominate his harrowing account of how his stinginess grew out of his own rough childhood; finally, it flows away in a stream of whisky-sentimentality which also sweeps away the last illusion of his own moral courage.[18]

Nor was humor lacking in this characterization. Hewes noted that Hanson "gets all the playful comedy out of scenes where he can pantomime dealing of cards, pouring whiskey, or niggardly turning on three light bulbs with the exaggerated abandon of a playboy millionaire." And "unforgettable" was the moment "in which he recites a line of Shakespeare with the futile stock gestures of an old-fashioned actor."[19] Hanson played James at full range. Despite the lighter moments in his performance, Hewes noted the audience's "sense of terror in the scenes where this pitiable self-centered old man must bellow in true rage. Here Mr. Hanson is Lear in a worn bathrobe."[20]

Ulf Palme, who played "Jim," has provided a description of his approach to the character in a letter he wrote to Carlotta O'Neill. He said that he felt the greatest pity for him, and that this pity emerged in his performance. He saw Jim as the family member who is most set aside and is most deeply in need of tenderness and love. He saw him as a happy and healthy child until the moment of his younger brother's birth, when he suffered the loss of love and security. He thought Jamie the weakest of the family, and thus the most cruel, the one who says the truth when the others fight around it. Palme tried to create Jim with great tenderness, stressing the emotional nakedness beneath his cynicism.[21] The critics responded to Palme's interpretation of the character, noting that even while drunk, he imparted "a kind of paradoxical human dignity," that of "a complex, tormented soul suffering from his own degradation." Jim was "a piece of noble human material that was being lost."[22] American critics generally felt that Palme's performance did not measure up to Jason Robards', but they recognized its quality. "Ulf Palme does not capture the undercurrent of suffering and personal distaste that Robards had revealed in the role of Jamie, the elder son, but he does play it with strength and intelligence," wrote Norman Nadel.[23] As Edmund, Jarl Kulle's first asset was that he resembled the young Eugene O'Neill. He also brought a certain toughness to the role that complemented the consumptive poet in Edmund. One critic described Kulle's Edmund as "infinitely experienced, unsteady, defiant, and helpless."[24] Another noted that Kulle played Edmund with "thoughtfulness and restraint," but this did not prevent him from making the carefully crafted and impeccably timed emotional outburst: "Utterly theatrical yet believable is the anguished shriek he utters as he furiously smashes his drunken brother in the face for jokingly referring to his drugged mother as 'the mad Ophelia.'"[25]

When *Lång dags färd mot natt* opened in Stockholm on 10 February 1956, Sweden proudly prepared for a landmark in theatre history. The king and queen were present, as was the American ambassador, and the full rank of Stockholm's literati and glitterati. As the curtain fell on the four-and-a-half-hour performance, reported *Time* magazine, "the audience rose and applauded for almost half an hour, while the cast took more than a dozen curtain calls."[26] Stephen Whicher wrote in his review for *The Commonweal* that *Long Day's Journey Into Night* might have succeeded in Sweden because "this heartsick pessimism goes down easier here than it would in the United States."[27] *Time* and *Newsweek* both made fun of what they saw as the Swedish taste for doom and gloom. *Newsweek* said that O'Neill's play "turned out to be just the sort of thing for audiences whose emotional stamina has been conditioned by bearing the overweight luggage of such of their countrymen as Henrik Ibsen and August Strindberg."[28] *Time* quoted the *Morgon-Tidningen*'s admiring description of "the most gripping picture of hell that has ever been seen in the theatre."[29] Once the play had been published on 20 February, however, even these wags changed their tune, and American critics began calling for an American production as soon as possible – a response that was just what Carlotta O'Neill could have hoped for. *Lång dags färd mot natt* ran in repertory at Dramaten until 1962, when it was taken to New York and the Seattle World's Fair along with productions of *Miss Julie* and *The Father*, and then retired after 130 performances, "a miracle in Swedish repertory theatre," as Tom Olsson has noted.[30] It was in fact the greatest success in the history of the Royal Dramatic Theatre, confirming the Swedish view of O'Neill as America's most important playwright and opening the door for the first production of the play in the language in which O'Neill had written it.

Lång dags färd mot natt, Stockholm, 1988; Brooklyn, 1991

Ingmar Bergman replaced Karl Ragnar Gierow as director of the Royal Dramatic Theatre in 1963. After a long association with the theatre, he offered his centenary tribute to O'Neill in the form of a radically reconceived production of *Long Day's Journey*, which opened at Dramaten on 16 April 1988. As the premiere production had reflected Dramaten's preeminence in naturalistic theatre in the 1950s, Bergman's production reflected the contribution that Sweden, largely through Bergman's own work in films, had made to the modernistic reconception of performance in the mid-twentieth century. Radically rejecting the reverence with which Ekerot had treated O'Neill's dialogue, Bergman broke away from the text, cutting it by about 20 percent. In doing so, he reduced Cathleen's part to a very few lines, cut the Harker story, which introduces the note of humor and conspiratorial camaraderie into the family's interaction, and cut nearly all of the literary allusions in Act 4. In doing so, he pared down the dialogue to the rhythmic interactions of accusation and reconciliation that form the basic architectonics of the play.

Peter Stormare, who played Edmund, said that, in reconceiving the play, Bergman had departed from naturalism because he "wanted to do it more like a dream that becomes a revelation in the night."[31] The set that Gunilla Palmstierna-Weiss developed to realize his concept was a simple platform with minimal furniture. The actors were harshly lit by spotlights, as if under interrogation, and surrounded by blackness. To deepen this impression, the theatre's ornate proscenium was shrouded in black. Expressionistic images were projected onto a cyclorama to indicate the dominant interior reality of each scene: the façade of the house; the window of the spare room; a closed double doorway; a large, greenish wallpaper pattern; the house enveloped in fog. Egil Törnqvist, who interviewed the designer, said that the forbidden darkness of the unseen back parlor was an important concept for the set design. He explained that, while one purpose of the raised platform was to bring the actors closer to the audience and emphasize the intimacy of the play, it was conceived as a "black 'raft' – a square, raised stage – surrounded by blackness, insisting that although the sun may enter the living room when the play opens, darkness surrounds it . . . the blackness of O'Neill's back parlour has, as it were, been extended" (T 376).[32] The set was also compared to the "black interior of an old-fashioned, funnel-shaped gramophone . . . an acoustic box, where every whisper is heard" (T 376). In Stockholm, for the last act, Bergman broke from O'Neill's single-set concept, placing the action on the veranda of the cottage. The intention was to place Edmund more in the context of the external world, particularly the sea and the fog. The impression to be conveyed was that of "a human aquarium" (T 376). When the production was brought to Brooklyn, the final act was staged in the windowless back parlor itself, emphasizing the difference between Mary's world in the first three acts and the world of the men in Act 4. The break between the two worlds was emphasized by Bergman's placing of a single intermission at the end of Act 3, thus treating the first three acts as a unit focused on Mary's drug addiction.[33]

For furniture, a symbolic minimalism was used. The set contained a round table with a cover at stage left, surrounded by "four chairs of different shape: four different human beings, four different fates" (T 376). At stage right, a worn, brown stuffed armchair served as a quotation of the original production as well as a functional piece of furniture. Two incongruous Greek columns in the corners concealed the liquor cabinet and the telephone. The projections loomed over this abstract representation of the Tyrones, expressionistic images of their preoccupations.

Masks and role-playing were an important part of the acting in this production, as Bergman emphasized the acting that each of the Tyrones did for the others. Jarl Kulle, who had played Edmund for six years, now portrayed James, Sr. as a "a big, boisterous child, in need of a mother . . . who is play-acting at home" (T 381). Some critics thought that his performance did not do enough to indicate the depths beneath the performance. Thommy Berggren, who, as

Jamie, gave the most highly praised performance, was described as "a grinning but all too clear-sighted boozer on the brink of despair."[34] Bibi Andersson, who at first appeared a bit too robust for Mary to an audience that was used to Inga Tidblad's high-strung frailty, proved convincing in the end.

To establish the overall concept of the family dynamic, Bergman inserted pantomime scenes at the beginning and the end of the play. As the actors entered, they slowly formed a sort of *tableau vivant* in which their inner realities were indicated through characteristic poses, and each was touching another with a gesture of love and intimacy. Then the group came apart and the play began, with the physicality of the opening extended as "the family members tried desperately to avoid facing what they clearly knew to be inevitable, clutching like drowning people to each other, embracing and kneeling to one another, stroking each other's hair, hands, and face, or sitting together on the floor (as Edmund and Mary do at one point) like small children."[35] The ending was choreographed in contrast to the beginning. Each of the characters slowly exited in a different direction, dissolving the family. In Stockholm, Edmund was the last to leave the stage, as a radiant tree was projected, symbolizing a new form of life-in-art being born from the Tyrones' anguish. Before he exited, he picked up a black notebook, which had been present throughout the play as an indication of his status as a budding writer, and from which he had read part of his transcendental modified monologue in Act 4, an interesting practical approach to the problem of the high-flown literarity of the lines as well as a visual thematic statement. In the Brooklyn production, Edmund remained on stage alone, and he actually opened the notebook and began to write, indicating concretely that the writer would create the play from this experience. Thus Bergman's interpretation of the play's tragedy was ultimately hopeful, emphasizing the modernist theme of the redemptive transformation of life by art that characterizes much of his cinema work. The production was considered a successful and provocative reinterpretation both in

Sweden and in Brooklyn, where it was received with bravos and a standing ovation.

GERMANY

Eines langen Tages Reise in die Nacht, Berlin, 1956

Carlotta O'Neill negotiated the German rights to *Long Day's Journey* shortly after the play opened in Stockholm. Oscar Fritz Schuh was granted the rights to the premiere in the German language, in a translation which he did with his wife Ursula Schuh. The German premiere was presented as part of the Berliner Festwochen, an international festival of the arts. Schuh's production lasted for four hours, and was considered a test of endurance by some of the audience. One critic called the play an "oratorio of disasters," complaining that nothing happens in it – it is just "the four Tyrones, talking, talking, talking."[36] For the most part, however, the praise of the critics was lavish, for the play, for the translation, and for the production. One summed up O'Neill's play as "a titanic attempt to free himself from the domestic evil of his youth."[37]

The most common description of *Long Day's Journey* in the German reviews was "novelistic." One critic suggested that O'Neill's gloomy "family-panorama" had more the quality of a novel in dialogue than of a play for the stage.[38] More penetratingly, Johannes Jacobi suggested that the "American" dramatic form of the "family play" ("Familien-stück") had been transformed by O'Neill into a dramatic form of the confessional biography. This was a drama that was couched in "everyday speech, but with form and depth-psychology – the tragedy of realism, in which the personality of the poet positively dominates."[39] Friedrich Luft made a similar statement in expressing his wonder that O'Neill was able to dramatize the "disaster of the home" in such realistic form, and without resorting to "Symbol-tricks."[40]

It was partly Schuh's translation and partly his direction that conveyed a simultaneous sense of realistic domestic drama and high tragedy. His direction was universally praised. Walther Karsch suggested that the production presented a four-hour education in the art of theatrical presentation, with every realistic detail and every psychological refinement that was possible.[41] Schuh's staging, he wrote, laid the lines of the play out clearly, his intellectual approach making the work "transparent" to the spectator. Georg Zivier wrote that Schuh and Caspar Neher, who did the costume and scene design, created the period on stage with a minute realism that departed from the quotidian only during the modified monologues. In Zivier's opinion, Schuh expended his greatest directorial talent on the acting, which was the real triumph of the production.

Without doubt, the Berlin production made *Long Day's Journey* Mary's play. Grete Mosheim was universally acclaimed for her performance in the role. Like Inga Tidblad, she was praised for the gradual way in which she indicated Mary's drifting away from reality and the detail with which she conveyed her morphine dependency. Karsch praised the way in which she conveyed the arc of the role, "at first embattled, and then ever more fidgety, agitated, and nervous as, from hour to hour, a thicker veil engulfed her until in the end she was carried off into the past." Karsch thought that Mosheim displayed an apparently inexhaustible abundance of nuance in expression, whether vocal, mimic, or gesticular. Nor was the performance lost in the details, he was quick to add. The character remained "ever complex," and Mosheim never gave in to the temptation of a mere pathological interpretation, which would have been much easier.[42] More than one critic pointed out Mosheim's ability to convey the varied aspects of Mary's character. One expressed her admiration at Mosheim's ability to be the convent-school pupil one minute, and the angry, uninhibited drug addict the next, a child-like girl and then an old woman.[43] Zivier said that it was admirable and touching at the same time when Mosheim shifted from natural behavior to that

12   Hans Christian Blech and Grete Mosheim

of the addict, with a flickering look and fluttering hands, always achieving the effect with the smallest nuance.[44]

Although the performances of the men were not considered in the same league with Mosheim's, they were praised for their contribution to the realistic whole. Paul Hartmann, who played James, achieved a moving characterization that was noted for its range, from the quiet affection he displayed in the scenes with Mary to the explosive quality of his arguments with his sons. The tone of his reminiscences was described as bordering on the sentimental, but not crossing the border.[45] One critic suggested, however, that while Hartmann was believable as a shadow of his former self – the ruin of a middle-class melodramatic actor – as husband and father, he was too much Paul Hartmann, "the classic gentleman."[46] As Edmund, Hans Christian Blech had "the furrowed expression of the consumptive and drinker"[47] and materialized in a convincingly realistic performance "the suffering and the smiling face, the ailing rebel in a bathrobe."[48] As Jamie, Heinz Drache created a convincing portrayal of the cynical Broadway wise guy who throws away his salary in bars and brothels but reveals himself to be a lost creature who suffers his share of the family agony.[49] In general, the production was seen by Berliners as pretty heavy theatre fare, but a triumphant tour de force for both O'Neill and Oscar Fritz Schuh and an amazing accomplishment for its actors, particularly Grete Mosheim.

In October, another production using the Schuhs' translation opened in Düsseldorf under the direction of Karl Heinz Stroux, with Elisabeth Bergner as Mary and Bernhard Minetti as James. *Eines langen Tages Reise in die Nacht* was thus well established before *Long Day's Journey* opened in New York, and it quickly found a place in the German repertoire. In November 1957 a production with Alma Seidler and Attila Hörbiger opened in Vienna. In 1959 it was staged in Oldenburg by Jochen Bernauer and in Kassel by Ulrich Hoffmann, where, again, Mary was at the center of the play. Luise Glau was particularly noted for her convincing realization of the addict in Mary, and the tragic sense with which she was able to invest her flight into the past.[50]

ITALY

Lunga giornata verso la notte, Milan; Turin; Rome, 1956–57

The third production of *Long Day's Journey* that opened before the New York premiere was done by the Eva Magni–Renzo Ricci Company in Italy. Ricci, who directed the production as well as playing James Tyrone, had little difficulty in securing the production rights through his agent Enrico Raggio. As he told an interviewer:

> I knew, as all theatre people knew, that O'Neill had left a posthumous work to be staged only after his death. My friends and theatrical associates informed me that it was available, but that, according to the

express wishes of the author the first to stage it would have to be the
Swedes . . . I looked into getting the permissions to stage it here in Italy
– which was quite easy in the end.[51]

Ricci's plan for the production included bringing the play to fifty
"piazze," provincial venues that major acting companies did not
normally visit, as well as the major cities of Turin and Rome after its
run in Milan. First, however, he took the wise course of a run of forty
performances after opening on 16 October 1956 in Milan's Piccolo
Teatro, a small theater with a reputation for literary quality. Ricci
noted that the theatre had "its own select public, from whom I expect
understanding and support" (PM). After its successful run in Milan,
the production moved on to the Teatro Eliseo in Turin on 7
December 1956, and to the Teatro Valle in Rome on 22 February
1957.

Ricci's approach to the play included some judicious cutting,
which eventually landed him in trouble with Carlotta O'Neill. The
New York Times review of the play reported that "a streamlined
'journey'" was offered to the Milanese, saying that the running
length "had been cut to three hours, not counting two thirty-minute
intervals."[52] Carlotta immediately cabled the agent Enrico Raggio
that cutting the play was "a violation of my contract with you.
Therefore you cannot continue presenting play as it is."[53] Ricci and
Company continued to perform the play as scheduled to "standing
room only" audiences, and Raggio's associate Neale Stainton at-
tempted to mollify Carlotta by assuring her that the *Times* report
was inaccurate. He told her that the Milan production took "four
hours plus," a time equivalent to that of the Quintero production
which was currently being previewed in Boston, and that the
"streamlining" mostly affected the normal Italian practices of curtain
calls at the end of each act and half-hour intervals between the acts.
He told her that, although there were some small cuts, the
production had preserved the themes, the plot, the characters, and
the development O'Neill would have wished and it had been
translated faithfully and accurately and without alteration except

where essential.[54] With this assurance, Carlotta made no further objections, and the show went on.

Ricci's interpretation of the play was based on his unique experience with O'Neill. Having staged *The First Man* two years before, he tended to look at *Long Day's Journey* more philosophically than autobiographically, as most of its other early directors did. The Italian critics and theatre artists had been more interested than most in O'Neill's spiritual quest plays of the late 1930s, particularly *Dynamo* and *Days Without End*, which dramatize the protagonists' dark nights of the soul and their personal search for a divinity to believe in. Ricci found *Long Day's Journey* a refreshing change from the earlier O'Neill plays in which he felt that "often a complicated theatricality covertly emerges," dominating the audience's experience of the play. In contrast, the realism of *Long Day's Journey* presented "truly four characters of a rich, complex humanity." He thought that the stark honesty of this drama, as opposed to the distracting theatricality of the earlier plays, "ought to strike the public, and make it suffer and think" (PM). Ricci's presentation emphasized the combination of what he saw as social realism in the play with the "interior" spiritual significance that he was primed by his earlier experience with O'Neill to see and to develop. The program notes for the Milan production reminded the audience that behind the Tyrones "there is not merely a completely private world, O'Neill's secret world":

> There is, doubtless, American society. Wouldn't anyone who looks closely at Edmund and James, for example, think back to the two sons of Billi [*sic*] Loman, Miller's traveling salesman? Their fall/failure takes place on the same terrain. Even if for O'Neill the causes are not sought on a concrete or real plane as for Miller, but in the sphere of the irrational and the individual. Here his religiosity also finds a place. (PM)

Ricci thought that from the beginning, O'Neill "set in opposition to the external and un-self-conscious presumption of the businessman,

of the self-made man, the abysses created in the individual conscience" (PM).

This was not to suggest that the psychological or the symbolic
was neglected in this interpretation. The program notes also made
it clear that the director considered *Long Day's Journey* more "self-
confession" than autobiography, declaring that O'Neill "wanted to
relive a moment of his life not only in its outward aspect, but
especially in the profound interior significance it had for him"
(PM). Symbolically, the fog was at the center of this production,
in which "the night that the morphine addict Mary approaches is
the fog that awaits all men, it is the immersion in a fog that wipes
out everything" (PM).

The reviews indicate that the Italian public agreed with Ricci's
interpretation of the play. One critic wrote with relief that "finally
[Ricci] has let us enjoy theatre in the truth of its dialectic and its
human inspiration, after many boring experiments of frigid Russian
academism," noting that "the public, recognizing this, paid tribute
by their warm and long praise of Renzo Ricci and the actors."[55]
Nicola Ciarletta placed *Long Day's Journey* in the context of the
spiritual quest of *Days Without End*, "when for a moment, it seemed
that the playwright was trying to rediscover the lost Catholic faith in
which he was raised."[56] Like the Germans, the Italian critics had only
one substantial complaint about the play: that it was novelistic. As
one critic in Turin put it, "the moralist, I would almost say, the
novelist, overtakes the dramaturge . . . Long Day's Journey has no
plot, no dramatic structure; there is no action, movement, no
catharsis. The characters, more like those in a novel than in a play,
remain exactly the same at the end of the drama as they were at the
beginning."[57]

Renzo Ricci placed the same value on honesty and naturalness in
his approach to the role of James Tyrone that he did to his direction
of the play. He was commended for the detail with which he attended
to the voice, gesture, and attitude of "the character who is supposed
to be a classically trained actor."[58] Several critics described the

quality of "humanity" with which he was able to imbue the character, and more than one identified its source as the ability to develop and synthesize the contradictory sides of James's nature. As the critic for Milan's *Il Giorno* put it: Ricci, "in the part of the old actor, drunken and avaricious, a mixture of egotism and paternal tenderness," created a "moving human figure."[59] One Turin critic found "his fatuousness" as Tyrone "sincere and painful, just as the author depicted him."[60]

Eva Magni's Mary was the only performance to come in for substantial negative criticism. One critic suggested that she was "at times overcome by the difficulty" of the role, although she attained moments of "vivid conviction."[61] While other critics agreed with this assessment, Magni's Mary was considered by at least one to be the "the most complete and moving" performance of her career. Like Ricci's, Magni's was a characterization built on naturalistic detail. One critic said that she emphasized "the crises and tics of the morphine addict" rather than the "sweet and dreamy vagueness in which she loses herself."[62] Others noted characterizing gestures such as rubbing her arthritic hands and playing with her hair. But at least one also noted the transcendent quality that pervaded her character-ization, so that Magni's rubbing her hands recalled Lady Macbeth as well as the troubled morphine addict.[63]

The acting of Glauco Mauri as Jamie and Gian Carlo Sbragia as Edmund was universally praised. Ricci's casting of the roles suggested a "dark pessimism" in Edmund and a "robust and vigorous" Jamie.[64] Mauri's Jamie was described as "excited, violent, and generous."[65] Sbragia's Edmund was praised for its range and "variability of tone," and the delivery of his modified monologue, which earned him "the most spontaneous and con-vincing of the two outbursts of applause that occurred during the performance."[66] The applause for the production was warm and abundant. One critic described "deafening applause" and many curtain calls.[67] The production was equally successful in Turin, and in Rome.

HISPANIC PRODUCTIONS

Viaje de un largo día hacia la noche, Buenos Aires, 1957

The first South American production of *Long Day's Journey* took place in Buenos Aires on 27 March 1957. This version was translated for the first time into Spanish by León Mirlas for the Francisco Petrone company, and was directed by Petrone, who also played James. Mirlas, the author of the comprehensive critical work *O'Neill y el Teatro Contemporáneo*, was one of the most distinguished South American critics of O'Neill's works at the time. Petrone's direction of the play, with Yordana Fain as Mary, Fernando Vegal as "Jaime," and Carlos Estrada as Edmund, was based on Stanislavskyan techniques that emphasized authenticity in the individual performances as well as the interactions between actors. They were praised for acting as an ensemble, reflecting the careful preparation of the group in their interactions, as well as for the precision of their individual physicalizations of the roles. Petrone's work was described by the critics as up to his usual high standard, displaying his technical capacity and efficiency as well as his robust temperament and his "animal vigor."[68] Fain was praised for the completeness and integrity with which she realized the varied shadings of Mary's personality, which was represented as not only "complex and abnormal, but susceptible to rapid and capricious psychological changes. From the woman who at the beginning of the work . . . encloses herself in a voluntary amnesia or in denying evidence to the woman who, in the final scene, uproots herself totally from her world, Yolanda Fain marks step by step the subtle metamorphoses that are being produced in this haunted being."[69] Fully developing the virtues of his Stanislavskyan approach to the production, Petrone was praised for the sincerity with which he portrayed James, the completeness of his "listening" to the other actors, and the fullness of his participation in the given circumstances of the scenes.[70]

Viaje de un largo día hacia la noche, Mexico City, 1957

In North America, the first production in Spanish, translated by Mary Martínez and José Luis Ibáñez, took place at the Teatro del Granero on 14 June 1957 under the auspices of the Unidad Artística y Cultural del Bosque and the Instituto Nacional de Bellas Artes. It was directed by Xavier Rojas, with Isabela Corona as Mary, Augusto Benedico as James, José Alonso as "Jimmy," and Jorge del Campo as Edmund. The critics received the production enthusiastically, noting with pride that it was the equal of the New York version.[71]

The star of the production was Isabela Corona, who received lavish praise for this performance, which was considered the culmination of a great career. She was particularly praised for the expressiveness of her face and body. As for the other actors, one critic noted that "the greatest praise we can give is to say that they are not overshadowed by the great performance" of Corona.[72] Benedico was praised for rising above his tendency to underplay, creating a vigorous, robust characterization of James, but tempering his strength with tenderness, although one critic thought that he was "excessively loud" in some of the scenes, given the small space of the Granero.[73] Del Campo was praised for exactness and clarity and Alonso was called "ardent and honest."[74] The sons were considered particularly effective in their confrontation scene, where they were convincingly drunken without overdoing it. Rojas' direction was credited with drawing exceptional performances from his actors as well as making expert use of the Granero's circular space in his most successful production to date. Antonio Lopez Mancera created an effectively minimal set for this space. The play itself was not received with the same unabated enthusiasm as the acting. One critic suggested that the final Act was "repetitive, excessively long, and consequently tired," and could easily be cut.[75] Overall, however, this production was considered a triumph for the company and a high point for twentieth-century Mexican theatre.

Long Day's Journey has been produced in Spain several times since the Madrid premiere in 1957, which was directed by Alberto Gonzalez Vergel. In 1988, the O'Neill Centenary was celebrated with a new production in a new translation by Ana Antón-Pacheco at the Teatro Español. Miguel Narros directed a cast that included Alberto Closas as James, Margarita Lozano as Mary, José Pedro Carrion as Jamie, and Carlos Hipolito as Edmund.

PORTUGAL AND BRAZIL

Jornada para a Noite, Porto; Lisbon, 1958
Longa Viagem Para a Noite, Lisbon, 1983

The crucial factors for the first productions of *Long Day's Journey* in Portuguese were the translations and the actors who played Mary – Dalila Rocha in Portugal and Cacilda Becker in Brazil – both of whom are recognized as among the great actresses of the century in their countries. The Portuguese production, staged first in Porto and then in Lisbon by Teatro Experimental do Porto (TEP), proved much the more fortunate in its translator. António Pedro, the TEP's dynamic founder and director, persuaded the eminent poet and critic Jorge de Sena to do the translation for his production. Recognizing the greatness of O'Neill's work and believing that Pedro and his company were capable of doing it justice, Sena undertook the task enthusiastically, even though the time frame in which he had to work was extremely short, and he was finally reduced, according to his wife, to sending daily batches of pages from Lisbon to Porto, a process that was interrupted for only three days by the birth of his sixth child.[76] Sena has written of *Long Day's Journey* as a "magnificent work, of appalling difficulty, devoid of even minimal concession to the public taste . . . long and breathtaking."[77]

The praise for Sena's translation was unanimous. One critic called it an "absolute model in its aural qualities, its impeccable rightness – be it in the translation of poetic intentions, or in the social and family details of the slang itself."[78] Another found in the translation "an excellent piece of work in which the human drama of those beings, hurt and broken through suffering . . . expresses what there is of poetry, of anguish, in those 24 hours of the psychological ruin of a family which marches toward the night, or toward death, without remedy."[79]

António Pedro was equally fortunate in Dalila Rocha and João Guedes, who played Mary and James, the lead actors in his distinctive theatre group. Pedro and the TEP were an important force in freeing the Portuguese stage from an academicism that had emphasized diction almost exclusively. He is credited with introducing the Portuguese theatre to Stanislavskyan acting techniques and other twentieth-century concepts of theatre artistry.[80] In staging *Long Day's Journey*, Pedro and his scene designer, Alvaro Portugal, created a set that combined ultra-realism in the furniture with expressionistic distortions in the angles of the walls and darkly twisted images of trees seen through the back window. Despite the theatre's proscenium arch, one critic noted that Portugal's thrust stage made the audience feel that it was "inside the house of the Tyrones,"[81] intimately involved in the experience of the play. The room was overwhelmingly bourgeois, with a formally patterned wallpaper and high ceilings outlined by a fancy double cornice – hardly one's image of a New London summer cottage. The furniture was spare, but it was formal and of good quality. It consisted primarily of an upholstered settee at stage left, a round antique card table toward the center, and an expensive secretary with bookshelves at stage right. The sole wall decoration, a portrait of Shakespeare, loomed over the room. A staircase was used effectively to indicate the semiotics of Mary's dissociation from the family. Overall, the set established the central metaphor of the house as a representation of a family that dwelt on the edges of sanity, trying to evade consciousness of its precarious condition while it presented a front of normality to the world.

Fernanda Gonçalves, who played Cathleen in the production,

remembered the enthusiasm with which Dalila Rocha entered into Pedro's conception of theatre in his acting and directing classes.[82] The critical response shows that the actors clearly exemplified Pedro's ideas about authenticity as well as physical fluidity and natural movement. "All those who figure in the production move on the stage not to represent, but to live the drama of that rich but disgraced family, that home without peace," wrote one critic:

> The acting of Dalila Rocha transcends, reaches above the normal, it . . . makes us believe this to be [the play's] principal role . . . She goes mad with such power of conviction and precise physiognomic gestures and nervous tics that the public remains suspended and on guard, and they await the end of each act uneasily, in order to determine whether or not the artist has maintained her mental faculties.[83]

Rocha's portrayal of Mary Tyrone was a major event in the Portuguese theatre of the 1950s, and considered by at least one critic to be "the greatest part of her artistic career."[84]

While Dalila Rocha clearly stood out, the other actors came in for praise as well. One critic wrote that Guedes enacted "the intriguing and contradictory gamut of feelings of the head of the family, sometimes anguished, sometimes compassionate, eager to justify himself to his wife or his son, sometimes eaten away by an odious avarice that turns him repulsive and brutal."[85] He also said that Alexandre Vieira, in the part of Edmund, established himself as "a magnificently gifted actor" by his forceful exteriorizing of emotion, his mastery of timing, and his vocal skill.[86] Another singled out Baptista Fernandes as Jamie, who, he thought, surpassed himself in spontaneity and accuracy of expression.[87]

The critical and public response was overwhelmingly positive, and the production was acclaimed in both Porto and Lisbon, receiving ovations and many curtain calls in both cities. It was recognized as "a great victory for Teatro Experimental do Porto" and for its approach to theatre.[88] The power of the production's influence and the strength of its memory was so great that it overshadowed the revival of *Long Day's Journey* that was done by the Teatro Nacional de D.

Maria II of Lisbon in 1983, in a new translation by Paulo Ferreira da Silva Teles called *Longa Viagem Para a Noite*. The director Jacinto Ramos took a much more symbolic approach to the play than Pedro had. As he explained it, "*Long Day's Journey into Night* is an autobiographical play in which O'Neill confers tragic stature on the members of his family personified in the Tyrone family. The general line of my direction aspires to respect this tragic dimension." The scenic space created by Paulo Guilherme, he explained, responded directly to "the exigencies of the conflict of relations in the work, leaving the center of the stage demarcated as an 'island' of light, a confessional from which no one departs with absolution."[89] This scenic space determined the direction of the modified monologues and gave the whole production a presentational, metatheatrical quality, while the acting was realistic. In addition, a musical score was composed by César Batalha in a "functional" mode, to accompany and reinforce the "evolution of the tragedy" throughout the performance. The production was not a success with either the critics or the public. One critic wrote a lengthy piece explaining just how the new production was inferior to the TEP production of twenty-five years earlier, which he called "one of the greatest productions of contemporary Portuguese theatre." He found the whole conception of Ramos' production inferior to Pedro's, suggesting that it indicated a regression in the Portuguese theatre, and faulting in particular the translation, the open set, the lighting, and the introduction of music.[90]

Jornada de um Longo Dia Para Dentro da Noite, Rio de Janeiro;
Porto Alegre; São Paulo, 1958

As it did in Portugal, the excitement of the theatre world over *Long Day's Journey* coincided in Brazil with the formation of a new theatre group, Teatro Cacilda Becker, which was named after the prestigious actress who was at the center of its productions, and was presided over by the theatrical genius Zbigniew Marian Ziembinski, known

affectionately to the Brazilian public as "Zimba." In 1957 Ziembinski was recognized as a theatre artist of great talent and wide
experience, with the "highest reputation and an influence over
Brazilian theatre that was almost mystical."[91] The formation of the
new theatre group with Cacilda Becker, Jorge Chaia, Fredi Kleemann, Walmor Chagas, and Kleber Macedo was an event in itself,
and it was announced with great fanfare on 5 December 1957 in the
Teatro Maria Della Costa in São Paulo, with full coverage from the
press, radio, and television, on the occasion of a public reading of the
group's new translation of *Long Day's Journey* by Helena Pessoa,
Jornada de um Longo Dia Para Dentro da Noite. The group originally
planned a premiere of the work in Rio, in early January of 1958, but
the premiere had to be postponed when they were reminded of a law
that had recently been enacted for the protection of Brazilian
authors, which decreed that the first production of any new theatre
organization had to be by a native author. Teatro Cacilda Becker
therefore chose Ariano Suassuna's *O Santo e a Porca* for its premiere,
delaying the production of *Long Day's Journey* until May of 1958.

This gave the group five months to work on *Long Day's Journey*,
which was rehearsed in repertory along with *O Santo e a Porca*.
Ziembinski's philosophical reading of O'Neill is evident in the
essay he printed in the program, in which he wrote of O'Neill's
"strange and tempestuous life" and his preoccupation with the
great questions of destiny, and of human guilt and responsibility.
He called the play a "cry of protest against the world in which we
live, a great 'J'Accuse,' and at the same time, a great comprehen-
sion of one's own culpability and a petition for pity . . . the
greatest modern drama."[92] Despite Ziembinski's obvious affinity
for O'Neill and the exhaustive preparation the cast underwent, the
production did not live up to their hopes for it. One major
problem with the production was clearly the translation by Helena
Pessoa, which was called "abominable" by critic Paulo Francis.
Perhaps related to this was what Bárbara Heliodora called Ziembinski's absolute unfamiliarity with the "American ambience,"

which she found evident in the physical, psychological, and emotional elements of the production.[93]

Although Ziembinski was praised for his "perfectly lucid"[94] direction, he made several choices that disrupted the integrity of the production. The characterization of the maid by Kleber Macedo was described as "unforgivable," a caricature of stupidity, boorishness, and noisy vulgarity that turned parts of the production into "a circus of Brazilianness."[95] This tone was completely out of keeping with Ziembinski's direction of the other actors. One critic said that the caricature in Macedo's performance greatly "dislocated" the play, because one of the merits of Ziembinski's direction otherwise was his sober tone and his avoidance of exaggeration or over-acting.[96]

The general consensus was that the production was a valiant effort, and "an event of major importance to the Brazilian theatre,"[97] but that the company was not yet ready for the task. Cacilda Becker confirmed this when she said later that she hoped to play the part of Mary again, after she had matured as an actress and as a woman.[98] Her performance was generally praised by the critics, who agreed that for the most part her acting achieved great emotional force, although at least one complained that she relied too much on external indications, such as a trembling of hands and body, to indicate her drugged condition, and that she fell at times into a mechanical and monotonous speech pattern.[99] Both Ziembinski as James and Fredi Kleemann as Jamie were praised for the quiet honesty of their performances, but Walmor Chagas was criticized for lapsing into "indifference" at times as Edmund.

This production was not a popular success, closing on 15 June 1958, after just a month of performances, although it traveled to Porto Alegre in August, and to São Paulo the following January. Nevertheless, for "its seriousness, for its high purpose, through the honesty by which it [sought] to serve a great, noble, and difficult text," it was recognized as deserving its audiences' applause and admiration.[100]

FRANCE AND BELGIUM

Long Voyage dans la Nuit, Paris, 1959

In his review of the Quintero production that had been brought to Paris' Théâtre des Nations in the summer of 1957, the French philosopher and critic Gabriel Marcel remarked that he hoped that "this remarkable play will be performed in French," noting that it would be necessary to "obtain authorization to make some essential cuts, especially in the first part of the last act." But would there be a French director brave enough to undertake this perilous task? Marcel confessed to having a few doubts on this point.[101] His concerns had long been anticipated by Carlotta O'Neill, who, from the beginning, had strong reservations about having the play produced in France at all. She had written to Karl Ragnar Gierow as early as February of 1956 that she could not picture anything more horrible than what the French would do to *Long Day's Journey*, complaining that in the last O'Neill production in France, *Desire Under the Elms*, Abbie had been dressed like a tart from the left bank.[102] Lars Schmidt, a young Swedish producer, sought the French rights immediately after the Swedish premiere, a request that Gierow advised Carlotta to refuse. His doubts were assuaged in June, when Schmidt presented a letter from A. M. Julien, the director of the Paris Theatre Festival, requesting permission to co-produce the play in a production featuring Edwige Feuillère, whom Gierow considered one of the best actresses in France.[103] In August, Gierow wrote again, advising Carlotta to let Julien produce the play in Paris and not to let Schmidt win his spurs as a producer with *Long Day's Journey*. His warnings came too late, for Carlotta had signed a contract with Schmidt in July, giving him and A. M. Julien the sole rights to produce *Long Day's Journey* in the French language. Under the terms of the contract, the producers agreed to obtain a first-rate translator of the play, subject to Carlotta's approval.[104]

The question of the play's length arose in August of 1957, when

Julien wrote to Carlotta, telling her that the recent Paris showing of the Quintero production had demonstrated that the play was too long for the French public. Edwige Feuillère had asked the producers to reduce the play by half an hour in order to make it "more acceptable to our public." Julien reminded Carlotta that O'Neill himself had cut *Mourning Becomes Electra* for its French production, and assured her that nothing would be done without obtaining her agreement, and that the cutting would be undertaken with discretion, respect, and care.[105] Carlotta did not allow this to happen, and the question of the Paris production stayed in limbo until May of 1958, when Gierow once again interceded with Carlotta on behalf of A. M. Julien. Carlotta wrote back that she would like to hear from Julien, but she was still adamant about cuts.

The A. M. Julien connection having failed to work out led to the play being finally produced in Paris by Lars Schmidt in November of 1959, in a translation by Pol Quentin, directed by Marcelle Tassencourt, with Jean Davy as James, Gaby Morlay as Mary, Michel Ruhl as Edmund, and Pierre Vaneck as Jamie. The script was cut to three hours for this production. Jacques Marillier's set was described as "lugubrious" by Betrand Poirot-Deipech in *Le Monde*, and Marcelle Tassencourt's staging "implacable," as each of the actors enacted "with scrupulousness the atrocity of O'Neill's nightmare." He described the play as a foggy day's journey from dawn to dusk in "the hideous room of a beach house," as "four monsters tear themselves apart or weep for their distress."[106] The critics stressed what they saw as a pitiless naturalism in the production, which was described as "an autobiographical play and also a clinical documentation of unmerciful precision of the mounting crisis of a morphine addict."[107]

The critics had high praise for the acting of Gaby Morlay as Mary. Jean-Jacques Gautier wrote that she herself constituted the true spectacle of the evening.[108] He said that she scored a tour de force in her creation of Mary: "Her pinched lips change the diction and volubility for which she is celebrated to the thick-tongued and anguished murmur of the intoxicated woman. Her eyes, her cheeks, her hands, never cease to be agitated, as if she had lost control of them . . . One fears for her."[109] Gautier noted the gradual way her expression grew more frightened and her voice more strident, her diction more jerky, as she successively embodied panic, suspicion, mistrust, and anger: "A staggering, shuddering being, she loses herself in a deluge of words, a torrent of recriminations that she wants to curb, but that flow from her mouth in spite of her, like a wave of foul beasts."[110]

Although this production was a star turn for Morlay, she did not completely eclipse the other actors. *L'Aurore* noted that Jean Davy played James with authority as "a domestic tyrant of shameful miserliness" and that Michel Ruhl and Pierre Vaneck made an excellent Cain and Abel.[111] Overall, the premiere of the French version was a powerful night in the theatre, although the production emphasized the more sensational aspects of the play, tending toward melodrama in its approach to the characters.

Long Voyage dans la Nuit, Charleroi, 1970

The March 1970 production in Charleroi, Belgium has been described in detail by Marc Maufort, who has shown that the emphasis in this production was clearly on the "tragedy of the elder Tyrones" (MM 123).[112] By this time, Carlotta O'Neill, only months away from her death at the age of 82, had long since ceased to care about cuts in O'Neill's plays. As Maufort notes, the cuts in the 1970 production were extensive, including such thematically central speeches as Edmund's modified monologues about the sea and the fog, and they reduced the size and importance of the sons' roles in the play, throwing off the balance of O'Neill's careful architectonics. Nevertheless, the critics detected and admired the "delicate balance established by the actors between the love and hatred characterizing the Tyrones' relationships" (MM 118).

One of the remarkable features of this production was the set, designed by André Masquelier. Far from a realistic rendering of the

O'Neill's New London cottage, this was a semi-abstract representation of a bourgeois drawing room, more redolent of European baroque style than turn-of-the-century cottage Americana. There was no wicker here, but elaborately carved plush chairs. The high, roofless walls, with large rectangular insets and cutouts, suggested a bourgeois mansion in the city rather than a country cottage. The set functioned symbolically as a kind of bourgeois prison, but it was not the secret, darkened parlor of the Quintero production.

The well-known Belgian actor Yvonne Garden, who played Mary, dominated the production, and established its aesthetic, which Maufort describes as a "poetic, suggestive realism," as well as O'Neill's musical architectonics through her "alternately tender, angered, and bold tones" (MM 121). Garden approached Mary's addiction in a "near-scientific" fashion, like Florence Eldridge treating her behavior as "near-psychotic" (MM 122). Christian Barbier was considered effective in representing James as a paternal, elderly figure, and of maintaining a believable state of inebriation throughout the performance, but he was not up to "the grandiloquent style of nineteenth-century American acting" (MM 123). While Gille Languais was a bit heavy-handed in his portrayal of Jamie, Jean-Michel Thibault was a credible Edmund, minus his most important speeches.

OTHER NOTABLE PRODUCTIONS

Long Day's Journey has been produced on six continents and in many languages since its Swedish premiere in 1956. While the vast majority of these productions have been in Europe and the Americas, O'Neill's play is also well known and well respected in Asia and Africa. Translated into Hebrew by Jacob Orland, the first Middle-Eastern production was in Tel Aviv in 1960, produced by the Israel National Theatre, and directed by Hy Kalus. Another production in Hebrew was directed by Michael Meacham at the Habimah in

Jerusalem in 1974. In 1986, the Jonathan Miller production with Jack Lemmon traveled to Tel Aviv for a short engagement of the production in English.

O'Neill's play was brought to Japan by Harold Clurman as part of a US State Department project in 1965. This cultural exchange resulted in two productions: one directed by Clurman in English, with American actors; and one directed by Tetsuo Arakawa in Japanese, with Japanese actors. Clurman described these productions as "two run-through rehearsals" with no scenery or "effects."[113] The *Japan Times* reported that Arakawa, who had served a sort of shadow apprenticeship to Clurman during production, studying his Western methods, had "learned his lesson magnificently, and this Kumo production is something of a landmark in Shingkei history."[114] Most recently, Tamiya Kuriyama directed *Long Day's Journey* at the New National Theatre in Tokyo in May 2000. In this balanced production, Masane Tsukayama was praised for "confidently commanding the stage with the dash and swagger of the matinee idol who swept Mary off her feet 36 years before" as James, and Kazuyo Mita was called "heartbreaking" as Mary, her descent into drugs convincingly "ghastly." Most noteworthy in the production was the power and strength with which Yasunori Danta invested Edmund, making his confrontation with his father in Act 4 "totally believable as well as surprising."[115]

During the Cold War era, Communist countries were slow to produce *Long Day's Journey*. In China, a centenary year *Long Day's Journey* was produced in 1988 at the Qian Xian Drama Theatre in Nanjing, directed by Zhang Fucheng, with Wang Ping as Mary. *Long Day's Journey* was first produced in Russia in 1988 as well, although it had productions in Budapest in 1963, directed by Endre Marton, and 1976, directed by Liviu Ciulei. Translated into Russian in 1980, the play was held up for eight years in the censor's office because drug addiction was a taboo subject on the Russian stage. In the atmosphere of new political and cultural openness at the end of the 1980s, it was finally produced at the second stage of the Maly Theater in Moscow, directed by Sergei Yashin, the theatre's first production of an American play. Not straying too far from the context of socialist realism, however, Yashin interpreted the play "as a social-psychological drama, believing with good reason that 'the history of one family reveals important aspects in the life of the American society.'"[116]

CHAPTER 4

MEDIA ADAPTATIONS

EMBASSY PICTURES, 1962

The best known and most significant film of *Long Day's Journey* is still the first, directed by Sidney Lumet, with Katharine Hepburn, Ralph Richardson, Jason Robards, Dean Stockwell, and Jeanne Barr in the roles of Mary, James, Jamie, Edmund, and Cathleen. It took some time for Carlotta O'Neill to agree to sell the film rights. As late as December of 1959, she was writing to her agent Jane Rubin that she would not permit anyone to produce the play "as a picture."[1] As she had with the play, she received many requests for the rights, from figures as different as Kirk Douglas and José Quintero. And as she had with the play, she finally made a surprising decision that might have been the best thing possible for O'Neill. She sold the rights to Ely Landau, a former television executive whose main accomplishment at this point was his *Play of the Week* series, which had televised adaptations of *Juno and the Paycock*, *The Cherry Orchard*, and *Don Juan in Hell*, as well as the recent four-hour version of *The Iceman Cometh*, directed by Sidney Lumet. Carlotta commented that her decision to option the motion picture and television rights to Landau was influenced by the artistic integrity displayed in his handling of *The Play of the Week*.[2]

With capital from Landau's partner Jack Dreyfus (of the Dreyfus fund) the film was budgeted at about $430,000, one-quarter of the typical studio budget for a similar film at the time. In order to save money, the director and the actors were all asked to take a fraction of their regular salaries, in exchange for a cut of the gross, should the movie prove profitable. Landau's original hope was to sign Katharine

126

Hepburn and Spencer Tracy for Mary and James. Hepburn, who was eager to play the part from the beginning, agreed to take a salary of $25,000, one-tenth of what she had been paid on her previous picture. Tracy refused to play James, however, giving the salary as the reason for his refusal, although Hepburn felt that he simply lacked the confidence in his acting to play James at that point in his career. Instead, Ralph Richardson got himself out of another film in order to take the part. As for the sons, according to Lumet, "Jason Robards – you couldn't have kept him away! And Dean we had like a shot, he was so eager right away."[3] Stockwell, fresh from his success in *Compulsion*, commented that this was the least he had ever been paid, even as a child actor.[4]

In choosing Sidney Lumet to direct the film, Landau was providing it with perhaps the ideal director to adapt O'Neill's work. At the center of his work on the film was the belief that when a literary work "is a masterpiece, it is a masterpiece for a reason. I don't think its structure can be tampered with." His aesthetic combined respect for the original work of art with a clear sense of his own medium and a confidence that the film he created would be a work of art on its own terms. Lumet was emphatic in stating that the film was "not, in any sense, a photographed stage play.": "It is a movie; the amount of technique was so prodigious, it was a technical tour de force in many ways. And all directed toward the one thing which I feel does make it 'cinematic.' It is a 'movie' if those people or that situation is defined in a way it *cannot* be defined by using any other form. That more than completed itself for me in *Long Day's Journey*" (L 20).[5]

Lumet's previous work had also provided him with the ideal training for the film. After years of directing for live television – a process that was like creating a weekly drama in the medium of film under severely constricted conditions as to space and sets – Lumet had recently directed five movies, including *12 Angry Men*, a technical tour de force which makes the constricted space of the jury room in which almost all the action takes place into a major asset for

13   Jason Robards, Katharine Hepburn, and Ralph Richardson in the
opening scene

creating the film's tense mood. With this experience, Lumet approached O'Neill's four-hour, single-set play with confidence, certain
that he could create an equivalent sense of the four Tyrones, trapped
in their existential hell of a house, in the medium of film.

Not surprisingly, Lumet decided to shoot the film essentially on
one set. "I don't feel you can break this play out in the conventional
movie sense," he said. "If you shoot a picture correctly, though, it
doesn't matter if you stay mostly in one room. This play will be
cinematic because of the depth with which O'Neill probes his
characters."[6] From the beginning of the play's Act 2, the entire film
takes place in the house. Lumet decided, however, to shoot the
opening sequences outside the house, in order to emphasize the
journey from day to night: "I wanted *literally* to take a 'long day's
journey into night.' I wanted to start with the brightest sunlight (in
fact, the opening title shot is against just the sun) and wind up with

the last shot of total blackness, just the lighthouse light sweeping the four people at the table" (L 21). The film's opening sequence, an extreme long shot of the house in the sunshine, as Cathleen comes out and walks briskly down the walk to check the mail, is a very effective contrast with the famous closing sequence, in which the four Tyrones sit around the table, and, in Lumet's words: "The camera pulls back slowly, and the walls of the room gradually disappear. Soon the characters are sitting in a black limbo, getting tinier and tinier as the light [from the lighthouse] sweeps across them. Fade out."[7]

Working closely with his photographer Boris Kaufman, Lumet worked out a progression for the light from bright day to black night, sunshine to fog, exterior to interior, hopeful promise to despair. The opening, rather cheerful, sequence is filmed on the lawn in bright sunshine, but, as Donald Costello has noted, Lumet shows disharmony during these early scenes by breaking up the light with shadows, dividing Mary and James from the boys as they go from the porch to the yard, and never framing all four of them in one shot: "As the plot begins, all seems quite well on the surface, but they are not together."[8] From the lawn, Lumet moves to the dingy garage for the testy scene between James and Jamie in which the worries about Edmund's illness and Mary's tenuous condition are first discussed, and then to the house for the scene between Edmund and Mary. Lumet has Edmund run out of the house and down to the beach, a brief burst of freedom, when he goes outside, leaving Mary to her "nap," a long shot framing Dean Stockwell's eloquently conveyed yearning for escape to the sea. He is imprisoned by the backyard wall when he has his conversation with Cathleen, and after he and Jamie come back inside and begin their day's drinking, the camera never leaves the house again.

In keeping with the film's modest budget, the exterior location was near the Manhattan studios where the set of the house was constructed. It was a house built in 1890, in the Bronx, facing Eastchester Bay, which was picturesquely dotted with boats. Lumet liked it because they could film at almost any angle without picking up anything that was not suitable to the time period, and he thought it was closer to the house that O'Neill's stage directions describe than Monte Cristo Cottage was at the time of the filming. Richard Sylbert's aim in decorating the interior set was to produce a realistic replica of the period that would plunge the audience into the Tyrones' world. He included many small touches that dated the house as 1912, such as the inglenook under the stairs, a vase with cigar bands pasted around it, wicker planters, shell-beaded curtains, Tiffany lamps, and oriental rugs, in addition to the inevitable wicker furniture and round card table. Katharine Hepburn pronounced the set "bone-chillingly marvelous" when she saw it.[9]

An important aspect of the set was the stairway, with its grill-work of wooden spindles and cross-bars. As Frank Cunningham has noted, Lumet "compels us to engage the stairs." We never see beyond the upstairs landing, but the stairs themselves become a visual representation of "the moral choices involved in human action – in this case, in self-abasement and self-humiliation,"[10] when Mary goes up for an injection. In keeping with the confinement motif that John Orlandello has analyzed, Mary is filmed through the grill, a simultaneous evocation of the addiction in which she is imprisoned and the convent where she would like to be closed off from the world.[11] During Act 4, when Edmund and James hear her moving upstairs and look up from the hall, they are filmed through the grill from the stairs above, emphasizing the barrier that has now been erected between them and Mary.

For Lumet, the set was the challenge. It was a source of great pride to him that no two set-ups in the movie were alike, despite the extremely restricted playing area and the fact that the action was all dialogue: "In camera placement, in camera positioning, in lens opening, in key light, in lens used, once 'Cut' was called, there was a brand new set-up for each shot in the picture" (L 24). Lumet is fond of saying that the camera is a "fifth character"[12] in the film, and it is indeed through the constantly shifting subjective point of view assumed by the camera that the film becomes a cinematic rather than a dramatic experience. The obvious instances of this are the memorable technical feats, such as the camera's pulling slowly out to the incredibly long shot at the end of the film, and then the shock of the extreme close-ups of the four faces, which were shot with different lenses: first Richardson and Robards with 18mm lenses; then Stockwell with a 25mm lens; and finally Hepburn with a 100mm lens – "a total reversal in the field, again for a deliberate and dramatic purpose" (L 27). Or the two 360° pans of the room as Mary circles desperately, saying, "if there was only some place I could go to get away for a day, or even an afternoon, some woman friend I could talk to . . ."[13] More important, however, was Lumet's making of a lens plot for the entire film, using the lenses to underline the emotional content of each scene. In Act 4, for example, the lenses became shorter and shorter in the confrontation between James and Edmund, ending with 18mm lenses to reflect "an increased hostility, an increased violence, an increase in the change of emotions the two characters were going through" (L 26). With Hepburn, who was filmed in long takes to give the sense of the character as "*legato*," the lenses got longer and longer, "so the outside world kept disappearing more and more" (L 24).

Camera angles made an even more dramatic way of inserting the "fifth character" into the scene. For Jason Robards and Ralph Richardson, the camera's angle of vision keeps dropping, making them, ostensibly from Edmund's point of view, loom larger than life. In Jamie's confessional scene, for example, Robards starts out on the floor, with the camera above him as he says, "I've known about Mama so much longer than you . . ." (*LDJIN* 163). As his anger and hostility build, however, both Robards and the camera move higher, so that when he gets to "You're only an overgrown kid! Mama's baby and Papa's pet!" (*LDJIN* 163), shot from below, he is no longer a drunken bum, but a powerful and threatening big brother. The opposite effect was achieved with Hepburn. As he shot her with longer and longer lenses, Lumet also had the camera move higher and higher above her, increasing the sense that she is lost and helpless.

The placement of the actors, the blocking, and the framing of the scenes consistently developed Lumet's interpretation of the play. He had thought that Quintero's production overemphasized the relationship between James and Jamie, largely because of the powerful performances by March and Robards. He thought that "if the play was about any of the four, it was about the mother . . . the fullest, and the most moving, tragic elements lie in the relationship of Mama and Edmund" (L 20). In keeping with this view, Hepburn is much more physical with Edmund than with the others, particularly Jamie. From the opening scene on the porch, where she embraces him and plays with the lapels of his jacket, her emotional connection to Edmund is the primary factor in her motivation. This is emphasized by the treatment of Edmund's revelation to Mary that he has to go to a sanatorium. Lumet had Hepburn slap Stockwell, and then embrace him, with the two actors moving to a *pietà* image as they sat on the wicker settee together, Mary cradling Edmund, and ending with his head on her breast. The emotional tie between mother and son was carefully undermined, however, at Edmund's line: "It's pretty hard to take at times, having a dope fiend for a mother!" (*LDJIN* 120), as the two look off in opposite directions, both lost in their pain, unable to connect finally.

Lumet and Landau made much of the fact that there was no screenwriter for the film, just O'Neill. While, as Donald Costello has shown, he cut approximately 25 percent of the dialogue, Lumet showed that he understood the architectonics of the play, and the importance of repetition to its rhythm and meaning.[14] As he said: "O'Neill is like life. It has to go around the same circle four times, but all the time it's like an awl which is biting deeper and deeper into the wood each time it goes around" (L 26). What he found, however, was that the camera could take the place of some of the repetition, so that he cut the references to James's miserliness from eighteen to ten, for example, and the references to Mary's lack of a home from ten to six.[15] He cut the first three-and-a-half pages, beginning the dialogue with Mary's ironically significant line, "Thank heavens, the fog is gone" (*LDJIN* 17), delaying the hints of Edmund's illness, James's miserliness, and Mary's addiction until after the cheerful scene with the four Tyrones. Besides the repetitions, Lumet also cut most of the references to any life outside the family circle, so the talk about Harker and his Standard Oil millions, about the Chatfields, and about McGuire is gone, as is Cathleen's talk about the other servants. There is also less detail about James's and Mary's families and about their wedding. Most of the quotations from Dowson, Wilde, and Swinburne are cut, as are half of each of Edmund's two speeches about the fog and his transcendent experiences in nature. The director's cut of the movie, at 175 minutes, thus preserves what Lumet felt to be O'Neill's aesthetic design, which was rooted in repetition, but adapts it to the cinematic medium where, he felt, after a certain point, less was more.

The nearly three-hour film was shot in thirty-seven days, following three weeks of rehearsal. Lumet said this was possible because his years in television had trained him to be very clear about technical matters before filming began. The lengthy rehearsal period was important for two reasons. One was that it established the rhythm of the film from the very beginning. As Lumet has said: "Essentially, the rhythm of the editing followed the rhythm of the shooting which was following the rhythm of the performances which were evolved in rehearsals" (L 25). The other was that it made an ensemble out of four very professional and experienced actors who worked very differently. Richardson worked from the language, noting that "in nearly every phrase, in nearly every speech, there's a pattern . . . It's all music, isn't it?"[16] Lumet learned to talk to him in these terms: "A little more bassoon, a little less violin, a little more cello, a little tympani here . . . it was immediately picked up and translated into acting" (L 21). Dean Stockwell, a Method actor, required detailed discussion of the character. With Robards and Hepburn, Lumet had to be flexible and tactful: "Jason likes to think of himself as an out-and-out technician. Of course, he's not. He's a totally inspired artist. With Jason . . . one doesn't talk about the most profound elements of it or the most moving. They are somehow understood between you. One deals largely on a technical level with him" (L 21). With Hepburn, Lumet tried to support an unschooled but extraordinary acting instinct with technical adjustments as well as "really profound, close, personal discussions between the two of us, *as* the two of us, of that character, of O'Neill" (L 22). The result was a remarkably integrated ensemble, despite the range of approaches.

The Lumet *Long Day's Journey* was chosen to represent the United States at the Cannes Festival in 1962, where it won Best Actor awards for the four principal actors. It was received with admiration by most American critics, who recognized what the filmmakers were trying to do, although they did not necessarily see it as entertainment. Lumet was exasperated by the number of critics who claimed, as Stanley Kauffmann put it, that "it is not a film. It is a play photographed,"[17] and with the ignorance of a statement like Arthur Knight's in *Saturday Review* that his approach "pointedly ignores the potential-ities of the film medium."[18] "You wanted to kill," he said, "because you knew any critic who would say that had no eye, did not belong in movies, should not be criticizing movies. He can't see what a lens does, he can't see what light is doing – sheer technical ignorance" (L 28). In the years since, however, the cinematic achievements of the film have been recognized, praised, and analyzed by a good many critics. The other major objection of reviewers was to "the talk, the acres and miles of O'Neill's probing, repetitious dialogue."[19] For the most part, the actors were praised, and as expected, the film found a small but enthusiastic audience, and made a small profit. It is now recognized as one of the classics of American filmmaking.

ITC/ABC TELEVISION, 1973

In June of 1972, Martin Starger, American Broadcasting Company's vice-president in charge of programming, announced the network's plans to produce several drama specials to upgrade the quality of programming for the next season. "We are definitely committed now to presenting the very best in drama for television," said Starger, "We are particularly proud to present O'Neill's masterpiece, based on Michael Blakemore's staging for the National Company and directed for television by Peter Wood."[20] The production, with the National's cast of Laurence Olivier, Constance Cummings, Denis Quilley, and Ronald Pickup, was adapted for television by Blakemore and Wood and taped in London in cooperation with the National Theatre and Britain's ITC. It was broadcast in Britain and the US in 1973, and was highly praised by critics, who lamented that in the US it attracted less than 10 percent of the viewing audience.

Peter Wood's production was a true television adaptation, not a taped stage play. Like Lumet before him, he introduced the camera as a "fifth character," a subjective point of view that directed the audience in its role as spectator of the Tyrones' tragic day and night. The production opens with a photo of the house, a rather weathered Victorian structure. A black-and-white still photograph of the O'Neill family on the porch at Monte Cristo is then shown, with Eugene at about age 10 sitting and reading, while a dandified Jamie and a rather tired-looking James look at the camera. Ella is absent. The camera then pans the porch of the set, showing the interior of the house through the two windows. What is presented is a middle-class Edwardian home, with Cathleen, in uniform, dusting the photographs that are arranged on a bureau scarf on the upright piano in the parlor. As she puts each photo down, a video vignette of each of the characters is shown, as Laurence Olivier, in his normal voice, explains who the characters are.

In the only opening-out of the set that Wood does, the middle scene in Act 1, between James and Jamie (29–41), is shot on the porch, and the interior is often shot through the two windows, a technique that suggests the stifling, confining nature of the house as well as the carefully guarded secrets that are contained in it and the somewhat voyeuristic curiosity that the invading camera invites in the audience. The rest of the set consists of a living room or library, where most of the action takes place, a confined space with two walls of books, furnished with a desk holding a large picture of Edwin Booth, a round table, four chairs, and a bookstand holding a folio edition of Shakespeare. An open archway leads to the parlor, which exudes turn-of-the-century middle-class taste. There are lace curtains at the windows, many pictures on the walls, a gramophone, the upright piano with the photographs of the family members and James as Monte Cristo, a small, round tea table, Mary's rocker, and another comfortable chair. Another open archway leads to the hall, facing the staircase and the front door to the right. A door with a frosted-glass pane opens onto the hall from the living room, and is used by Wood several times to suggest the family's attempts to create barriers and to keep secrets. This set suggests a well-ordered, middle-class Edwardian household rather than the dreary, haphazard beach cottage that many productions depict, and this milieu contributes to the characterizations that are developed, particularly Mary's.

Wood's use of the camera both determines and serves the production's overall interpretation of the play. This Tyrone family does its best to evade the worst truths about itself, putting on a brave face of normality, both to the outside world and to each other. In the course of the production, the protective strategies they have developed are breaking down, and the spectator is allowed to penetrate the protective shield of the house's four walls as each of the characters is exposed to the scrutiny of the others. One of the ways Wood establishes this motif is by shooting the interior of the house through the windows. At various times, James, Mary, and Jamie are all shot this way. As they look out of the window partly to evade the scrutiny of the others, they are instead exposed to the spectator by the camera. The camera also emphasizes the spying on each other that the Tyrones do. As Jamie comes up to the house for lunch, he looks through the window at Edmund taking a drink before he climbs through and says, "Sneaking one, eh" (53). As James and Jamie discuss Mary and Edmund secretly out on the porch, the camera follows their covert gestures toward the windows. Wood makes a point of Mary's separation from them as well as her confinement in the long shot of the porch that ends this scene, with James and Jamie on either side of the window, and Mary behind it, looking out.

In the scene between Mary and Edmund that ends Act 1, Wood employs a prop – a bowl of apples – as well as the camera, to show Mary's increasing distance from Edmund. When James and Jamie go down to the hedge, Mary comes inside and sits at the table in the living room, beginning to pare the apples, as if for a pie. She sits thinking worriedly for a while, glancing toward the stairway, then she gets up and goes toward the hall, as if she is headed upstairs. She is distracted by Edmund's coming down. During their conversation, Edmund sits at the table with her, helping to core the apples. When Edmund goes outside, he sits on the porch, on the other side of the window that frames the back of Mary's head, as she sits at the table, trapped by Edmund's presence, but in no way comforted by it. Instead of heading up the stairs, as almost every other Mary Tyrone has done, Wood has Constance Cummings sit at the table again, pick up the knife, and start paring the apples. The camera focuses tightly on her hands as she hacks away more and more wildly at the apple. At the opening of Act 2, Edmund comes in and sees two mutilated apples on the table, turning brown. The visual image is completed when Cathleen comes in and bundles up the ruined apples in newspaper to throw away, marking the end of Mary's attempt to resume her domestic role.

Wood also makes constant use of camera angles and the placement of characters to emphasize the dynamics of the relationships in each scene. In the scene between James and Jamie on the porch, for instance, the approach–avoidance conflict of father and son is emphasized by Jamie's sitting sideways on a bench and pretending to read a newspaper while James paces back and forth into the leaf shadows on the side of the porch. The power relationship between the characters is made clear in this scene, as well as in Jamie's confession scene with Edmund, through the camera angles and the relative height at which the actors are placed. In the confessional scene, Jamie begins sitting in a chair, with Edmund kneeling on the floor in front of him. The power relationship is reversed when Jamie kneels in front of Edmund as he confesses that he will do his damndest to make Edmund fail. The scene ends with Edmund sitting in the chair and Jamie sitting on the floor beside him, passed out with his head on Edmund's hand, having passed his power over to his brother by exposing his jealousy and resentment.

Wood did not cut a great deal from the dialogue, but the cuts he made shape the interpretation of the play significantly. A good deal of Mary's scene with Cathleen in Act 3 (98–100, 101–03, 104, 105) and her complaints at the opening of Act 2, scene 2 (71–72) were cut, as was Edmund's speech about the fog, most of the Baudelaire quotation, the Macbeth story, Edmund's prose poem, about half of his speech about transcendence, and his "stammering" speech. Cutting the repetitions and most of the complaints in Mary's speeches made her a much more appealing character, which was in keeping with Constance Cummings' portrayal of Mary as a refined and delicate, but straightforward and basically honest woman. Her Mary is not "performing" constantly, as was the case with Eldridge's and Hepburn's. She delivers her lines as direct expressions of her thoughts and feelings, in a gentle, rather flat Midwestern voice. She does not portray Mary as abstracted and dissociated in Act 3, but only as more animated and chatty than usual. It is not until Act 4 that she has drifted off, and even then her acting is "real" in the subjective moment in which Mary finds herself. In keeping with this characterization, Wood uses a voiceover when Mary expresses her thoughts at the end of Act 3 so that she is not talking to herself, but thinking.

The same quality of understated quiet pervades Denis Quilley's performance as Jamie, perhaps the most unusual interpretation of the four because he avoids the full-out passion that has marked the portrayal of Jamie in Act 4 since Jason Robards played the role. Quilley plays Jamie as an avoider of conflict. He pretends to read the paper to avoid a face-to-face confrontation when he is talking with his father, and he literally runs away from Mary when he goes upstairs to get dressed in Act 2, scene 2, waiting in the parlor till she has passed by so he does not have to talk to her. His face betrays genuine concern for Mary and for Edmund, but his speeches are quiet and controlled. He tries to cover his bitter cynicism with a gay, smiling manner, and even his confession to Edmund is played more as a warning against an almost inevitable sibling rivalry than as an expression of bitter self-loathing. His Jamie is more cruel than tortured. The "hophead" line, for example, is said smoothly into Edmund's face rather than shouted in pain. He is a quiet alcoholic rather than a roaring drunk. His speech is not even slurred in Act 4, but he shudders with each drink he takes, and passes out swiftly with the "K. O." drink, suggesting a consistently high level of alcohol in his blood. This Jamie does not evoke pity for an outsized suffering and self-loathing. Quilley's characterization is more an exposure of an all-too-human bitterness, jealousy, and cruelty mixed with love and vulnerability.

With the cuts in his speeches, Ronald Pickup is left only one real proof of his status as a poet – the remaining part of the "transcendence" speech, which marks him as a much more hopeful character than the "fog" speech, and the prose poem about the trollop crying into her stale beer. Like Cummings' and Quilley's, his is a quiet, straightforward performance, although he is a forceful Edmund, who is believably enraged when he shouts his father down, accusing him of wanting to send him to the state sanatorium and lying about it. His characteristic mode, however, is that of listening and observing, and Pickup is brilliant in the many close-up reaction shots that Wood places throughout the production. Like the audience, Edmund is mostly watching, and is often filmed looking through the window, standing in the door frame, or looking through the glass door, studying his family.

Laurence Olivier's performance as James has been praised for its virtuosity. It is a characterization that seems to begin with his voice. Like Fredric March, Olivier thought that James should have an Irish brogue, and that the brogue should become more marked when he remembers the past. He does this very effectively with the first of his modified monologues, when he talks about his family's poverty (147–48). Wood establishes the concept that James is acting for Edmund in this speech by having Edmund sit at the table in the living room while James, framed by the proscenium arch of the parlor doorway, tells the story of his childhood. This scene is a feat, for Olivier manages to convey that James is both sincere and acting at the same time. He is genuinely weeping at the end of the speech and Edmund is genuinely affected by it, but there is still a quality of recitation, of performance, about his delivery of it. This quality disappears when he goes on to his confession about selling out for success, something that, as he tells Edmund, he has never admitted to anyone else (149). One of the ways Olivier conveys its naturalness is by using a natural voice, a quiet, conversational tone with a slight Irish lilt delivered in a simple manner. This underplaying gives the speech perhaps the greatest import of any in the play, partly because it is played against two other voices that Olivier gives Tyrone, the very artificial nineteenth-century "actorly" tone with which he quotes Shakespeare, and the rather strange, "hearty" speech he uses to indicate the habitual act that James puts on before his family, a hoarse, exaggerated voice with an accent that sounds peculiarly like that of Wallace Beery in *Treasure Island*. He pronounces "compliment" "com-plē-ment," and "prettier," "purtier." This speech is alienating, and makes James seem more bumptious than he is, but played against it, his confession is more deeply revelatory and affecting.

Olivier's James dominates the production, partly because he retains almost all of his lines, while those of Edmund and Mary are cut substantially. But he is also the emotional center of the production. Unlike Fredric March and Ralph Richardson, who played James as a man who is fighting desperately to keep his emotions under control, Olivier lets them give way. This is not a dignified, courtly figure, but an emotional man with a temper whose peasant crudeness is just below the surface of his carefully learned social behavior. His outbursts at his sons are temper tantrums. His reaction to Mary's relapse is naked grief, which he struggles to cover with his "hearty" manner. His first exclamation "Mary!" (74) in Act 2, scene 2 is almost a shriek. His second, when she starts upstairs, he delivers weeping, with head in hand. He drops his mask with the boys as he shouts, weeping, "I wish she hadn't led me to hope this time. By God, I never will again!" (78). He grabs Mary around the waist and buries his face in her belly as he says the next "Mary!" and his "Dear Mary! . . . won't you stop now?" (85) is delivered as a wounded cry. His "You won't even try?" (85) is not a question, but a weeping accusation, and he cries, "Oh, God!" when she evades this with "Try to go for a drive this afternoon" (85). He is just as overt when he inflicts pain, as in Act 4, when he gets angry and shouts at Edmund, "if you hadn't been born she'd never" (142). He howls in agony when he realizes what he has said, and beats on his forehead as if he were playing King Lear, which, in a sense, he is. The dignity that he achieves in his simple recounting of the story of his career is crucial to his portrayal of the character. Like Edmund, the audience goes from feeling contemptuous of this man, to pitying him, to respecting him – to understanding and forgiving him, as O'Neill put it.

Peter Wood's closing shot repeats the motif of the opening, this time reversing the process of penetrating the walls around the Tyrones. All four of them are seated at the table as Mary finishes her final speech. The camera moves in to a close-up of Mary as she says, "I fell in love with James Tyrone and was so happy for a time" (176). Wood follows this with close-ups on James, Jamie, Edmund, and Mary, then a long shot of the four. The camera slowly pans around the room, then, as the credits run, it tracks through the parlor, past the front door, and down the hall, finally shooting the four of them through the frosted-glass panels of the door to the living room. The image fades to the black-and-white of a photograph, and then blacks out.

ABC VIDEO ENTERPRISES, 1982

The 1981 Richard Allen Center Production that is discussed in Chapter Two was adapted to video the following year, produced by David A. Lown for ABC Video. It was taped at the Glen Warren Studios in Canada and first broadcast on the ARTS cable channel on 23 November 1982. It was later re-broadcast in three segments for *A&E Classroom*. As director, Geraldine Fitzgerald was replaced by William Woodman, who had been artistic director of Chicago's Goodman Theater for five years before coming to New York to direct daytime soap operas. There were also two new members in the cast. Ruby Dee replaced Gloria Foster as Mary, and Thommie Blackwell replaced Al Freeman, Jr. as Jamie.

For this production, about one third of the dialogue was cut, and some was rewritten, although most of the rewriting consisted of transposing words, phrases, and sentences. The major cuts were most of Edmund and Jamie's literary quotations and substantial chunks from their Act 4 modified monologues. Most of the repetitions of the play's major motifs of Mary's desire for a home, James's miserliness, Jamie's disappointments to his parents, Mary's fears for Edmund, were cut, although enough of them remain to make it clear that they are recurring subjects among the family. All of the references to the Tyrones' Irishness were cut, in keeping with the overall aim in the production to create the Tyrone family's experience within a milieu that is distinctly African-American. As the maid, Rhetta Hughes speaks with a "Negro" accent appropriate to 1912. Woodman opens up the play for two brief scenes at the beginning of Act 3 that show the Tyrones down town. In the first, the camera pans a row of shops and moves in on Cathleen coming out of the pharmacy with Mary's prescription. The second shows Jamie and Edmund coming out of a saloon, and Edmund giving Jamie some money. A few passers-by appear on the street, none of them white, establishing that the Tyrones live within an African-American community. Beyond this, nothing is done to make a point of their ethnicity. The play is simply enacted as the experience of a particular family that happens to be African-American.

In designing the set, Woodman and art director Eldon Elder chose to use two rooms for their playing area rather than the confined single room that O'Neill describes. After a panoramic shot of the harbor that moves in on the house, the porch, and finally the window, the first Act opens in a sun room that is surrounded by windows and is very bright. It is paneled in narrow horizontal strips of natural light wood. It has a bright oriental carpet on the floor, and the spacious room is furnished with a wicker chaise longue covered with bright blue chintz, a round card table with two wicker chairs, a rocking chair, and a straight-backed chair. There is a door to the porch, an open doorway leading to the hall, through which the stairway is visible, and a glass door to the dining room. Throughout the first scene, the dining room is visible through the open door, the mantel with its silver candlesticks and the elegantly covered table establishing the household's bourgeois lifestyle.

In Act 2, scene 2, rather than have the family come back into the sun room from the dining room, Woodman places Mary, Edmund, and James around the dining-room table. A long shot briefly shows Jamie drinking in the sun room before the camera moves in to a three-shot of the others. When Mary gets up from the table, the camera shoots through the glass door from Jamie's point of view as he stands looking at her and then slowly opens the door to James and Edmund with the line "Another shot in the arm!" (75). This helps to emphasize Jamie's isolation from the rest of the family.

Acts 3 and 4 also begin in the dining room. Mary's scene with Cathleen takes place at a small tea-table placed next to the fireplace, and Cathleen drinks her bourbon from a fine china cup. Mary comes into the sun room when she sends Cathleen off, and runs nervously back and forth from the front door into the room when she hears the men returning. Act 4 opens with James seated at the dining-room table, drinking by himself in semi-darkness. He and Edmund remain there until James suggests the casino game, and they move into the sun room. This room, quite brightly lit to begin with, is of course darkened when James turns out the bulbs in the chandelier, but is brightened almost into daylight when Jamie comes in and turns the lights on again. The change of scene and the variation in the lighting makes for visual interest in the scenes, but it sacrifices the sense of dreary confinement that is crucial to the impact of Acts 3 and 4, particularly during Jamie's modified monologue.

While some of the elements of the stage production remain in the performances, the introduction of Ruby Dee and Thommie Blackwell make for a fundamental shift in interpretation. Gloria Foster's Mary had been compared to Lady Macbeth. Hers was the tragedy of a *grande dame* brought down. Ruby Dee's Mary is warm and down-to-earth, a loving woman who finds herself in the grip of a force that is beyond her control and tries to make the best of it. Her performance has a clear arc of regression, from mother to child. In the first scene, she is nervous and busy, clearly worried about Edmund and trying hard to escape her worry through activity and denial. She talks too fast, and she bustles around the room attending to her men – handing James the newspaper, putting a cushion behind Edmund's back, lifting his feet onto a footstool. She is also physically affectionate, particularly with James. They enter laughing, in an embrace, and he pulls her down into his lap, playfully hugging her on the line, "Your eyes are beautiful, and well you know it" (28).

Ruby Dee's portrayal of the morphine effect is naturalistic, effectively taking over the character after the end of Act 1. When Mary enters at the beginning of Act 2, her speech is markedly slower and slurred; her quick, nervous movements have become loose-limbed, exaggerated gestures. As the day goes on and the level of morphine in her system increases, she becomes increasingly volatile; the indifference and detachment that she is seeking alternate with outbreaks of awareness and emotion. Thus she does not avoid looking the men in the eyes as she talks to them, simply looking away when they show their knowledge that she has resumed the drug. She weeps on James's chest when she says, "I tried so hard! I tried so hard!

Please believe – !" (69), but she immediately recovers her detachment as they go in to lunch. In Act 2, scene 2, as the family sits around the lunch table, her animation has returned. She delivers her complaints about James breathlessly and thoughtlessly, her voice rising to anger during her speech about Dr. Hardy. In Act 3, after she has taken more morphine, her speech is again slurred and slow, she is light-headed and giggly, and she has become physically unstable, literally, as Cathleen says, as if she'd "a drop taken" (104). She giggles rather than taking offense at the idea of her going on the stage, when she talks about meeting James, and when she pulls the trick of adding water to the whiskey bottle. When she tries to say the "Hail Mary," she topples over onto the floor, and then laughs as she says, "You expect the Blessed Virgin to be fooled by a lying dope fiend reciting words!" (107).

When she hears the men coming back, her condition approaches hysteria as she runs back and forth from the door to the sun room three times, repeating "I'd rather be alone," her voice rising and her arms clasped as she looks wildly about. Then she collapses into the rocker, saying quietly, "I'm so glad they've come! I've been so horribly lonely!" (108). Her emotional volatility reaches a peak when Edmund reminds her of her father's death from consumption and she lunges at him, pummeling his chest as she says, "I hate you when you become gloomy and morbid! I forbid you to remind me of my father's death, do you hear me?" (120). The usually passive Edmund grabs her arms and throws her toward the table as he says, "It's pretty hard to take at times, having a dope fiend for a mother!" (120), the most intense moment in the production. It is quickly deflated a moment afterward, when Edmund, standing stiffly away from her, says, "Forgive me, Mama. I was angry. You hurt me" (120), and she simply wanders away to the window, listening to the foghorn. In Act 4, Dee plays Mary as having completely regressed into childhood. She talks in a low, pouty voice like that of a spoiled child, quite a bit younger than the high-school senior that she is impersonating. She is completely detached, her face that of a bewildered child, and her childishness is emphasized by her virginal white nightgown.

Ruby Dee's performance, integrated and well-motivated in itself, does not fit well with Earle Hyman's more technical, language-centered performance as James. The most remarkable thing about Hyman is the virtuosity with which he approaches James's speeches. He makes full use of his great vocal range, from the lowest bass when he is the great actor intoning Shakespeare in true nineteenth-century melodramatic style, to the highest tenor when he is voicing hurt and irritation with his sons. Unlike the others', Hyman's modified monologue is not cut very much, but he finds it necessary to say it at breakneck speed, so that when James is confiding in Edmund one of his most personal truths he sounds like an actor rolling off a well-practiced set piece, with perfect diction and well-modulated tones. Played against Peter Francis-James's and Ruby Dee's very natural diction, the effect is jarring, with the perhaps unintended result that James seems never to be sincere, but always to be acting, even in moments of intimacy. What is more, neither Hyman nor Thommie Blackwell as Jamie ever appear very drunk, certainly not to the extent of its affecting their diction. In contrast with Dee's Mary, Blackwell is barely affected by his day of drinking, even as he succumbs to "the old K.O."

Woodman develops an interesting spatial design for the sons. Jamie is isolated from the family physically. Not only is he placed in another room in Act 2, scene 2, but as soon as he sees that Mary has begun taking drugs again, he cuts himself off, lurking in the corners of the room, covering his eyes, literally walking away from the rest of the family. It is not until the scene with Edmund, when he approaches him to warn him, that a kind of reconciliation is made for Jamie. The scene ends with the brothers on the floor, Jamie holding Edmund in his arms. Edmund is treated as the passive observer of the family, with suggestions that he has been emotion-ally damaged by his mother's alternating indifference and smothering. His response to hostility is usually to withdraw, and he is most often placed sitting or standing, staring straight ahead, in the midst of the family battles. He also erupts from time to time, however, as when he throws Mary across the room on the "dope fiend" line and when he finally shouts at James that he is a "stinking old miser" (145) and collapses to the floor in a fit of coughing. Woodman adds these outbreaks to the ones against Jamie that are in the stage directions, on "another shot in the arm" (75) and "The Mad Scene. Enter Ophelia!" (170), to show Edmund as an emotional man who has repressed his feelings almost to the extent of paralysis. Edmund's violent outbreaks from this characteristic passivity signal a danger in his personality that is not often brought out in performance.

While this production brings out some interesting aspects of the individual characters, it never quite succeeds in becoming an integrated interpretation of the play. Ruby Dee's interpretation of Mary follows a clear trajectory from mother to child, concern to indifference, sunshine to fog, but the overall trajectory of the production is not nearly as clear. The set does not help to produce the effect of encroaching darkness. The other actors do not approach the state of drunken oblivion with any kind of consistency. The performances never mesh into an ensemble.

SHOWTIME/ PBS, 1987; 1988

The 1986 Jonathan Miller production of *Long Day's Journey* was taped for television at the CFTO studios in Scarborough, Ontario under a joint agreement between the US cable network Showtime and the US Public Broadcasting Service. Under the agreement, Showtime paid a healthy percentage of the production costs in return for the right to broadcast the show before PBS. Consequently, *Long Day's Journey* premiered on the *Broadway on Showtime* program in April 1987. After being repeated several times on the for-profit network, it was broadcast for free in May 1988 as part of PBS's

American Playhouse series and distributed as a video cassette by American Playhouse.

The video retains the essential approach and interpretation of the stage version, but Jonathan Miller being a talented and experienced television director, it also makes effective use of the camera to emphasize particular nuances. Miller carried over his technique of overlapping many of the lines from the stage production, and he had the actors, particularly Bethel Leslie as Mary, speak some of their dialogue at top speed, so that, although the video runs for only about three hours, it is the most complete rendition of the play available. The only substantial cuts are most of Edmund's quotations in Act 4 (132–35). Most of the overlapping of speeches takes place in the first two acts of the play, as the family members interact with each other. Although they are not paying attention to the content of each other's complaints, the overlapping gives a sense of their engaging with one another emotionally on familiar ground. There is less of this free-for-all in Acts 3 and 4, when Mary is pursuing her drug-induced solipsistic state and when James, Edmund, and Jamie are actually telling each other things for the first time, and paying attention to them. Although the overlapping technique is effective in conveying these dynamics of the family's life together, the breakneck pace of the speeches, particularly Leslie's, is less effective, particularly when she recites a speech such as her "none of us can help the things life has done to us . . ." (61) and her modified monologues in Act 3 with the same flat intonation and speed as the "Hail Mary" she recites by rote. As Jamie, Kevin Spacey is more successful with the quick-paced start of his confession in Act 4 because he varies the pace in his modified monologue, using the contrasts to delineate his emotional trajectory. Peter Gallagher and Jack Lemmon speak pretty much at normal speed throughout the play, which emphasizes the centrality of Edmund and James in this production.

The set for the video is minimal. Its horizontally paneled walls and sparse, shabby furniture are dimly lit by John Rook, mainly through translucent windows in the first three acts and the chandelier in the fourth, to produce the sepia tones of an old photograph. The unit set is unusual in that it includes a grand piano at stage right and the stairway is centrally placed on the set, behind the round table and chairs and the wicker settee where most of the action takes place. Miller placed a camera on the landing, which angles down on Leslie and Gallagher at the end of Act 1 and on Leslie and Lemmon at the end of Act 3. As Leslie walks by the camera on her way upstairs, Gallagher is left at the bottom of the stairs looking up, a shot that is repeated with Lemmon. Gallagher delivers the last lines of Act 1 into a void, and then says "Mama!," a cry that isn't heard, and has a coughing fit as he leaves. This moment foreshadows the end of the play, when, just before Mary's final line he says again, "Mama!" and Leslie looks at his face and says "Who?" before she puts her arms around the seated Lemmon from the back and says she fell in love with James Tyrone and was so happy for a time. The camera shoots Leslie from above as she goes up the stairs at the end of Act 3 and Lemmon says "Up to take more of that God-damned poison" (123). After she disappears from view, Lemmon is shot from above, looking small and pathetic as he shouts in a heartbroken anger, "Mary!" and is left alone. This shot is reprised in Act 4, when Lemmon is shot from above through the chandelier, as he turns on all the lights in his vain and short-lived gesture against his terror of poverty.

Miller also makes effective use of the long shot, showing the whole depth of the set as the Tyrones move dispiritedly into the dining room after the men have discovered Mary's relapse. Just the end of the dining table is visible in the shot, as Lemmon stands behind Leslie's chair, taking refuge in the habit of middle-class etiquette as he pulls it out for her and Gallagher gets heavily to his feet. Miller also uses the long shot to indicate the dynamics between the characters in a scene. For example, in Act 2, scene 1, when Jamie realizes that Mary has relapsed by the first sound of her voice, but Edmund does not, Miller places Bethel Leslie on the stairs above the boys, Gallagher at far stage right and in front of her, and Spacey at center stage, looking straight at the camera, his devastation clear to see.

Miller goes to a close-up on Spacey as he turns to look at his mother, the accusation in his face the only concern at this point, and then a close-up on Spacey's back as he resolutely turns away. The double triangulation of the scene – Jamie between the mother who has failed him and the brother he loves, hates, and blames; Edmund between the useless hope he places in his mother and the despairing cynicism of his brother – brings out the full implications of Mary's speech about respecting their father. Several times, Miller uses the long shot to place the speaking character between two reactors, creating an overall effect of the intermeshed subjective lives of the Tyrones. More often, he makes use of the close-up reaction shot, as during the Act 4 monologues, when there are five reaction shots of Gallagher during Lemmon's modified monologue about his acting career and three of Lemmon during Gallagher's modified monologue about the sea. Both Gallagher and Lemmon provide crucial information in these close-ups, so the viewer is ready to accept Edmund's statement that he understands his father much better and James's that his son has the makings of a poet in him when they come.

Although Miller takes great pains to show the Tyrone family as an organic unit and its members as deeply enmeshed in each others' psyches, it is clear that this is James's show. If only because he is the only actor who speaks almost all his lines at a normal speed, Jack Lemmon is the one the audience attends to. He also makes a constant accompaniment of mutterings, sighs, and grunts to the other characters' dialogue, and his approach to the part involves a great deal of business with props that create constant motion, such as combing his hair, going through his mail, pouring coffee and drinking it, and fussing with his glasses and a handkerchief. In Act 4, he takes off his belt and slaps the table with it when he talks about thrashing Edmund. The effect of this business is to create a nervous James, but not so much a fussy as an evasive one. Lemmon plays James Tyrone as an angry man. He is angry with Mary, with Jamie, and with Edmund. He places his hand on his belly to indicate the physical pain that they exacerbate with every conflict. He tries to get away from his family when they make him angry, and he uses objects and activity to distract himself from his anger, but he is not always successful.

In Act 2, scene 2, for example, when James and Mary discuss the automobile, Lemmon quickly moves from concern about his wife to anger at the waste of his money. His speech about the expense builds in vehemence so that his lines about "the same old waste that will land me in the poorhouse" (84) is delivered angrily, and the next dialogue, which Miller overlaps, is an eruption of anger between the two of them. Lemmon then heads toward the stairs, and the rest of his momentum in the scene is toward flight. His line "You won't even try" (85), which is usually whispered while James takes Mary in his arms, is delivered here as an accusation from the landing of the stairs, and two close-ups on Lemmon during Mary's complaint about her social ostracism after marrying an actor show his anger and resentment. He comes down the stairs briefly, but heads back up again when Mary starts complaining about life on the road, then comes down and kisses her hands when he says "For God's sake, forget the past!" (87). When she responds angrily with her "The past is the present" speech, he leaves her and sits in a chair in the foreground, facing front, while she stands behind him. Finally, Edmund's appearance gives him the escape he has been seeking throughout the scene, and he meets him on the landing for the dialogue about the $10.00 gift, which Lemmon makes clear is a mistake that he decides to follow through on.

In Act 4, Lemmon and Peter Gallagher play James and Edmund as far more alienated than is usual. The opening conflict about turning out the light is not dismissed with bantering affection after the belt incident; both mutter their apologies half-heartedly. This opening skirmish about James's miserliness is escalated in the argument about James's responsibility for Mary's addiction, and Edmund's line that he cannot help liking his father in spite of everything is not met with a grin. Lemmon delivers the line "You're no great shakes as a son. It's a case of 'A poor thing but mine own'" (143) with a long, cold, contemptuous look, and Gallagher turns away. When Lemmon says the lines about Edmund's not having to go to the state sanatorium, Gallagher does not face him, but is shot through the window as he stares out, with Lemmon behind him. When Lemmon tries to take his arm, he breaks away and grabs a drink. During the speech about James's childhood, Gallagher does not soften, responding as though this were all an old story in which he was not very much interested, inserting "I know," saying some of the lines along with Lemmon, and correcting him with "it was Christmas" when Lemmon says his mother got the $1 tip on Thanksgiving. It is only during the speech about James's career that Gallagher begins to show sympathy for his father, and even then he maintains a distant, observer's stance.

On the other hand, beneath the outright hostility between James and Jamie, Lemmon and Spacey portray a tacit understanding, as when they shift into a well-practiced act to shield Mary from their talk about her relapsing in Act 1 and when they communicate silently after Tyrone gets off the phone with Dr. Hardy in Act 2. Lemmon's James Tyrone is not the dignified paterfamilias of Fredric March, Ralph Richardson, or Earle Hyman, but, like Laurence Olivier, a very human instance of "man beset." He is a man who really does love his family "in spite of everything," but can't help feeling both guilt and anger. Lemmon underscores his ordinariness by numerous small changes in his lines that make them less distinctive, less Irish and "actorly," and more prosaic. For example, he changes James's line after his speech about the money-maker, "Maybe you'll only feel more contempt for me. And it's a poor way to convince you of the value of a dollar" (151), to "You'll probably only resent me all the more. It's really not a very good way to teach you the value of a dollar."

Bethel Leslie's Mary is on the earthy, pragmatic, Geraldine Fitzgerald model. In the opening scenes, she behaves affectionately and naturally with James, even giving him an impish look when he declares that land is "safer than the stocks and bonds of Wall Street swindlers" (15). She shows flashes of anger in the first act that show why the men are exchanging worried glances about her, and these escalate into eruptions later as she loses her inhibitions, slapping Edmund and shouting bitterly at James. For the most part, however, Leslie plays Mary's drug reaction as an increasing indifference to her listeners as she rattles on at breakneck speed about the past in a flat, monotonous voice. Unlike most productions, this one includes almost all of Mary's lines, but they are delivered without nuance or emphasis. The only exception to this is the final scene, when Leslie, whom Miller has wearing her wedding dress rather than carrying it, plays with her hair and speaks the lines about the convent in a childish voice that sounds more like a child of seven than the senior in high school she is remembering. Like Ruby Dee's, her final state comes off as infantile, giving a strange cast to her final lines about falling in love with James Tyrone.

Kevin Spacey's Jamie is angry like his father, but in an adolescent way. He evades his anger through mockery and joking, such as adding animal sound effects to the Shaughnessy story when Edmund tells it and constantly mocking James when he talks. Miller also has Spacey play an obvious Oedipal subtext. Jamie filches a cigar from his father, puts on his glasses and sits in his chair in Act 1. In Act 2, he enters with the cigar in his mouth, and keeps it there when he sneaks James's whiskey. His emotional tie to his mother is evident in his look of complete devastation when he sees that she has relapsed and his crying when he tells Edmund about catching her in the act with a "hypo." In one of the most satisfying performances of the Edmund–Jamie scene in Act 4, Spacey and Gallagher convey a deep bond between the brothers, beginning with the unspoken sympathy beneath their giggling together on the settee over the Mamie Burns episode. The brothers stay in sync as the mood changes quickly when Edmund punches Jamie for the "hophead" remark. By the end of the confession, both brothers are crying, but the confession is not cathartic. Miller places Gallagher at the window, and Spacey passed out on the settee, so that Edmund has been distanced from his brother, as he has from his father, although he understands them better.

This is in keeping with Gallagher's generally dark interpretation of the role. His Edmund is clearly exhausted and ill as well as sick at heart. Miller's coaching on the symptoms of tuberculosis is evident in his performance. Edmund becomes progressively more tired, lies down when he can, and has coughing fits whenever he gets up. He is also visibly drunk in Act 4, and sits shivering in his pea coat after his walk in the fog. Distanced by both James's and Jamie's confessions, he is finally cut off from the family when Mary responds with "Who?" to his "Mama!" Both Jonathan Miller and the cast liked to talk about the humor in the play and the familial bond the Tyrones exemplify, but this is in essence a very dark interpretation of *Long Day's Journey*, in which understanding does not necessarily bring forgiveness, and forgiveness does not necessarily bring peace. What Miller accomplishes here is to bring out the painful and inexplicable emotional ties that unite the Tyrone family, and their inability to break free of them "in spite of everything."

CINEPLEX ODEON FILMS, 1996

The 1994 Stratford, Ontario production was so successful that it was repeated at the Stratford Shakespeare Festival the following year, and then Rhombus Media, a Toronto-based production company known for its performing arts films, acquired the film rights. *Long Day's Journey* was filmed in Toronto on a very tight budget of $2.1 million, released by Cineplex Odeon films, and later broadcast on the CBC network in Canada and Bravo cable network in the US. Because of the limited budget, the 173-minute film had to be shot in thirty days, a heroic schedule for actors and director. In approaching the conception of the film which is, according to the credits, "inspired by" the Stratford production directed by Diana Leblanc, David Wellington did not interfere with the actors' approaches to their roles. Having seen the Stratford production fifteen times, he worked with the play as they had realized it, telling an interviewer:

"They're very gifted, intuitive people . . . and the last thing they need is clutter in the way they're thinking and the way they work."[21] The adaptation from stage to film was another matter, however, and Wellington's approach to the film demanded absolutely minimal acting. As Martha Henry, who played Mary, said: "He's been after all of us, and especially me, to bring it way down . . . And finally, you have no choice, you have to trust the director – that he knows what he's seeing and that he's getting what he's seeing."[22]

The performances are so understated that the actors, particularly Henry, murmur rather than speak their lines, and the virtuoso William Hutt, as James, often speaks with perfect emphasis at a level that is just beyond a whisper. The aesthetic reason for this is more than just the transfer from stage to screen. This interpretation treats the Tyrones as fundamentally a family with a secret. They speak in low tones and conspire together as if in constant danger of being overheard, which they sometimes are. Like Sidney Lumet's and Peter Wood's, Wellington's production employs the camera as a "fifth character," peering voyeuristically through windows and doorways, picking up the listener in the background as well as the speakers. The camera's subjectivity is established during the opening credits, as James and Mary engage in their seemingly meaningless, desultory conversation. The camera begins by slowly panning the entire set, created by John Dondertman in great detail on the plan of the Monte Cristo Cottage, which he and Wellington, along with several of the actors, flew to New London to visit in preparation for the production. The effect is that of an outsider slowly taking in the Tyrone family's private world.

Unlike the dreary minimalism of most productions, this set is a museum-like material representation of upper-middle-class North American life in 1912. It is brightly lit in Acts 1 and 2, and plentifully furnished with good, well-cared for furniture, oriental rugs, and paintings on the walls. Like Monte Cristo Cottage, the set has a front door opening to a hall and staircase. An open archway leads to the parlor, painted white, which contains the piano. Another archway leads to the sun room at stage right, paneled in light wood, with the familiar round table and chairs and sofa, although this is an expensive upholstered sofa, rather than the usual wicker and chintz settee. A door with panes of frosted glass leads to the dining room upstage, which has a heavy, dark dining table and sideboard, fine white linen, and expensive china. Not only is the house evidence of the Tyrones' prosperity, and perhaps Mary's conventional taste, it is also an environment particular to them. There are a number of theatrical photographs on the walls. Portrait photographs of Shakespeare and of the young James O'Neill in costume are conspicuous, and are strategically framed with James and with Mary in several shots. The bookcases and the piano also figure prominently in early scenes, establishing their significance for the family.

After the slow panning of the opening has established the Tyrones' environment, Wellington uses a sequence of visual synecdoches to suggest the threat of disruption that is harbored within this seemingly calm and ordered home. The camera shows a series of tight, off-center close-ups, several on Mary's arthritic hand, which Martha Henry forms almost into a claw and emphasizes throughout the film by holding it in front of her, constantly rubbing it and calling attention to it, a metonymic representation of the morphine addiction that has twisted her soul and caused her to lose her faith. The camera also focuses briefly on the newspaper that James is reading, a reference to O'Neill/Edmund's brief tenure on the *New London Telegraph*, on the piano, and on various parts of Mary's body – her torso, her waist, her hand touching her hair, and her ear, emphasizing her nervous movements. Later in the scene, as she becomes more and more upset about Edmund, the camera follows Mary's nervous movement, first tracking her pacing around the room, and then, after James and Jamie go outside, panning the set as she moves frantically from room to room until Edmund comes down the stairs.

Mary's imprisonment in the house is emphasized by Henry's looking out of windows, and her being photographed through them from the outside. For example, she says her speech about the Chatfields looking first through the blinds of one window, and then running to another to peer through the curtains. She is shot from the outside through the blinds, an obvious prison-bar effect, and then from the back as she strains to see through the filmy curtains covering the window. When the men leave her at the end of Act 2, she is shot through the screen door, another barrier, and then the camera moves behind and above her as she finally sits bent over on the stairs, saying, "Mother of God, why do I feel so lonely?" (95). A similar closed-in effect is achieved during Edmund's speech about the fog in Act 4, although for him it is ultimately liberating. He is first shot through the window in a long shot showing the porch in the fog. As he talks about finding peace in the fog, the camera moves in to a clear close-up and is followed by an inside shot as he tells his father, "I'm talking sense" (131). The camera is angled several times from above or below the stairs in order to diminish or emphasize the characters, and they are often shot through the doorway in their conspiratorial moments, as if about to be discovered.

Aided by Ron Sures's melancholy score, the mood of the film is languid and sad rather than volatile. There is very little laughter in this version, and the few times that Hutt and Henry raise their voices in anger are startling amidst the almost laconic interactions of the family during the first two acts. One might say that these Tyrones are more Canadian than Irish, and this is emphasized by their diction. Hutt and Henry speak with just the hint of a brogue in Act 1, and none of the actors make any attempt to disguise their Canadian accents. When Tom McCamus tells the Shaughnessy story, he imitates him in the accent of a rough Canadian farmer rather than that of an Irish immigrant. In Act 4, Hutt heightens his brogue a bit during his reminiscences, but the most interesting use of the accent is Henry's brogue in the final scene when Mary is speaking as her convent-girl self. This is a very effective device, which, in addition to emphasizing her dissociation from the present, helps Henry to suggest youthful innocence with her lilting tones, and yet avoid the childish quality that too often enters this scene when actors try to suggest youth.

Henry becomes progressively more languid and detached as Mary drifts into her drugged state, but her dreaminess is broken by moments of anger, weeping, and physically reaching out to James and Edmund. Until Act 4, Hutt underplays James, and the focus is centered on the bond between Mary and Edmund. This is underscored by Henry's constant attempts to engage Edmund physically. She hugs him, plays with his hair, rocks him in the rocking chair, holds his head on her breast, whispers in his ear, and pats his head, constantly trying to keep him with her and away from Dr. Hardy through a strange mixture of flirtation and mothering that has clear Oedipal overtones. McCamus breaks away from her several times, whenever he tries to get her to understand that his illness is serious while she insists that all he needs is his mother to nurse him. The one time she breaks away from him is when Edmund tries to draw her to him so he can see her eyes and tell whether she has relapsed. The trajectory of their relationship is Edmund pulling away from the comfort of Mary's illusory world and into the real world. His final lines to her, "Mama! It is not a summer cold! I've got consumption!" (174), isn't so much the plea of "*a bewilderedly hurt little boy,*" as O'Neill's stage directions have it, as the culmination of a struggle between mother and son, and a last offer to Mary to join him in facing the world.

Hutt's James is businesslike and self-controlled, clipped in speech and stern with the boys in Act 1. He softens throughout the play, with moments of authentic emotion such as his heartfelt "For the love of God, for my sake and the boys' sake and your own, won't you stop now?" (85) to Mary, which is followed by the startling anger of his shouted "I hope you'll lay in a good stock ahead" (86). He is on the verge of tears when he pleads with Mary in Act 3, "Mary! Can't you forget – ?" (113) after she tells Edmund about his drinking. These glimpses of James's emotional nature prepare the way for the scene with Edmund in Act 4. His soft intonation of the line, "A poor

14   Tom McCamus as Edmund, William Hutt as James

thing but mine own'" (143) conveys a depth of affection for his son, to which Edmund responds. Hutt and McCamus play the speech about James's childhood as if Edmund is hearing it for the first time, and both of them are moved by it. When Hutt asks him what he thinks he got for his work in the machine shop, McCamus shakes his head slightly and murmurs, "I don't know" (148). When Hutt repeats James's mother's line, " 'Glory be to God, for once in our lives we'll have enough for each of us!' " he weeps. Hutt also weeps when he tells the Edwin Booth story, and both he and McCamus respond to each other with a new candor at the end of his confession scene. McCamus goes and switches out the hall light when Hutt turns out the extra bulbs in the chandelier, a gesture of respect and sympathy.

The part of Edmund is emphasized in this production as observer, judge, and truth-teller, not as victim. McCamus has few coughing fits, and the ones he has are mild. In fact he seems to have more energy than any of the other characters. In Act 4, he stands and declaims his modified monologue as if it were poetry, not seeming the least bit tired after his long walk in the fog. During Jamie's modified monologue, the only one that is cut considerably, Edmund is the one in control, being much less drunk than his brother. Peter Donaldson plays Jamie as a believable alcoholic, without the tortured depths of Robards' or Spacey's performances. He is a sloppy drunk, confessing unsavory things about himself to warn his brother, not Cain confessing to Abel. Wellington has cut most of the lines about the Mamie Burns episode, so there is no chance for the bond between the brothers to be established before the confession. McCamus plays Edmund as disgusted with Jamie when he first comes in. They do have a giggling fit together over James's "within reason" line, and when Donaldson says that he picked Fat Violet, McCamus literally falls on the floor laughing. After he slaps him down for the "hophead" line, McCamus lifts Donaldson's head and cradles it for a moment and he hugs him when he says, "I love your guts. I'd do anything for you" (163). The first half of Jamie's confession is cut, from that point: to "Listen, Kid, you'll be going away" (165), so that his modified monologue is a relatively brief confession of his feelings of love and hate, ending with his trying to sit on a chair and landing on the floor. The effect is to present Jamie as truly a "drunken hulk" of a man who is past hope and Edmund as a sympathetic observer, rather than to create a moment of confession, epiphany, and disillusionment between two brothers who have a deep emotional bond between them.

In the final scene, with the appearance of a ghost-like Mary, wearing white with her hair down and her wedding veil over her head, Edmund appears to be the strongest of the family, as James reverts to a stoic dignity and Jamie looks on in an alcoholic stupor. Martha Henry's rendition of the monologue brings Mary to peace in the past, and she delivers her final line with the emphasis on "happy" rather than "for a time." After close-ups on McCamus, Donaldson, and Hutt, the men watching Mary, the camera shoots the family through the window, and then pulls slowly out, showing the wall of the house and the porch in the fog. As with Wood's production, the effect is to reestablish the spectator's point of view as external to that of the suffering family inside and somewhat voyeuristic. The Tyrone family secrets are once more enclosed within the walls of their ordinary-looking, middle-class house.

NOTES

1 The New York premiere

1 Eugene O'Neill Work Diary, 1939–43, BEINECKE, rpt. *Eugene O'Neill at Work*, ed. Virginia Floyd (New York: Ungar, 1981): 281.

2 Work Diary, 1939–43, rpt. Floyd 292.

3 Eugene O'Neill to Georg Jean Nathan, 15 June 1956. Travis Bogard and Jackson R. Bryer, *Selected Letters of Eugene O'Neill* (New Haven: Yale University Press, 1988): 506–07.

4 Judith E. Barlow, *Final Acts: The Creation of Three Late O'Neill Plays* (Athens: University of Georgia Press, 1985): 72.

5 Work Diary, 1939–43, rpt. Floyd: 296.

6 Eugene O'Neill to Bennett Cerf, 13 June 1951, Bogard and Bryer: 589.

7 Bennett Cerf to Eugene O'Neill, 15 June 1951, BEINECKE.

8 *Inscriptions: Eugene O'Neill to Carlotta Monterey O'Neill* (New Haven: privately printed, 1960): n.p.

9 Quoted in Louis Sheaffer, *O'Neill: Son and Artist* (Boston: Little, Brown, 1973): 635.

10 Jane Rubin to Carlotta Monterey O'Neill, 27 January 1954, BEINECKE.

11 Donald S. Klopfer, Random House, Inc. to Jane Rubin, 30 March 1954, BEINECKE.

12 Carlotta Monterey O'Neill, Diary, 13? July 1954, BEINECKE, rpt. Barlow: 179 n. 41. It should be noted that Carlotta recopied her diaries in the early 1960s, editing the entries.

13 Karl Ragnar Gierow and Pat M. Ryan, "*LDJ* Was the 'Wrong' Play," *Theatre Survey* 29 (May 1988): 107. Gierow thought that his later acquaintance with Carlotta O'Neill demonstrated that her reputation was undeserved.

14 Carlotta Monterey O'Neill to Dag Hammarskjöld, 14 June 1955, BEINECKE.

15 Carlotta Monterey O'Neill to Karl Ragnar Gierow, 16 June 1956, BEINECKE.

16 Carlotta Monterey O'Neill to Karl Ragnar Gierow, 19 Aug. 1955, BEINECKE.

17 "Stockholm to See Last O'Neill Play," *New York Times* 5 Jan. 1956: 26. Dramaten had produced nine of O'Neill's plays at this point.

18 Carlotta Monterey O'Neill to Blevins Davis, 18 May 1956, BEINECKE.

19 Jo Mielziner to Carlotta Monterey O'Neill, 24 Feb. 1955, BEINECKE.

20 Jo Mielziner to Carlotta Monterey O'Neill, 25 May 1956, BEINECKE.

21 "Schools May See Drama by O'Neill," *New York Times* 11 May 1956: 24.

22 Lewis Funke, "Billy Rose Joins Quest for O'Neill Play," *New York Times* 3 June 1956: sec. 2, 1.

23 "Sponsors for Reading Tour of O'Neill's Play Set," *New York Times* 17 June 1956: sec. 2, 1.

24 Mildred Dunnock to Carlotta Monterey O'Neill, 18 June 1956, BEINECKE.

25 Carlotta Monterey O'Neill to Lewis Funke, 26 June 1956, BEINECKE. Published in the *New York Times*, 1 July 1956: sec. 2, 1.

26 Statement to the Drama Editor, *New York Times*, 27 July 1956, BEINECKE.

27 Sheaffer, *O'Neill: Son and Artist*: 634. See also Arthur Gelb and Barbara Gelb, *O'Neill*, enlarged edition with a new epilogue. (New York: Harper & Row, 1973): 862 and Gelb and Gelb, *O'Neill: Life With Monte Cristo* (New York: Applause, 2000): 14.

28 Ibid.: 635.

29 Barlow: 74.

30 Eugene O'Neill to Eugene O'Neill, Jr., 28 April 1941; Bogard and Bryer: 517.

31 Work Diary, 1939–43, BEINECKE; quoted in Barlow: 74.

32 Dorothy Commins, *What Is an Editor?: Saxe Commins at Work* (Chicago: University of Chicago Press, 1978): 54.

33 Quoted in Sheaffer: 666–67.

34 Jane Rubin to Carlotta Monterey O'Neill, 4 Feb. 1955, BEINECKE.

35 Jane Rubin to Carlotta Monterey O'Neill, 14 Mar. 1956, BEINECKE.

36 Seymour Peck, "Talk with Mrs. O'Neill," *New York Times*, 4 Nov. 1956: sec. 2, 3.

37 See his accounts in José Quintero, *If You Don't Dance They Beat You* (1974; New York: St. Martin's, 1988): 205–06; José Quintero, "Postscript to a Journey," *Theatre Arts* 41 (Apr. 1957): 29; Mamie Crichton, "A Call from the Widow in Black Meant Fame," *Scottish Daily Express* 9 Sep. 1958; and Leonard Harris, "Quintero Given Blessing by Mrs. Eugene O'Neill," *New York World-Telegram & Sun* 19 Feb. 1964.

38 See "Carlotta and the Master," *New York Times* 1 May 1988: sec. 6, 56.

39 Mel Gussow, "José Quintero's Long Journey Back," *New York Times* 28 Jan. 1974: 34.

40 It should be noted that Ted Mann relates a different version of events in which both he and Quintero were present in Carlotta's apartment, along with Jane Rubin (Sheila Hickey Garvey, "'Not for Profit': The History of the Circle in the Square." Ph. D diss., New York University, 1984: 179–83). His presence at the meeting is supported by the version told in Lewis Funke's theatrical gossip column, "News and Gossip on the Rialto" *(New York Times* 23 July 1956: sec. 2, 1), which reports that all three producers went to see Carlotta.

41 Contract between Carlotta Monterey O'Neill and José Quintero, Theodore Mann, and Lee Connell, 11 July 1956, BEINECKE.

42 José Quintero, "Postscript to a Journey": 29.

43 Helen Ormsbee, "Likes Acting with Husband: Miss Eldridge Shares Career," *New York Herald Tribune* 1 Sep. 1957.

44 "Postscript to a Journey": 29.

45 Ibid. In an interview with Ward Morehouse before the show opened, Quintero said, "I had read 150 actors for the role of the young O'Neill and I finally took Bradford to Mrs. O'Neill for her approval. She had wanted the okay on that particular part."("Broadway After Dark," Newark *Star Ledger* 23 Oct. 1956.)

46 Elinor Hughes, "'I Hope I'm Good Enough': Young Actors Get Key Roles in Last Eugene O'Neill Play," *Boston Herald* 15 Oct. 1956.

47 *New York Times* 26 Aug 1956, clipping file, NYPL. As Fig. 3 shows, Monte Cristo Cottage has no widow's walk.

48 Phyllis Funke, "José Quintero and the Devil of Success," *Wall Street Journal* 15 May 1974: 20.

49 This and subsequent page references cited as "Q" are to José Quintero, *If You Don't Dance They Beat You* (1974; New York: St. Martin's, 1988).

50 Morehouse, "Broadway After Dark."

51 Barbara Gelb, "Quintero in the Square," *New York Times* 16 Feb. 1964: sec. 2, 3.

52 This and subsequent page references cited in the text as "M" refer to Edwin Joseph McDonough, *Quintero Directs O'Neill* (New York: a capella books, 1991).

53 Emory Lewis, "Journey Uptown With O'Neill," *Cue* 3 Nov. 1956: 13.

54 Gilbert Millstein, "José Quintero," *Theatre Arts* 44 (May 1960): 12.

55 Millstein: 12.

56 David Hays, *Light on the Subject* (New York: Limelight, 1989): 5.

57 The drawings have been reproduced in Virginia Floyd, *Eugene O'Neill at Work*: 295.

58 There is a color photograph of the set in the *New York Sunday News* 24 March 1957. David Hays's original watercolor drawing of the set, inscribed to José Quintero, is in the BEINECKE.

59 Hays: 76.

60 Wolcott Gibbs, "Doom," *New Yorker* 32 (24 Nov. 1956): 121.

61 A second script belonging to Fredric March is in the Fredric March Collection at the Wisconsin State Historical Society, Madison, Wisconsin.

62 Holograph notes laid into Fredric March's script for *LDJIN*, with underlinings and holograph notes, Monte Cristo Cottage, New London, Connecticut.

63 José Quintero, "On Stage," *Playbill* August 1975: 23.

64 Ibid.: 23–26.

65 Ibid.: 23.

66 The phrase was attributed to Laurence Olivier by Elliot Martin: "He said, 'Freddie took the actor home. I'm going to be a common man.' And so he was. He played a little fussbudget in the home. I think that was wrong because everything you ever read about James O'Neill, the pictures you see, they were all declamatory. He just wanted to be different from Freddie" (McDonough: 56).

67 Holograph notes laid into Fredric March's script for *LDJIN*, with underlinings, Monte Cristo Cottage, New London, Connecticut.

68 Quintero: "On Stage" 23.

69 Brooks Atkinson, "Theatre: Tragic Journey," *New York Times* 9 Nov. 1956, *NYTCR*.

70 Florence Eldridge, "Reflections on *LDJIN*: First Curtain Call for Mary Tyrone," *Eugene O'Neill: A World View*, ed. Virginia Floyd (New York: Ungar, 1979): 286–87.

71 Ormsbee.

72 Eldridge, "Reflections on *LDJIN*": 286.

73 Ibid.

74 Gussow: 34.

75 Eldridge, "Reflections on *LDJIN*" 286. Judith E. Barlow offers a persuasive analysis of the relationship between Carlotta and Mary Tyrone in "Mother, Wife, Mistress, Friend and Collaborator: Carlotta Monterey and *LDJIN*" in *Eugene O'Neill and the Emergence of American Drama* (ed. Marc Maufort. Amsterdam: Rodopi, 1989: 123–31).

76 R. J. L., "Eugene O'Neill's Last Play," *New Haven Register* 30 Oct. 1956.

77 Kenneth Johnson, "Robards: He's Like Hotspur, Noted for Fire and Storm," *Boston Globe Magazine* 5 Apr. 1958: 12.

78 Mel Gussow, "Robards and a Long Career's Journey," *New York Times* 22 Dec. 1975: 44.

79 Arthur Gelb, "Long Journey Into Light," *New York Times* 25 Nov. 1956: sec. 2, 3.

80 Barbara Gelb, "A Touch of the Tragic," *New York Times Magazine* 11 December 1977: 126.

81 Henry Hewes, "O'Neill: 100 Proof – Not a Blend," *Saturday Review* 39 (24 Nov. 1956): 30.

82 Walter Kerr, "'LDJ,'" *New York Herald Tribune* 18 Nov. 1956.

83 Kenneth Johnson, "Robards: He's Like Hotspur, Noted for Fire and Storm," *Boston Globe Magazine* 5 April 1958: 12; and Tom Killen, "Jason Robards and the O'Neill Connection," *Westport News* 14 Oct. 1981: 22.

84 Ormsbee.

85 Barbara Gelb: 125–6.

86 Alta Maloney, "'LDJ' O'Neill Drama, Wilbur," *Boston Traveler* 16 Oct. 1956.

87 Guy, "LDJIN," *Variety* 16 Oct. 1956.

88 Elinor Hughes, "'LDJIN,'" *Boston Herald* 16 Oct. 1956.

89 Cyrus Durgin, "'LDJ' O'Neill's Last, Great Play," *Boston Daily Globe* 16 Oct. 1956.

90 Elliot Norton, "O'Neill Play Needs Cut," *Boston Sunday Advertiser* 21 Oct. 1956.

91 Elinor Hughes, "'LDJ' an Absorbing Emotional Drama," *Boston Sunday Herald* 21 Oct. 1956.

92 Eldridge, "Reflections": 287.

93 John Chapman, "'LDJIN' A Drama of Sheer Magnificence," *New York Daily News* 8 Nov. 1956, *NYTCR*.

94 Brooks Atkinson, "Theatre: Tragic Journey," *New York Times* 9 Nov. 1956, *NYTCR*.

95 "Triumph From the Past," *Newsweek* 48 (19 Nov. 1956): 117.

96 John McClain, "Superb Cast Supplements O'Neill Genius," *New York Journal American* 8 Nov. 1956, *NYTCR*.

97 Tom Donnelly, "A Long Journey Worth Taking," *New York World-Telegram* 8 Nov. 1956, *NYTCR*.

98 Richard Watts, Jr., "A Superb Drama by Eugene O'Neill," *New York Post* 8 Nov. 1956, *NYTCR*.

99 Walter Kerr, "'LDJIN,'" *New York Herald Tribune*, 8 Nov. 1956, *NYTCR*.

100 John Chapman, "'LDJIN' Is Great Event in Our Theatre," *Sunday News* 18 Nov. 1956: sec. 2, 1.

101 Walter Kerr, "'LDJ,'" *New York Herald Tribune* 18 Nov. 1956.

102 Land, "LDJIN," *Variety* 6 Feb. 1957.

103 "O'Neill's 'Long Day' Goes to Paris," *Boston Record* 22 Feb. 1957.

104 "'Journey' By O'Neill Is Staged in Paris," *New York Times* 3 July 1957: 14.

105 Thomas Quinn Curtiss, "'LDJ' a Hit," *New York Herald Tribune*, Paris edition, 4 July 1957.

106 Jean-Jacques Gautier, "Le long voyage dans la nuit," *Le Figaro* 4 July 1957.

107 "'Journey' a Long Night's Paris Hit," *Variety* 10 July 1957.

108 "Chi Bally Keeps 'Journey' on Road," *Variety* 21 Jan. 1958.

109 Claudia Cassidy, "On the Aisle," *Chicago Tribune* 7 Jan. 1958: sec. 2, 13.

110 Richard L. Coe, "Great Drama: A Week Only," *Washington Post* 18 March 1958.

111 Cassidy: 13.

112 Van Allen Bradley, "Eugene O'Neill Is Real Star of 'LDJ,'" *Chicago Daily News* 7 Jan. 1958: 16.

113 Ibid.

114 "Force of O'Neill's Drama 'Of Old Sorrow' Overrides Defects," *Chicago Sun-Times* 7 Jan. 1958: 34.

115 Dudley Nichols to Carlotta Monterey O'Neill, 29 April 1958, BEINECKE.

2 Productions in English

1 "Big US Share in 1958 Festival," Press Release, Festival News Service, 19 Mar. 1958.

2 *New York Times* 26 Mar. 1958, clippings file, NYPL.

3 New York *Journal American*, 26 Mar. 1958, clippings file, NYPL and letter, Audrey Wood to Carlotta O'Neill, 18 June 1956, BEINECKE.

4 Anthony Cookman, "A Playwright's Personal Drama," *The Tatler & Bystander* 8 Oct. 1958: 82.

5 W. A. Darlington, "O'Neill Play Tautened," *Daily Telegraph* (London), BEINECKE.

6 Tynan, "Massive Masterpiece," *The Observer* (London) 28 Sep. 1958.

7 Tynan, "Massive Masterpiece"; see also R. B. M. "O'Neill Takes Us on His 'LDJIN,'" *Stage* (London) 2 Oct. 1958.

8 Cookman: 82.

9 Ronald Mavor, "Quality of Truth Bars Criticism," *The Scotsman* 9 Sep. 1958.

10 "Bold Experiment on the Edinburgh Stage," *The Times Weekly Review* (London) 11 Sep. 1958: 13.

11 Felix Barker, "A Play for Everyone Who Thinks," *Evening News*, clippings file, BEINECKE.

12 Ibid.

13 Cecil Wilson, "This Grim Game of Unhappy Families," *Daily Mail* 2 Oct. 1958.

14 Laurence Olivier, *On Acting* (New York: Simon and Schuster, 1986): 245.

15 Ibid.: 244–45.

16 Ibid.: 247.

17 According to Elliot Martin, Olivier told him, "'Freddie took the actor home. I'm going to be a common man'" (Edwin J. McDonough, *Quintero Directs O'Neill* [New York: a capella books, 1991]: 58.)

18 Harold Hobson, "Olivier's Triumph," *The Sunday Times* (London) 2 Jan. 1972: 14.

19 Jeremy Kingston, "Theatre," *Punch* 262 (5 Jan. 1972): 27.

20 Pit, "LDJIN," *Variety* 22 Dec. 1971: 37.

21 Irving Wardle, "Olivier Fascinating in London 'LDJ,'" *New York Times* 23 Dec. 1971: 16.

22 Helen Dawson, "O'Neill's Show Shop," *The Observer* (London) 2 Jan. 1972: 24.

23 Hugh Leonard, "Long Day's Journey Into Night,'" *Plays and Players* 19.5 (Feb. 1972): 48.

24 Pit: 37.

25 Leonard: 48.

26 Wardle: 16.

27 Clive Barnes, "The Theater: 'LDJ,'" *New York Times* 7 Sep. 1972: 53.

28 Leonard: 67.

29 Wardle: 16.

30 Dawson: 24.

31 R. B. Marriott, "National Company Are Masterly in O'Neill Masterpiece," *The Stage and Television Today* 30 Dec. 1971: 13.

32 Wardle: 16.

33 Dawson: 24.

34 Ibid.

35 Barnes: 53.

36 Martin Hoyle, "LDJIN," *Financial Times* 9 Apr. 1984, *LTR*.

37 Robin Thornber, "LDJIN," *The Guardian* 15 Mar. 1985, *LTR*.

38 C. L. Dallat, "Confession Is Enough," *Times Literary Supplement* 19 July 1996: 4.

39 Michael Coveney, "Guilt-Edged Agony Slumbers," *The Observer* (London) 24 Feb. 1991: 61.

40 Sheridan Morley, "LDJIN," *Herald Tribune* 29 May 1991, *LTR*.

41 Ibid.

42 Quoted in Edward L. Shaughnessy, *Eugene O'Neill in Ireland: The Critical Reception* (New York: Greenwood, 1988): 104.

43 "Abbey Theatre Turns to O'Neill," *The Times* (London) 1 May 1959.

44 J. J. F., "A Long Day with Tyrone Family," *Evening Herald* (Dublin) 29 Apr. 1959.

45 A. R., "Eugene O'Neill at the Abbey," *The Irish Times* 29 Apr. 1959.

46 "Abbey Theatre Turns to O'Neill."

47 Gerald Mayhead, "One of the Year's Best," *The Herald* (Melbourne) 15 Nov. 1973: 31.

48 Geoffrey Hutton, "A Great Writer's Last Testament," *The Age* (Melbourne) 15 Nov. 1973.

49 Howard Palmer, "A Horrifying Family Brew," *The Sun* (Melbourne) 15 Nov. 1973.

50 Mayhead: 31.

51 "O'Neill Play is Important Event," *The Gazette* 28 Feb. 1959: 24.

52 Ibid.

53 Herbert Whittaker, "Showbusiness," *Toronto Globe and Mail* 3 Mar. 1958.

54 "O'Neill Play."

55 Lawrence Sabbath, "Stage Director O'Neill Expert," *The Gazette* 7 Mar. 1959.

56 Rupert Caplan, "Montreal's Link with O'Neill," *Montreal Star* 7 Mar. 1959: sec. 2, 1.

57 Sabbath.

58 Pierre Saucier, "Caplan donne une version envoûtante de la tragédie célèbre d'Eugene O'Neill," *La Patrie du Dimanche* 15 Mar. 1959: 126.

59 Ibid. This and subsequent translations from the French are mine.

60 Ibid.

61 Video interview with Arvin Brown and Geraldine Fitzgerald, 20 July 1971, Billy Rose Theatre Collection, New York Public Library for the Performing Arts.

62 Tom Burke, "Geraldine's Long Journey," *New York Times* 13 June 1971: sec. 2, 1.

63 Video interview 20 July 1971.

64 Ibid.

65 Ibid.

66 Burke: sec. 2, 7.

67 Video interview 20 July 1971.

68 Burke: sec. 2, 7.

69 Ibid.

70 Video interview 20 July 1971.

71 George Gent, "Ryan Sees Something of Himself in O'Neill's People," *New York Times* 5 Apr. 1971: 45.

72 T. E. Kalem, "Doom Music," *Time* 97 (3 May 1971): 62.

73 Martin Gottfried, "'LDJIN,'" *Women's Wear Daily* 23 Apr. 1971.

74 Walter Kerr, "Do the Tyrones Live Here?," *New York Times* 2 May 1971: sec. 2, 3.

75 Video interview 20 July 1971.

76 Marshall Hahn, "Anytime is Ripe for an O'Neill," *New Haven Register* 21 Mar. 1971: D, 1.

77 Harold Clurman, "Theatre," *The Nation* 212 (10 May 1971): 606.

78 Jack Kroll, *Newsweek* 77 (10 May 1971): 122.

79 Howard Taubman, "Theater: O'Neill at Houston's Alley," *New York Times* 27 June 1963: 25.

80 Clive Barnes, "The Theater: 'LDJIN,'" *New York Times* 31 Mar. 1971: 67.

81 Mel Gussow, "Robards and a Long Career's Journey," *New York Times* 22 Dec. 1975: 44.

82 Ibid.

83 Douglas Watt, "A Divided Homefront," *New York Daily News* 29 Jan. 1976, *NYTCR*.

84 Gussow: 44.

85 Watt.

86 Martin Gottfried, "An Endless 'Night' in Brooklyn," *New York Post* 29 Jan. 1976, *NYTCR*.

87 "Off Broadway," *New Yorker* 51 (9 Feb. 1976): 80.

88 "Robards Returns to O'Neill's 'Journey,'" *New York Times* 25 Jan. 1976: sec. 2, 5.

89 Ibid.

90 Ibid.

91 Mark Czarnecki, "The Reign of Dissension," *MacLean's Magazine* 93 (20 Oct. 1980): 69.

92 Robert Coe, "Everybody's Autobiography," *Soho Weekly News* 27 Dec. 1979: 47.

93 David Savran, *The Wooster Group, 1975–1985: Breaking the Rules* (Ann Arbor: UMI, 1986): 146.

94 Quoted in Carol Lawson, "Broadway Celebrates Eugene O'Neill's Birthday," *New York Times* 27 Mar. 1981: C2.

95 Ibid.

96 Mel Gussow, "Theater: Black Cast Stages O'Neill," *New York Times* 3 Mar. 1981, C10.

97 "'Long Day's' Worth the Journey," *New York Post* 4 Mar. 1981, *NYTCR*.

98 "LDJIN," *New York* 14 (20 Apr. 1981): 56.

99 Christopher Sharp, "'LDJIN,'" *Women's Wear Daily* 3 March 1981, *NYTCR*.

100 Gussow: C10.

101 David Sterritt, "Splendid Black Version of O'Neill Drama," *Christian Science Monitor* 23 Apr. 1981, *NYTCR*.

102 Gussow: C10.

103 Program, *LDJIN*, National Asian American Theatre Company, 4–23 Nov. 1997.

104 Quoted in Lesley Valdes, "LDJ Onto Broadway," *Wall Street Journal* 11 Apr. 1986: 25.

105 Quoted in David Rieff, "A Shorter 'Day's Journey,'" *Vanity Fair* (May 1986): 109.

106 Michael Leech, "Miller's Journey," *Plays and Players* 1 Sep. 1986: 13.

107 Quoted in Sheila Hickey Garvey, "Rethinking O'Neill," *The Eugene O'Neill Newsletter* 10 (Winter 1986): 16.

108 Leech: 13.

109 Garvey: 16.

110 Brian Lee, "Accelerating the Decline," *Times Literary Supplement* 15 Aug. 1986: 891.

111 Jack Kroll, "Jack's Journey," *Newsweek* 5 May 1986, *NYTCR*.

112 Garvey: 17.

113 Valdes: 25.

114 Ibid.

115 Quoted in Samuel G. Freedman, "Lemmon Relives the Past in O'Neill's 'Journey,'" *New York Times* 27 Apr. 1986, sec. 2, 1.

116 Ibid.

117 "LDJIN," *Daily Mail* (London) 4 August 1986, LTR.

118 "'Day's Journey' to Glory; B'way at Its Greatest," *New York Post* 29 Apr. 1986, *NYTCR.*

119 "Stage: A New 'LDJ,'" *New York Times* 29 Apr. 1986, *NYTCR.*

120 "Role Playing, Self Reference, and Openness," *The Hudson Review* 39 (Autumn 1986): 473.

121 Garvey: 19.

122 Ibid.

123 "'Journey' Notice Up; Fourth Straight Flop for O'Neill Revival," *Variety* 18 June 1986: 93–94.

124 Linda Winer, "'A LDJ' Revisited," *Newsday* 15 June 1988, *NYTCR.*

125 Clive Barnes, "Though the Past, Darkly," *New York Post* 15 June 1988, *NYTCR.*

126 Winer.

127 Holly Hill, "O'Neill's 'Journey' Doesn't Make It," *The Advocate* (Stamford) 15 June 1988: C10.

128 Douglas Watt, "'Journey' of a Lifetime," *Daily News* 24 June 1988, *NYTCR.*

129 Frank Rich, "The Stars Align for 'LDJ,'" *New York Times* 15 June 1988: C21.

130 William A. Henry III, *Time* 27 June 1988, *NYTCR.*

131 Ibid.

132 Kenneth Tynan, "Message from Manhattan," *The Observer* (London) 26 May 1957.

133 Rich: C21.

134 Ibid.

135 Edwin Wilson, "O'Neill's Redeeming Values," *Wall Street Journal* 8 July 1988, *NYTCR.*

136 Richard Hummler, "Public Says No, No O'Neill Again; Fifth Straight B. O. Flop on B'way," *Variety* 27 July 1988, 63.

137 Linda Ben-Zvi, *LDJIN, The Eugene O'Neill Newsletter* 12.1 (Winter 1988): 64–66.

138 A. James Fisher, "*LDJIN,*" *The Eugene O'Neill Newsletter* 12.3 (Winter 1988): 50–51.

139 Joan E. Vadeboncoeur, "'LDJIN,'" *Herald-Journal* 20 Nov. 1988.

140 Vit Wagner, "Shadows of Their Former Play," *Toronto Star* 6 August 1995, Final Edition: B4.

141 David Richards, "Casting a Fearless Eye on a Sacred Text," *New York Times* 9 June 1994: C16.

142 Ibid.: C15.

143 Ibid.: C16.

144 Keith Garebian, "Following the Arts," *Journal of Canadian Studies* 31.2 (Summer 1996): 172.

145 Geoff Chapman, "Martha Henry Returns Gloriously Triumphant," *Toronto Star* 1 June 1994: D2.

146 Ibid.

147 John Bemrose, "A Great Actor Comes Home," *MacLean's Magazine* 107 (27 June 1994): 50.

148 Garebian: 172.

149 Ibid.

150 C. L. Dallat, "Confession is Enough," *Times Literary Supplement* 20 (19 July 1996): 20.

151 Bronwyn Eisenberg, "An Interview with Director Laird Williamson on *LDJIN*," *Words on Plays: LDJIN* (San Francisco: American Conservatory Theater, 1999): 36–46.

3 Productions in translation

1 "Royal Dramatic Theatre of Sweden Opens One-Week Engagement," Press Release, 13 Apr. 1962: 2.

2 Bengt Ekerot, "Propaganda tragedi i teaterarbete: några funderingar," *Teaterkonst* 1 (1956): 18. Translated in Lennart A. Björk, "The Critical Reception of Eugene O'Neill in Sweden 1923–1963," Ph.D. diss. Princeton, 1966, 120.

3 Ibid.

4 Martin Strömberg, "En familj går under på Dramaten," *Stockholms-Tidningen* 11 Feb. 1956. Translated in Björk: 127.

5 "Stockholm to See Last O'Neill Play," *New York Times* 5 June 1956: 26.

6 Carlotta Monterey O'Neill to Georg Magnusson, 20 Feb. 1956, BEINECKE.

7 Stephen Whicher, "O'Neill's Long Journey," *The Commonweal* 16 Mar. 1956: 615.

8 Åke Janzon, "Lång dags färd mot natt," *Bonniers Litterära Magazin* 25 (1956): 238. Translated in Björk: 124.

9 Henry Hewes, "O'Neill and Faulkner via the Abroad Way," *Saturday Review* 39 (20 Oct. 1956): 58.

10 Ebbe Linde, "Teaterhistoria på Dramaten," *Dagens Nyheter* 11 Feb. 1956. Translated in Björk: 123.

11 Walter Kerr, "Royal Swedish Theater *'Long Day's Journey . . .'*" *New York Herald Tribune* 16 May 1962, *NYTCR*; see also, John Chapman, "O'Neill Packs Punch in Swedish," *New York Daily News* 16 May 1962, *NYTCR* and Whitney Bolton, "Theatre," *New York Morning Telegraph* 21 May 1962, *NYTCR*.

12 Melvin Maddocks, "Swedes in New York," *Christian Science Monitor* 19 May 1962.

13 Hewes: 58.

14 Kerr, 16 May 1962.

15 Hewes: 58. See also, "Theatre Uptown," *Village Voice* 24 May 1962: 13.

16 "The Royal Dramatic Theatre of Sweden," Swedish Information Service, 1962: 2.

17 Gunnar Unger, "Dramaten: Världpremiär blev stor seger," *Kvällsposten* 2 Feb. 1956. Translated in Björk: 125.

18 Pem, "Lång lysande kväll," *Göteborgs-Posten* 4 Nov. 1956. Translated in Björk: 125.

19 Hewes: 58.

20 Ibid.

21 Ulf Palme to Carlotta Monterey O'Neill, 21 Feb. 1956, BEINECKE.

22 Sten Selander, "O'Neills postuma drama," *Svenska Dagbladet* 11 Feb. 1956. Translated in Björk: 126.

23 Norman Nadel, "'Long Day's Journey' Played by Swedish Company at Cort," *New York World-Telegram & Sun* 16 May 1962.

24 Ivar Harrie, "En förkrossande teaterkväll," *Expressen* 11 Feb. 1956. Translated in Björk: 126.

25 Hewes: 58.

26 "O'Neill's Last Play," *Time* 67 (20 Feb. 1956): 89.

27 Whicher: 615.

28 "Theater: O'Neill's Last," *Newsweek* 47 (20 Feb. 1956): 92.

29 "O'Neill's Last Play."

30 Tom Olsson, "O'Neill and the Royal Dramatic," in *Eugene O'Neill: A World View*, ed. Virginia Floyd (New York: Ungar, 1979): 50.

31 Quoted in Roger W. Oliver, "Bergman's Trilogy: Tradition and Innovation," *Performing Arts Journal* 14 (Jan. 1992): 81.

32 This and subsequent page references cited in the text as "T" refer to Egil Törnqvist, "Ingmar Bergman Directs 'LDJIN,'" *New Theatre Quarterly* 5.20 (Nov. 1989): 374–83.

33 Oliver: 80.

34 Lars Linder, *Dagens Nyheter* 17 Apr 1988, quoted in Lise-Lone Marker and Frederick J. Marker, *Ingmar Bergman: A Life in the Theater* (Cambridge: Cambridge University Press, 1992): 272.

35 Marker and Marker: 274.

36 Eric Burger, "Kein Licht scheint in dieser Finsternis," *Kurier* (Berlin) 27 Sep. 1956. This and subsequent translations from the German are mine.

37 Friedrich Luft, "Unerbittlich und wahrhaft wie die klassische Tragödie," *Welt* (Berlin-Hamburg) 27 Sept. 1956.

38 Georg Zivier, "Berliner Festwochen 1956," *Morgenpost* (Berlin) 27 Sep. 1956.

39 Johannes Jacobi, "Berlin ist eine Reise wert," *Die Zeit* (Hamburg) 4 Oct. 1956.

40 Luft.

41 Walther Karsch, "Ein Abend großer Schauspielkunst," *Der Tagesspiegel/Feuilleton* 27 Sep. 1956.

42 Ibid.

43 Dora Fehling, "Die Hölle sind wir selbst," *Telegraf* (Berlin) 27 Sep. 1956.

44 Zivier.

45 Ibid.

46 Jacobi.

47 Wanderscheck, "Vier verdammte Seelen um einen runden Tisch," *Hamburger Abendblatt* 27 Sep. 1956.

48 Zivier.

49 Wanderscheck.

50 Willi Fehse, "O'Neill aus dem Nebel des Rausches," *Die Abendpost* (Frankfurt) 28 Feb. 1959.

51 Quoted in program, *Lunga giornata verso la notte*, Milan, 1956. Subsequent references appear in the text as "PM." This and subsequent translations from the Italian are by Mary Gallucci.

52 "Streamlined Version," *New York Times* 17 Oct. 1956: 40.

53 Cable from Carlotta O'Neill to Enrico Raggio, 17 Oct. 1956, BEI-NECKE; rpt. "End of a 'Journey,'" *New York Times* 18 Oct. 1956.

54 Neale Stainton to Carlotta O'Neill, 17 Oct. 1956, clippings file, BEINECKE.

55 F. G. "Le Prime del Teatro," *Il Popolo Italiano*, clippings file, BEINECKE.

56 Nicola Ciarletta, "Un dramma postumo di O'Neill al Teatro Eliseo," *Il Paese*, BEINECKE.

57 L. G., "'Lunga giornata verso la notte' di O'Neill applaudita a Torino," *Il Popolo Nuovo* 8 Dec. 1956.

58 E. P., "Lunga giornata verso la notte," *Corriere Della Sera* 17 Oct. 1956.

59 Roberto De Monticelli, "Si chiamano Tyrone ma sono gli O'Neill," *Il Giorno* 17 Oct. 1956.

60 F. B., "Lunga giornata verso la notte di Eugenio O'Neill al 'Carignano'," *La Nuova Stampa* 8 Dec. 1956.

61 Aggeo Savioli, "Lunga giornata verso la notte," *L'Unita* 23 Feb. 1957.

62 Contini, Ermanno, "Lunga giornata verso la notte," *Il Messaggero* clippings file, BEINECKE.

63 L. G., "'Lunga giornata verso la notte' di O'Neill applaudita a Torino."

64 Savioli.

65 Giorgio Prosperi, "Le Prime a Roma," *Il Tempo* 23 Feb. 1957.

66 Ibid.

67 Savioli

68 "Amarga y Cruel es la Obra Póstuma de Eugene O'Neill," *La Prensa* 28 Mar. 1957: 9. This and subsequent translations from the Spanish are by George Monteiro.

69 "Intenso Drama Autobiográfico en el T. Odeón," *La Nacion* 29 Mar. 1957: 9.

70 "Intenso": 9.

71 "Gran Exito de la Obra de Eugene O'Neill," *Excelsior* 27 June 1957: B3.

72 Wilberto Canton, "Viaje de un largo dia hacia la noche," *Excelsior* 30 June 1957, *Diorama de la Cultura*: 3.

73 Antonio Magaña Esquivel, "Estrenos en Junio," *Suplemento Semanario de El Nacional* 14 July 1957: 13.

74 Canton: 3.

75　Esquivel: 13.

76　Mécia de Sena, "Introdução," *Jornada para a Noite* (Lisbon: Edições Cotovia, 1992): 9.

77　Jorge de Sena, "'Jornada para a Noite,' de Eugene O'Neill, pelo Teatro Experimental do Porto," in *Do Teatro em Portugal* (Lisbon: Edições 70, 1988): 191. This and subsequent translations from the Portuguese are by George Monteiro.

78　U[rbano] T[avares] R[odrigues], "Jornada para a Noite," *Diário de Lisboa* 12 Apr. 1958, 13.

79　K., "Primeras Representações," *O Primeiro de Janeiro* 5 Jan. 1958: 7.

80　"Breve Introdução," *Dalila Rocha: Homenagem* (Lisbon: Fundação António de Almeida, 1998): 11.

81　K., "Primeras Representações,": 7.

82　"Fernanda Gonçalves," in *Dalila Rocha: Homenagem*: 69.

83　"Teatro Experimental do Porto," *O Comércio do Porto* 5 Jan. 1958: 4.

84　Ibid.

85　R[odrigues]: 13.

86　Ibid.

87　K., "Primeras Representações,": 7.

88　Ibid.

89　"O'Neill no Teatro Nacional," *Diário de Notícias* 7 June 1983: 37.

90　"Viagem ao fim da noite," *Diário de Lisboa* 20 June 1983: 19.

91　Yan Michalski, *Ziembinski e o Teatro Brasileiro* (São Paulo: Editora Hucitec, 1995): 243.

92　Program for *Jornada de um Longo Dia Para Dentro da Noite*, Teatro Cacilda Becker, Rio de Janeiro, 1958.

93　"Jornada por um Ambiente Desconhecido," Suplemento Dominical, *Jornal do Brasil* 25 May 1958.

94　Paulo Francis, "A Tragédia de O'Neill," *Diário Carioca* 18 May 1958.

95　Ibid.

96　Henrique Oscar, "Viagem de um Longo Dia Para Dentro da Noite," *Diário de Notícias* 21 June 1958.

97　Francis.

98　Michalski: 250.

99　Oscar.

100　Ibid.

101　"Gabriel Marcel" in *Eugene O'Neill's Critics: Voices from Abroad*, ed.

Horst Frenz and Susan Tuck (Carbondale: Southern Illinois University Press, 1984): 75.

102 Carlotta O'Neill to Karl Ragnar Gierow, 16 February 1956, BEINECKE.

103 Karl Ragnar Gierow to Carlotta O'Neill, [20 June 1956], BEINECKE.

104 Contract between Carlotta Monterey O'Neill and Lars Schmidt, 18 July 1956, BEINECKE.

105 A. M. Julien to Carlotta O'Neill, 29 Aug. 1957, BEINECKE.

106 Bertrand Poirot-Deipech, "Long Voyage vers la Nuit," *Le Monde* 28 Nov. 1959: 13. This and subsequent translations from the French are mine.

107 "Gaby Morlay: un drame de la drogue pour sa rentrée chez Hébertot," *L'Aurore* 27 Nov. 1959: 4.

108 Jean-Jacques Gautier, "'Long voyage vers la nuit,'" *Le Figaro* 28–29 Nov. 1959: 18.

109 Ibid.

110 Ibid.

111 G. Joly, "Long voyage vers la nuit," *L'Aurore* 30 Nov. 1959: 4.

112 This and subsequent references designated "MM" are to "Eugene O'Neill and Poetic Realism: Tragic Form in the Belgian Premiere of *Long Day's Journey Into Night*," *Theatre Survey* 29.1 (1988): 117–25. References for quotations from this source in the following text are given as page numbers in parentheses.

113 Harold Clurman, "Notes from Afar: Part I," *The Nation* 201 (16 Aug. 1965): 85.

114 M. E., "Kumo's O'Neill Production Well Learned from Clurman," *The Japan Times* 8 Sep. 1965: 12.

115 Jerry Rudd, "'Long Day's Journey' a Harrowing Trip," *The Daily Yomiuri* (Tokyo) 18 May 2000: 13.

116 "American Plays on Soviet Stage," TASS 1 Feb. 1988.

4 Media adaptations

1 Carlotta O'Neill to Jane Rubin, 5 Dec. 1959, BEINECKE.

2 Ibid.

3 Quoted in Robin Bean, "The Insider," *Films and Filming* 11.9 (June 1965): 13.

4 Eugene Archer, "Long Day of 'Night' in the Bronx," *New York Times* 22 Oct. 1961: sec. 2, 7.

5 This and subsequent page numbers cited in the text as "L" refer to Dale Luciano, "Long Day's Journey Into Night: An Interview with Sidney Lumet," *Film Quarterly* 25.1 (Fall 1971): 20–33.

6 Joseph Morgenstern, "Filming O'Neill's House of Anguish," *New York Herald Tribune* 22 Oct. 1961.

7 Sidney Lumet, *Making Movies* (New York: Vintage, 1995): 16–17.

8 Donald P. Costello, "Sidney Lumet's Long Day's Journey Into Night," *Literature & Film Quarterly* 22.2 (1994): 88.

9 Lumet: 103.

10 Frank R. Cunningham, *Sidney Lumet: Film and Literary Vision* (Lexington: University Press of Kentucky, 1991): 132.

11 Orlandello analyzes the imprisonment motif in *O'Neill on Film* (Rutherford, NJ: Associated University Presses, 1982): 133–35.

12 Sidney Lumet, "On a Film 'Journey,'" *New York Times* 7 Oct. 1962: sec. 2, 7.

13 Eugene O'Neill, *Long Day's Journey Into Night* (New Haven: Yale University Press, 1956): 46. Subsequent page references appear in the text.

14 While Lumet's estimate of the cuts ranged from 7 to 17 pages of the 177-page script, Costello has counted 749 lines that were cut out of a total 2,849 lines (79).

15 See Costello for a careful analysis of the cuts.

16 Quoted in John Crosby, "Katherine [*sic*] Hepburn Thrilled with Making O'Neill Movie," *Boston Sunday Globe* 26 Nov. 1961.

17 Stanley Kauffmann, "Fate *Accompli*," *Show* (Nov. 1962): 33.

18 "Total Recall," *Saturday Review* 45 (6 Oct. 1962): 30.

19 Archer Winsten, "'Journey' Arrives at Tower East," *New York Post* 10 Oct. 1962: 71.

20 Quoted in Albin Krebs, "A. B. C., in a Shift, Plans Series of Serious Dramatic Specials," *New York Times* 28 June 1972: 91.

21 Quoted in John Bemrose, "Long Day's Film Journey," *Maclean's Magazine* 109 (15 Jan. 1996): 60.

22 Ibid.

PRODUCTION CHRONOLOGY

1956

Date: 10 February
Country: Sweden *City:* Stockholm *Theatre:* Kungliga Dramatiska
   Teatern
Director: Bengt Ekerot *Designer:* Georg Magnusson *Producer:*
   Kungliga Dramatiska Teatern
James: Lars Hanson *Mary:* Inga Tidblad
James, Jr.: Ulf Palme *Edmund:* Jarl Kulle
Cathleen: Catrin Westerlund
Notes: world premiere; translation Sven Barthel; costumes Gunnar
   Gelbort; ran in repertory until 1962

Date: 25 September
Country: Germany *City:* Berlin *Theatre:* Theater am
   Kurfürstendamm, Haus der Freien Volksbuhne
Director: Oscar Fritz Schuh *Designer:* Caspar Neher
James: Paul Hartmann *Mary:* Grete Mosheim
James, Jr.: Heinz Drache *Edmund:* Hans Christian Blech
Cathleen: Ilse Kiewiet
Notes: German premiere; translation Ursula und Oscar Fritz Schuh

Date: 16 October
Country: Italy *City:* Milan *Theatre:* Piccolo Teatro
Director: Renzo Ricci *Designer:* Luciano Damiani *Producer:*
   Renzo Ricci
James: Renzo Ricci *Mary:* Eva Magni
James, Jr.: Glauco Mauri *Edmund:* Gian Carlo Sbragia

Cathleen: Anna Nogara
Notes: Italian premiere; translation Amleto Micozzi; costumes Ezio Frigerio

Date: 27 October
Country: Germany   *City:* Düsseldorf   *Theatre:* Düsseldorfer Schauspielhaus
Director: Karl Heinz Stroux   *Designer:* Ita Maximowna
James: Bernhard Minetti   *Mary:* Elisabeth Bergner
James, Jr.: Klausjurgen Wussow   *Edmund:* Martin Benrath
Cathleen: Inge Rassaerts
Notes: translation Ursula and Oscar Fritz Schuh

Date: 7 November 1956–27 March 1958
Country: US   *City:* New York   *Theatre:* Helen Hayes
Director: José Quintero   *Designer:* David L. Hays   *Producer:* Leigh Connell, Theodore Mann, José Quintero
James: Fredric March   *Mary:* Florence Eldridge
James, Jr.: Jason Robards, Jr.   *Edmund:* Bradford Dillman
Cathleen: Katherine Ross
Notes: American premiere, 390 performances; costumes: Motley (Elizabeth Montgomery); lighting: Tharon Musser; tryouts at Wilbur Theatre, Boston, week of 15 October 1956; Shubert Theatre, New Haven, 29 October–3 November; Albert Morgenstern replaced Dillman

1957

Date: 5 January
Country: Denmark   *City:* Copenhagen   *Theatre:* Det Konglige Teater
Director: Erling Schroeder   *Designer:* Espen Hansen
James: Henrik Bentzon   *Mary:* Karin Nellemose
James, Jr.: Jørn Jeppesen   *Edmund:* Fritz Helmuth
Cathleen: Birgit Sadolin

Date: 27 March–21 April
Country: Argentina   *City:* Buenos Aires   *Theatre:* Odeón
Director: Francisco Petrone   *Designer:* Mario Vanarelli and German
  Gelpi   *Producer:* Fernando Botti
James: Francisco Petrone   *Mary:* Yordana Fain
James, Jr.: Fernando Vegal   *Edmund:* Carlos Estrada
Cathleen: Miryam Van Wessen
Notes: ran for more than 100 performances; translated for first time
  into Spanish by León Mirlas

Date: 14 June
Country: Mexico   *City:* Mexico City   *Theatre:* Teatro del Granero
Director: Xavier Rojas   *Designer:* Antonio Lopez Mancera
  Producer: Unidad Artística y Cultural del Bosque and Instituto
  Nacional de Bellas Artes
James: Augusto Benedico   *Mary:* Isabela Corona
James, Jr.: José Alonso   *Edmund:* Jorge del Campo
Cathleen: Nancy Cárdenas
Notes: "Viaje de un largo dia hacia la noche" translation Mary
  Martínez and José Luis Ibáñez

Date: 2–6 July
Country: France   *City:* Paris   *Theatre:* Théâtre Sarah Bernhardt
Director: José Quintero   *Designer:* David L. Hays   *Producer:* Leigh
  Connell, Theodore Mann, José Quintero and the American
  National Theatre and Academy (ANTA)
James: Fredric March   *Mary:* Florence Eldridge
James, Jr.: Jason Robards, Jr.   *Edmund:* Bradford Dillman
Cathleen: Katherine Ross
Notes: Lights: Tharon Musser; Costumes: Motley (Elizabeth
  Montgomery); special appearance of American premiere company

Date: 24 September 1957?
Country: Austria   *City:* Vienna   *Theatre:* Akademie Theater

Director: Joseph Glücksmann   *Designer:* Gottfried Neumann-
  Spallart   *Producer:* Vorstellung des Burgtheaters
James: Attila Hörbiger   *Mary:* Alma Seidler
James, Jr.: Alexander Trojan   *Edmund:* Andreas Wolf
Cathleen: Inge Brückleimer
Notes: translation Ursula and Oscar Fritz Schuh

1958
Date: 6 January
Country: US   *City:* Tour: Cleveland, Detroit, Chicago, San
  Francisco, Los Angeles, Pittsburgh, St. Louis, Philadelphia,
  Washington D. C., Baltimore
Director: José Quintero   *Designer:* David L. Hays   *Producer:* Leigh
  Connell, Theodore Mann, José Quintero
James: Anew McMaster   *Mary:* Fay Bainter
James, Jr.: Roy Poole   *Edmund:* Chet Leaming
Cathleen: Liz Thackston
Notes: Tour of the original production, with new cast; after
  disastrous engagements in Cleveland and Detroit, the tour was
  on the point of being cancelled; positive notices in Chicago,
  especially from Claudia Cassidy, ensured a six-week run there,
  and saved the tour

Date: 4 April
Country: Portugal   *City:* Porto   *Theatre:* Sá da Bandeira
Director: António Pedro   *Designer:* Alvaro Portugal   *Producer:*
  Teatro Experimental do Porto
James: João Guedes   *Mary:* Dalila Rocha
James, Jr.: Baptista Fernandes   *Edmund:* Alexandre Vieira
Cathleen: Fernanda Gonçalves
Notes: also produced in Lisbon, 11 April; translated by Jorge de Sena

Date: 15 May
Country: Brazil   *City:* Rio de Janeiro   *Theatre:* Teatro Dulcina

Director: Zbigniew Ziembinski   *Designer:* Gianni Ratto   *Producer:*
  Teatro Cacilda Becker
James: Zbigniew Ziembinski   *Mary:* Cacilda Becker
James, Jr.: Fredi Kleemann   *Edmund:* Walmor Chagas
Cathleen: Kleber Macedo
Notes: traveled to Porto Alegre, 26 August 1958; São Paulo, 7
  January 1959

Date: 28 September
Country: UK   *City:* Edinburgh and London   *Theatre:* Globe
Director: José Quintero   *Designer:* David L. Hays   *Producer:* New
  Watergate Presentations and H. M. Tennent, in association with
  Leigh Connell, Theodore Mann, and José Quintero
James: Anthony Quayle   *Mary:* Gwen Ffrangcon-Davies
James, Jr.: Ian Bannen   *Edmund:* Alan Bates
Cathleen: Etain O'Dell
Notes: British premiere; it should also be noted that the Globe
  production is the London premiere.

1959
Date: 11 February
Country: Germany   *City:* Oldenburg   *Theatre:* Oldenburger
  Schlossbuhne
Director: Jochen Bernauer
James: Raimund Bucher   *Mary:* Dorothea Constanz
James, Jr.: Piet Clausen   *Edmund:* Edgar Wiesemann
Cathleen: Marlene Achtermann

Date: 20 February
Country: Germany   *City:* Kassel   *Theatre:* Hessische Staatstheater
Director: Ulrich Hoffmann   *Designer:* Lothar Baumgarten
James: Ernst von Klipstein   *Mary:* Luise Glau
James, Jr.: Hans Häckermann   *Edmund:* Karl Maldek
Cathleen: Evelyn Matzura

Date: 9 March
Country: Canada   *City:* Montreal   *Theatre:* Orpheum
Director: Rupert Caplan   *Designer:* Robert Prévost   *Producer:* Le
    Théâtre du Nouveau-Monde
James: Ian Keith   *Mary:* Mildred Dunnock
James, Jr.: Michael Kane   *Edmund:* Roland Hewgill
Cathleen: Eileen Clifford
Notes: Canadian Premiere

Date: 28 April
Country: Ireland   *City:* Dublin   *Theatre:* Queen's Theatre
Director: Frank Dermody   *Designer:* Tomas MacAnna   *Producer:*
    Abbey Players
James: Pilib Ó Floinn (Philip O'Flynn)   *Mary:* Ria Mooney
James, Jr.: Tomas P. MacCionaith (T. P. McKenna)
Edmund: Uinsionn Ó Dubhlainn (Vincent Dowling)
Cathleen: Caitlin Ni Bearain (Cathleen Barrington)
Notes: Irish premiere; an orchestra under the direction of John
    Reidy played music by Mozart as an overture and by Purcell and
    Ó Riada at the two intermissions; revived in 1962

Date: 2, 3 October
Country: Australia   *City:* Adelaide   *Theatre:* University Theatre
Director: Robin Lovejoy   *Designer:* Wendy Dickson   *Producer:*
    Elizabethan Theatre Trust Productions and The University
    Theatre Guild
James: Frank Waters   *Mary:* Dinah Shearing
James, Jr.: Ron Haddrick   *Edmund:* Neil Fitzpatrick
Cathleen: Patricia Conolly
Notes: Australian premiere

Date: 26 November
Country: France   *City:* Paris   *Theatre:* Théâtre Hébertot

Director: Marcelle Tassencourt   *Designer:* Jacques Marillier
   Producer: Lars Schmidt
James: Jean Davy   *Mary:* Gaby Morlay
James, Jr.: Pierre Vaneck   *Edmund:* Michel Ruhl
Notes: Translation Pol Quentin

Country: France   *City:* Paris   *Theatre:* Théâtre de l'Atelier
James: Georges Wilson   *Mary:* Suzanne Flon
James, Jr.: Bernard Verley   *Edmund:* Jose-Maria Flotats

Country: UK   *City:* Bristol   *Theatre:* Royal
Director: Peter Wyngarde   *Designer:* Patrick Robertson   *Producer:*
   Bristol Old Vic
James: William Hutt   *Mary:* Dorothy Reynolds
James, Jr.: Ronald Hines   *Edmund:* John Charlesworth
Cathleen: Susan Lawrence

1960
Country: Israel   *City:* Tel Aviv   *Theatre:* Habimah
Director: Hy Kalus   *Designer:* Roda Relinger   *Producer:* Israel
   National Theatre
James: A. Meskin   *Mary:* H. Rovina
James, Jr.: H. Buchman   *Edmund:* S. Bar Shavit
Cathleen: D. Friedland
Notes: Hebrew translation: Jacob Orland

Date: 5 October
Country: Canada   *City:* Toronto   *Theatre:* Crest
Director: Leon Major   *Designer:* Michael Johnston
James: David Hooks   *Mary:* Gwen Ffrangcon-Davies
James, Jr.: James Douglas   *Edmund:* George Luscombe
Cathleen: Pat Tully

1961
Date: 14 April
Country: Sweden   *City:* Goteborg   *Theatre:* Folkteatern
Director: Mats Johansson   *Designer:* Kaj Englund   *Producer:* Sven
    Barthel
James: Ulf Johanson   *Mary:* Margareta Bergfelt
James, Jr.: Carl-Hugo Calander   *Edmund:* Coran Graffman
Cathleen: Mona Astrand

1962
Date: 30 April–12 May, Seattle; 15 and 17 May, New York
Country: US   *City:* Seattle; New York   *Theatre:* World's Fair
    Playhouse; Cort
Director: Bengt Ekerot   *Designer:* Georg Magnusson   *Producer:*
    Seattle World's Fair and Roger L. Stevens
James: Georg Rydeberg   *Mary:* Inga Tidblad
James, Jr.: Ulf Palme   *Edmund:* Jarl Kulle
Cathleen: Catrin Westerlund
Notes: costumes: Gunnar Gelbort; in Swedish, played in repertory
    at the World's Fair with Strindberg's *The Father* and *Miss
    Julie*

Date: October
Country: US
Director: Sidney Lumet   *Designer:* Richard Sylbert   *Producer:* Ely
    Landau
James: Ralph Richardson   *Mary:* Katharine Hepburn
James, Jr.: Jason Robards, Jr.   *Edmund:* Dean Stockwell
Cathleen: Jeanne Barr
Notes: Embassy Picture Corporation Film; photographer: Boris
    Kaufman; Music: André Previn; production design, Richard
    Sylbert; line producer George Justin

1963

Date: June
Country: US   *City:* Houston   *Theatre:* Alley
Director: Nina Vance   *Designer:* Paul Owen   *Producer:* Alley
  Theater
James: Moultrie Patten   *Mary:* Virginia Payne
James, Jr.: Lew Wayland   *Edmund:* Ray Stricklyn
Cathleen: Bettye Fitzpatrick

Country: Hungary   *City:* Budapest   *Theatre:* Teatro Nemzetti
  Szinhaz
Director: Endre Marton
James: Ferenc Bessenyer   *James, Jr.:* Farenc Kallai

Country: US   *City:* Williamstown, Mass.   *Theatre:* Adams
  Memorial
Director: Tom Brennan   *Designer:* Robert E. Darling   *Producer:*
  The Williamstown Theatre
James: Louis Zorich   *Mary:* Olympia Dukakis
James, Jr.: James Noble   *Edmund:* Michael Ebert
Cathleen: Margaret Ladd
Notes: costumes: Marney Welmers; lighting: Carol Foy

1965

Country: Japan   *City:* Tokyo   *Theatre:* Dai-Ichi Seimei Hall
Director: Harold Clurman   *Producer:* United States Information
  Service
James: William Prince   *Mary:* Ruth White
James, Jr.: Roy Scheider   *Edmund:* Ira Lewis
Notes: technical advisor: Paul Morrison

Date: 7 March
Country: Northern Ireland   *City:* Belfast   *Theatre:* Lyric
Director: Denis Smyth   *Designer:* Ivan Armstrong

James: Jack McQuoid   *Mary:* Heather Gibson
James, Jr.: Peter Adair   *Edmund:* Ron. Nichol
Cathleen: Ida Faris

Date: 26 March
Country: Greece   *City:* Athens   *Theatre:* National Theatre of
    Greece
James: T. Fyssoun   *Mary:* Katina Taxinou
James, Jr.: D. Horn   *Edmund:* Al. Minotis
Cathleen: Hel. Hatziargyri

Date: 7–14 September
Country: Japan   *City:* Tokyo   *Theatre:* Dai-Ichi Seimei Hall
Director: Tetsuo Arakawa   *Producer:* Kumo Gekidan
James: Shigeru Koyama   *Mary:* Haruko Kato
James, Jr.: Noboru Nakaya   *Edmund:* Hiroyuki Sugi
Cathleen: Tadae Sano

1967
Date: May
Country: US   *City:* San Francisco   *Theatre:* Marines' Theater
Director: Byron Ringland   *Producer:* American Conservatory
    Theatre
James: Ramon Bieri   *Mary:* Angela Paton
James, Jr.: Patrick Tovatt   *Edmund:* David Grimm
Cathleen: Izetta Smith

Date: 5 June
Country: Ireland   *City:* Dublin   *Theatre:* Abbey
Director: Frank Dermody   *Designer:* Alan Barlow   *Producer:* Abbey
    Players
James: Philip O'Flynn   *Mary:* Angela Newman
James, Jr.: Patrick Laffan   *Edmund:* Vincent Dowling

Cathleen: Deirdre Purcell

Notes: production toured Galway, Sligo, Athlone, Waterford, Limerick, Cork, Carrickmore, and Belfast before opening in Dublin

1969

Country: Ireland   *City:* Dublin

Director: P. J. O'Connor   *Producer:* Radio Telefís Eireann

James: Anew McMaster   *Mary:* Pegg Monahan

James, Jr.: Seamus Forde   *Edmund:* Frank O'Dwyer

Notes: radio adaptation re-broadcast in 1977 and 1982

Country: US   *City:* Baltimore   *Theatre:* Center Stage

James: William Prince   *Mary:* Vivian Nathan

James, Jr.: Carlton Colyer   *Edmund:* Tom Brannum

1970

Date: 20–31 March

Country: Belgium   *City:* Charleroi   *Theatre:* Charleroi Music Academy

Director: Jacques Fumière   *Designer:* André Masquelier   *Producer:* Théâtre de l'Ancre

James: Christian Barbier   *Mary:* Yvonne Garden

James, Jr.: Gilles Languais   *Edmund:* Jean-Michel Thibault

1971

Country: US   *City:* Washington, D. C.   *Theatre:* Hartke Theater

Director: Leo Brady   *Designer:* James D. Waring

James: Michael Higgins   *Mary:* Helen Hayes

James, Jr.: Robert Milli   *Edmund:* Jason Miller

Cathleen: Peggy Cosgrave

Date: 19 February–28 March

Country: US   *City:* Hartford   *Theatre:* Hartford Stage

Director: Jacques Cartier   *Designer:* Santo Loquasto   *Producer:* The
   Hartford Stage Company
James: Robert Pastene   *Mary:* Teresa Wright
James, Jr.: Tom Atkins   *Edmund:* John Glover
Cathleen: Tana Hicken

Date: 21 April–21 August
Country: US   *City:* New York   *Theatre:* Promenade
Director: Arvin Brown   *Designer:* Elmon Webb and Virginia
   Dancy   *Producer:* Edgar Lansbury, Jay H. Fuchs, Stuart Duncan,
   Joseph Beruh
James: Robert Ryan   *Mary:* Geraldine Fitzgerald
James, Jr.: Stacy Keach/ Tom Atkins   *Edmund:* James Naughton
Cathleen: Paddy Croft
Notes: moved to Cherry Lane Theatre 10 August

Date: 21 December
Country: UK   *City:* London   *Theatre:* New Theatre
Director: Michael Blakemore   *Designer:* Michael Annals   *Producer:*
   The National Theatre Company
James: Laurence Olivier   *Mary:* Constance Cummings
James, Jr.: Denis Quilley   *Edmund:* Ronald Pickup
Cathleen: Maureen Lipman/ Jo Maxwell-Muller
Notes: "American advisor": Donald Ogden Stewart

1973
Date: 10 March
Country: UK/ US
Director: Peter Wood   *Designer:* Michael Annals   *Producer:* ABC
   Television, The National Theatre, and ITC
James: Laurence Olivier   *Mary:* Constance Cummings
James, Jr.: Denis Quilley   *Edmund:* Ronald Pickup
Cathleen: Maureen Lipman

Notes: television adaptation by Michael Blakemore and Peter Wood; art director, Peter Roden; lighting, John Rook

Date: August
Country: US   *City:* Cambridge, MA   *Theatre:* Loeb Center
Director: Pirie MacDonald   *Designer:* Franco Colavecchia
James: Robert Pastene   *Mary:* Eleanor Wilson
James, Jr.: James Pickering   *Edmund:* Richard Blackburn
Cathleen: Darcy Pulliam

Date: 14 November–8 December
Country: Australia   *City:* Melbourne   *Theatre:* St. Martin's
Director: Rodney Fisher   *Designer:* Michael Pearce   *Producer:* South Australian Theatre Company
James: Brian James   *Mary:* Patricia Kennedy
James, Jr.: Neil Fitzpatrick   *Edmund:* Alan Becher
Cathleen: Carole Skinner
Notes: production originated in Adelaide

1974
Date: October
Country: Israel   *City:* Jerusalem   *Theatre:* Habimah
Director: Michael Meacham   *Designer:* Joe Karl
James: Shimon Finkel   *Mary:* Miriam Zohar
James, Jr.: Misha Asheaoff   *Edmund:* Alex Peleg
Notes: Hebrew translation: Ada Ben Nahum

1975
Country: US   *City:* Ashland, Oregon   *Theatre:* Angus Bowman Theatre
Director: Jerry Turner   *Designer:* Richard L. Hay   *Producer:* The Oregon Shakespeare Festival
James: Michael Kevin Moore   *Mary:* Jean Smart

James, Jr.: Denis Arndt   *Edmund:* William M. Hurt
Cathleen: Katherine James

Country: US   *City:* Philadelphia   *Theatre:* Walnut Street
Director: Richard Maltby, Jr.   *Designer:* David Ballou   *Producer:*
  Philadelphia Drama Guild
James: Robert Pastene   *Mary:* Geraldine Fitzgerald
James, Jr.: Philip Kerr   *Edmund:* John Glover
Cathleen: Regan O'Connell

Date: October
Country: US   *City:* Washington, D. C.   *Theatre:* Kreeger
Director: Martin Fried   *Designer:* Karl Eigsti   *Producer:* Arena Stage
James: James Broderick   *Mary:* Leora Dane
James, Jr.: Stanley Anderson   *Edmund:* Mark Metcalf
Cathleen: Halo Wines

Date: 11 December–3 January 1976
Country: US   *City:* Indianapolis   *Theatre:* Indiana Repertory
  Theatre
Director: Thomas Gruenewald   *Designer:* John Lee Beatty
  Producer: Indiana Repertory Theatre
James: Edward Binns   *Mary:* Nancy Coleman
James, Jr.: Steven Ryan   *Edmund:* T. Richard Mason
Cathleen: Priscilla Lindsay
Notes: costumes: Barbara Medlicott; lighting: Michael Watson

Date: December
Country: US   *City:* Washington, D. C.   *Theatre:* Kennedy Center
Director: Jason Robards   *Designer:* Ben Edwards   *Producer:*
  Kennedy Center
James: Jason Robards   *Mary:* Zoe Caldwell
James, Jr.: Walter McGinn   *Edmund:* Michael Moriarty

Cathleen: Lindsay Crouse
Notes: costumes: Jane Greenwood

1976
Date: 28 January
Country: US   *City:* Brooklyn, NY   *Theatre:* Brooklyn Academy of
    Music
Director: Jason Robards   *Designer:* Ben Edwards   *Producer:* Xerox
    Corporation American Bicentennial Production
James: Jason Robards   *Mary:* Zoe Caldwell
James, Jr.: Kevin Conway   *Edmund:* Michael Moriarty
Cathleen: Lindsay Crouse
Notes: costumes: Jane Greenwood

Date: 18 November–19 December
Country: US   *City:* Chicago   *Theatre:* Goodman
Director: George Keathley   *Designer:* Joseph Nieminski   *Producer:*
    Goodman Theatre Center
James: Edward Binns   *Mary:* Frances Hyland
James, Jr.: Drew Snyder   *Edmund:* John V. Shea
Cathleen: Sonja Lanzener
Notes: previews began 12 November; costumes: Virgil Johnson;
    lights: F. Mitchell Dana

Date: 2–19 December
Country: US   *City:* New York   *Theatre:* Manhattan Conservatory
Director: Nora Hussey
James: Hazen Gifford   *Mary:* Mary Jay
James, Jr.: Edmund Davys   *Edmund:* Philip Casnoff
Cathleen: Pat Murphy

Country: Hungary   *City:* Budapest   *Theatre:* Teatral Bulandra
Director: Liviu Ciulei   *Designer:* Dan Jitianu   *Producer:* Liviu
    Ciulei

James: Toma Caragiu   *Mary:* Clody Bertola
James, Jr.: Victor Rebengiuc   *Edmund:* Florian Pittiş
Cathleen: Marianna Mihuţ

1977
Date: 24 January
Country: US   *City:* Milwaukee   *Theatre:* Hancher Hall
Director: Irene Lewis   *Designer:* R. H. Grahman   *Producer:*
    Milwaukee Repertory Theatre Company
James: Robert Barr   *Mary:* Regina David
James, Jr.: Ronald Frazier   *Edmund:* Anthony Heald
Cathleen: Rose Pickering
Notes: produced with *Ah, Wilderness!*; costumes: Susan Tsu

Date: 18 February–2 April
Country: US   *City:* Los Angeles   *Theatre:* Ahmanson
Director: Peter Wood   *Designer:* Carl Toms   *Producer:* Center
    Theatre Group
James: Charlton Heston   *Mary:* Deborah Kerr
James, Jr.: Andrew Prine   *Edmund:* Robert Burke
Cathleen: Nora Heflin
Notes: lighting: H. R. Poindexter

Date: 3 May
Country: US   *City:* Boston   *Theatre:* Shubert
Director: Michael Kahn   *Designer:* Howard Bay   *Producer:*
    Massachusetts Center Repertory Company; Stephen A. Mindich,
    John Zurich, Jonathan R. Yates, and Janice Cashell
James: José Ferrer   *Mary:* Kate Reid
James, Jr.: Len Cariou   *Edmund:* Ben Masters
Cathleen: Laurie Kennedy
Notes: costumes: Pearl Somner; the actors played for Equity
    minimum to raise money for a professional theatre in
    Boston

1978
Date: 7 April
Country: US   *City:* New York   *Theatre:* Greenwich Mews
Director: Sonia Moore   *Designer:* Stephen Palestrant   *Producer:*
   American Stanislavski Theatre
James: Gay Reed   *Mary:* Darell Brown
James, Jr.: Peter Sherayko   *Edmund:* Mark McKenna
Cathleen: Donna Caulkins
Notes: costumes: Jo Anne Nikovits

1980
Date: October
Country: Canada   *City:* Stratford, Ontario
Director: Robin Phillips   *Designer:* Susan Benson   *Producer:*
   Stratford Shakespeare Festival
James: William Hutt   *Mary:* Jessica Tandy
James, Jr.: Graeme Campbell   *Edmund:* Brent Carver

1981
Date: 8 January–1 February
Country: US   *City:* New York   *Theatre:* Apple Corps Theatre
Director: David O. Glazer   *Designer:* Daniel Reeverts, III
   Producer: Apple Corps Theatre
James: Frederick Watters   *Mary:* Vera Lockwood
James, Jr.: John Raymond   *Edmund:* Robert L. Sanders
Cathleen: Cindie Lovelace
Notes: costumes: Grace Hunter Tannehill; lighting: Wayne S.
   Lawrence

Country: US   *City:* New York   *Theatre:* Anspacher/ Public Theater
Director: Geraldine Fitzgerald   *Designer:* John Scheffler   *Producer:*
   Joseph Papp, Hazel J. Bryant, and The Richard Allen Center for
   Culture and Art Production
James: Earle Hyman   *Mary:* Gloria Foster

James, Jr.: Al Freeman, Jr.   *Edmund:* Peter Francis-James
Cathleen: Samantha McKoy
Notes: African-American cast; costumes: Myrna Colley-Lee; lights:
  Paul Mathiesen

1982

Date: 23, 27 November
Country: US
Director: William Woodman   *Designer:* Eldon Elder   *Producer:*
  David A. Lown and ABC Video Enterprises
James: Earle Hyman   *Mary:* Ruby Dee
James, Jr.: Thommie Blackwell   *Edmund:* Peter Francis-James
Cathleen: Rhetta Hughes
Notes: based on Richard Allen Center production; aired on the
  ARTS and A&E cable networks

1983

Date: 3 June
Country: Portugal   *City:* Lisbon   *Theatre:* Teatro Nacional de D.
  Maria II
Director: Jacinto Ramos   *Designer:* Paulo Guilherme   *Producer:*
  Varella Silva
James: Rogério Paulo   *Mary:* Lígia Telles
James, Jr.: Mário Pereira   *Edmund:* Carlos Daniel
Cathleen: Luz Franco
Notes: translation Paulo Ferreira da Silva Teles; music César
  Batalha

Date: November
Country: UK   *City:* Nottingham   *Theatre:* Siddons
Director: Gregory Doran   *Designer:* Trevor Pitt   *Producer:*
  Nottingham Playhouse
James: John Turner   *Mary:* Carol Teitel
James, Jr.: Eric Allan   *Edmund:* George Winter

1984

Date: 5–9 April
Country: UK *City:* London *Theatre:* Arts Theatre
Director: Ludovica Villar-Hauser *Designer:* Jane Cameron
  Producer: Villar-Hauser Productions
James: Trevor Martin *Mary:* Darlene Johnson
James, Jr.: Michael Deacon *Edmund:* Sean Mathias
Cathleen: Wendy Miller

1985

Date: 14 February
Country: Ireland *City:* Dublin *Theatre:* Abbey
Director: Patrick Laffan *Designer:* Alpho O'Reilly *Producer:*
  Abbey Players
James: Godfrey Quigley *Mary:* Siobhan McKenna
James, Jr.: Desmond Cave *Edmund:* Stephen Brennan
Cathleen: Brid Ni Neachtain

Date: 13–26 March
Country: UK *City:* Manchester *Theatre:* Royal Exchange
Director: Braham Murray *Designer:* Johanna Bryant
James: James Maxwell *Mary:* Dilys Hamlett
James, Jr.: Jonathan Hackett *Edmund:* Michael Mueller
Cathleen: Victoria Hastead

1986

Date: 28 April–29 June
Country: US *City:* New York *Theatre:* Broadhurst
Director: Jonathan Miller *Designer:* Tony Straiges *Producer:*
  Emanuel Azenberg, The Shubert Organization, Roger Peters,
  Roger Berlind, and Pace Theatrical Group, Inc.
James: Jack Lemmon *Mary:* Bethel Leslie
James, Jr.: Kevin Spacey *Edmund:* Peter Gallagher
Cathleen: Jodie Lynne McClintock

Notes: costumes: Willa Kim; lighting: Richard Nelson; previewed at Duke University 3–15 March; opened 26 March at National Theatre, Washington, D. C.; opened 4 August in London and 30 October in Tel Aviv

Date: 14 November–10 January 1987
Country: Belgium   *City:* Bruges   *Theatre:* Korrekelder
Director: Julien Schoenaerts   *Designer:* Julien Schoenaerts
    Producer: Korrekelder Theatre Company and Antwerp Arenbergschouwburg Company
James: Julien Schoenaerts   *Mary:* Reinhilde Decleir
James, Jr.: Carl Ridders   *Edmund:* Norbert Kaart
Cathleen: role deleted
Notes: Dutch translation Julien Schoenaerts

1987
Date: 13 April
Country: US
Director: Jonathan Miller   *Designer:* Tony Straiges   *Producer:* Michael Brandman, Emanuel Azenberg, Iris Merlis; Broadway on Showtime/American Playhouse, PBS
James: Jack Lemmon   *Mary:* Bethel Leslie
James, Jr.: Kevin Spacey   *Edmund:* Peter Gallagher
Cathleen: Jodie Lynne McClintock
Notes: lighting: John Rook; art director Harley Moden; editor: Gary L. Smith; premiered on the Showtime cable network, and repeated on PBS's *American Playhouse*, 4 May 1988

1988
Date: 5 January–12 February
Country: US   *City:* Denver   *Theatre:* Denver Center Theater
Director: Malcom Morrison   *Producer:* Denver Center Theater
James: James Lawless   *Mary:* Carol Mayo Jenkins
James, Jr.: Michael Winters   *Edmund:* Jamie Horton

Date: 22 March–21 May
Country: US   *City:* New Haven   *Theatre:* Yale Repertory Theatre
Director: José Quintero   *Designer:* Ben Edwards   *Producer:* Yale
    Repertory Theatre
James: Jason Robards   *Mary:* Colleen Dewhurst
James, Jr.: Jamey Sheridan   *Edmund:* Campbell Scott
Cathleen: Jane Macfie
Notes: costumes: Jane Greenwood; played in repertory with *Ah,
    Wilderness!* as part of a "Eugene O'Neill Centennial Celebration"

Date: 16 April
Country: Sweden   *City:* Stockholm   *Theatre:* Kungliga Dramatiska
    Teatern
Director: Ingmar Bergman   *Designer:* Gunilla Palmstierna-Weiss
    Producer: Kungliga Dramatiska Teatern
James: Jarl Kulle   *Mary:* Bibi Andersson
James, Jr.: Thommy Berggren   *Edmund:* Peter Stormare
Cathleen: Kicki Bramberg
Notes: production traveled to the Brooklyn Academy of Music,
    opening there on 14 June 1991

Date: 11 June–23 July
Country: US   *City:* New York   *Theatre:* Neil Simon
Director: José Quintero   *Designer:* Ben Edwards   *Producer:* Ken
    Marsolois, Alexander H. Cohen, and the Kennedy Center for
    the Performing Arts, in association with Yale Repertory
    Theatre
James: Jason Robards   *Mary:* Colleen Dewhurst
James, Jr.: Jamey Sheridan   *Edmund:* Campbell Scott
Cathleen: Jane Macfie
Notes: costumes: Jane Greenwood; lighting: Jennifer Tipton

Date: October
Country: Spain   *City:* Madrid   *Theatre:* Teatro Español

Director: Miguel Narros   *Designer:* Andrea D'Odorico   *Producer:*
  Teatro Español
James: Alberto Closas   *Mary:* Margarita Lozano
James, Jr.: José Pedro Carrion   *Edmund:* Carlos Hipolito
Cathleen: Ana Goya
Notes: translation Ana Antón-Pacheco

Date: 18 November
Country: US   *City:* Syracuse, NY   *Theatre:* Syracuse Stage
Director: William Woodman   *Designer:* Gary May   *Producer:*
  Syracuse Stage
James: Tony Mockus   *Mary:* De Ann Mears
James, Jr.: P. J. Benjamin   *Edmund:* Steven Dennis

1990
Date: 5–23 December
Country: US   *City:* Seattle   *Theatre:* Poncho Forum
Director: Michael Engler   *Designer:* Andrew Jackness   *Producer:*
  Seattle Repertory Theatre
James: William Biff McGuire   *Mary:* Marion Ross
James, Jr.: John Procaccino   *Edmund:* Patrick Breen
Cathleen: Katie Forgette

1991
Date: 19 February Bristol; 21 May London
Country: UK   *City:* Bristol, Sheffield, Glasgow, Nottingham,
  Manchester, Bradford, Newcastle, Cardiff, London   *Theatre:*
  Bristol Old Vic/ Lyttelton
Director: Howard Davies   *Designer:* John Gunter   *Producer:* Royal
  National Theatre and the Bristol Old Vic
James: Timothy West   *Mary:* Prunella Scales
James, Jr.: Sean McGinley   *Edmund:* Stephen Dillane
Cathleen: Geraldine Fitzgerald

1992

Date: 13 September
Country: France   *City:* Paris   *Theatre:* Madeleine
Director: Patrice Kerbrat   *Designer:* Nicolas Sire
James: Jean Desailly   *Mary:* Simone Valere
James, Jr.: Christophe Allwright   *Edmund:* Jean Pennec

1994

Date: 25 May (preview)–17 September
Country: Canada   *City:* Stratford, Ontario   *Theatre:* Tom Patterson
Director: Diana Leblanc   *Designer:* Astrid Janson   *Producer:*
   Stratford Shakespeare Festival
James: William Hutt   *Mary:* Martha Henry
James, Jr.: Peter Donaldson   *Edmund:* Tom McCamus
Cathleen: Martha Burns
Note: lighting by Louise Guinand

1995

Date: 6 January–12 February
Country: US   *City:* Washington, D. C.   *Theatre:* Fichlander
Director: Douglas C. Wager   *Designer:* Ming Cho Lee   *Producer:*
   Arena Stage
James: Richard Kneeland   *Mary:* Tana Hicken
James, Jr.: Casey Biggs   *Edmund:* Rainn Wilson
Cathleen: Holly Twyford

1996

Date: 24 May–16 July
Country: US   *City:* Cambridge, MA   *Theatre:* Loeb Drama Center
Director: Ron Daniels   *Designer:* Michael H. Yeargan   *Producer:*
   American Repertory Theatre
James: Jerome Kilty   *Mary:* Claire Bloom
James, Jr.: Bill Camp   *Edmund:* Michael Stuhlbarg
Cathleen: Emma Roberts

Notes: costumes: Catherine Zuber; lighting: Frances Aronson;
 previewed in Stamford, Conn. with Dan O'Herlihy as James.

Date: July
Country: UK   *City:* London   *Theatre:* Young Vic
Director: Laurence Boswell   *Producer:* Theatre Royal Plymouth
James: Richard Johnson   *Mary:* Penelope Wilton
James, Jr.: Mark Lambert   *Edmund:* Paul Rhys
Notes: music: Mick Sands

Date: September
Country: Canada
Director: David Wellington   *Designer:* John Dondertman
  Producer: Cineplex Odeon Films; Daniel Iron and Niv Fichman
James: William Hutt   *Mary:* Martha Henry
James, Jr.: Peter Donaldson   *Edmund:* Tom McCamus
Cathleen: Martha Burns
Notes: made by Cineplex Odeon Films in conjunction with
 Rhombus Media; broadcast by the CBC and Bravo television
 networks; music by Ron Sures

1997
Date: 4–23 November
Country: US   *City:* New York   *Theatre:* The Mint Space
Director: Stephen Stout   *Designer:* Sarah Lambert   *Producer:*
 National Asian American Theatre Company
James: Ernest Abuba   *Mary:* Mia Katigbak
James, Jr.: Paul Nakauchi   *Edmund:* Andrew Pang
Cathleen: Jody Lin
Notes: Asian-American cast

1998
Date: 25 February
Country: US   *City:* Houston   *Theatre:* Alley

Director: Michael Wilson   *Designer:* Tony Straiges   *Producer:* Alley
  Theatre
James: David Selby   *Mary:* Ellen Burstyn
James, Jr.: Ian Kahn   *Edmund:* Rick Stear
Cathleen: Krista Forster

Date: 22 March
Country: US   *City:* New York   *Theatre:* Irish Repertory Theatre
Director: Charlotte Moore   *Designer:* Akira Yoshimura
James: Brian Murray   *Mary:* Frances Sternhagen
James, Jr.: Paul Carlin   *Edmund:* Paul McGrane
Cathleen: Rosemary Fine
Notes: original music by Jason Robert Brown

Date: 31 March
Country: Ireland   *City:* Dublin   *Theatre:* Gate
Director: Karel Reisz   *Designer:* Robin Don   *Producer:* Gate
  Theatre
James: Donald Moffat   *Mary:* Rosaleen Linehan
James, Jr.: David Herlihy   *Edmund:* Andrew Scott
Cathleen: Sonya Kelly

1999
Date: 25 February–1 April
Country: US   *City:* Hartford   *Theatre:* Hartford Stage
Director: Michael Wilson   *Designer:* Tony Straiges   *Producer:* The
  Hartford Stage Company
James: David Selby   *Mary:* Ellen Burstyn
James, Jr.: Andrew McCarthy   *Edmund:* Rick Stear
Cathleen: Derdriu Ring

Date: 14 April–2 May
Country: US   *City:* San Francisco   *Theatre:* Geary Theater

Director: Laird Williamson   *Designer:* Kate Edmunds   *Producer:*
   American Conservatory Theater
James: Josef Sommer   *Mary:* Pamela Payton-Wright
James, Jr.: Marco Barricelli   *Edmund:* Jason Butler Harner
Notes: lighting: Peter Maradudin

2000
Date: 11–31 May
Country: Japan   *City:* Tokyo   *Theatre:* New National Theatre
Director: Tamiya Kuriyama   *Designer:* Yukio Horio
James: Masane Tsukayama   *Mary:* Kazuyo Mita
James, Jr.: Kazuyuki Asano   *Edmund:* Yasunori Danta
Notes: lighting: Jiro Katsushiba; sound: Joji Fukagawa

DISCOGRAPHY

Performance

Brown, Arvin, dir. *Long Day's Journey Into Night*. Sound Recording. Caedmon TRS 350. 1972. 33 1/3 rpm record. Program notes by Louis Sheaffer.

Long Day's Journey Into Night. New York; Caedmon, 1972. Caedmon #CDL 5350. 4 cassettes.

[Reading of the play based on the Promenade Theatre production, with Robert Ryan, Geraldine Fitzgerald, Stacy Keach, James Naughton, and Paddy Croft.]

Robards, Jason. Dramatic Readings from Eugene O'Neill's *Long Day's Journey Into Night*, *A Moon for the Misbegotten*, *The Hairy Ape*, *The Iceman Cometh*. Sound recording. Columbia OL 5900. 1963. 33 1/3 rpm record. Program notes by Arthur Gelb.

[Excerpts from the plays read by Robards.]

Interpretation

Bryer, Jackson R. *Long Day's Journey Into Night*. Sound Recording. Modern Drama Series. De Land FL: Everett/Edwards, 1971. 1 cassette.

Robards, Jason. [Eugene O'Neill's *A Long Day's Journey Into Night*]. Washington, D. C.: Voice of American Music Collection, Library of Congress, 1976. 2 reels.

[Robards discusses the play at a Kennedy Center Symposium, 14 January 1976.]

Stein, Howard. *Long Day's Journey Into Night*. Sound Recording. World Literature Series. De Land FL: Everett/Edwards, 1976. 1 cassette, 37 minutes.

VIDEOGRAPHY

Productions

Brown, Arvin, dir. *Long Day's Journey Into Night*. Video Recording. 1971. New York Public Library for the Performing Arts. NCOB 10. 190 minutes.

[Video recording of the Promenade Theatre production, with Robert Ryan, Geraldine Fitzgerald, Tom Atkins, James Naughton, and Paddy Croft.]

Broadway Magazine # 126. 1988. New York Public Library for the Performing Arts. NCOX 941. 29 min.

[This includes a short video-taped excerpt from the 1988 production with Colleen Dewhurst and Jason Robards directed by José Quintero, as well as an interview with Dewhurst.]

Ed Sullivan Show, CBS Television. 5 January 1958. Museum of Television and Radio, New York.

[Taped live for the television show, this contains most of Act 2, scene 2 as performed by Fredric March, Florence Eldridge, Jason Robards, and Albert Morgenstern in the original New York production directed by José Quintero.]

Lumet, Sidney, dir. *Long Day's Journey Into Night*. Video Recording. Republic Pictures Home Video, 1992. 30th Anniversary Digitally Mastered Reissue of 1962 Film with Trailer. 2 videocassettes, 180 minutes.

[1962 film with Ralph Richardson, Katharine Hepburn, Jason Robards, Dean Stockwell, Jeanne Barr.]

Miller, Jonathan, dir. *Long Day's Journey Into Night*. Video Recording. American Playhouse, 1988. 1 videocassette. 180 minutes.

[Based on the 1986 New York production, with Jack Lemmon, Bethel Leslie, Kevin Spacey, Peter Gallagher, Jodie Lynne McClintock.]

Wellington, David, dir. *Long Day's Journey Into Night*. Video Recording.

Videography 209

Cineplex Odeon Films Canada/ Rhombus Media, 1996. 1 videocassette. 177 minutes.

[Based on the 1994 Stratford Shakespeare Festival production with William Hutt, Martha Henry, Peter Donaldson, Tom McCamus, Martha Burns.]

Wood, Peter, dir. *Long Day's Journey Into Night*. Video Recording. ITC/ National Theatre of Great Britain Production. ABC Television. 10 March 1973. Museum of Television and Radio, New York.

[National Theatre production adapted for television by Michael Blakemore, with Laurence Olivier, Constance Cummings, Denis Quilley, Ronald Pickup, Maureen Lipman.]

Woodman, William, dir. *Long Day's Journey Into Night*. Video Recording. ABC Video/ A&E Classroom. 1982. 146 min. Museum of Television and Radio, New York.

[Based on the 1981 Richard Allen Center Production, with Earle Hyman, Ruby Dee, Thommie Blackwell, Peter Francis-James, Rhetta Hughes.]

Interpretation

Brown, Arvin and Geraldine Fitzgerald. Joint Interview on *Long Day's Journey Into Night*. 20 July 1971. New York Public Library for the Performing Arts. NCOW 3. 35 min.

BIBLIOGRAPHY

[Note that the abbreviations *LDJIN* and *LDJ* are substituted for *Long Day's Journey Into Night* and *Long Day's Journey* in the titles of reviews.]

Major Archives

BEINECKE. Eugene O'Neill Papers. YCAL MSS 123. Yale Collection of American Literature, Beinecke Rare Book and Manuscript Library, Yale University, New Haven, Connecticut.

NYPL. Billy Rose Theatre Collection, New York Public Library for the Performing Arts, New York.

SHEAFFER. Louis Sheaffer–Eugene O'Neill Collection, Charles E. Shain Library, Connecticut College, New London, Connecticut.

Books

Barlow, Judith E. *Final Acts: The Creation of Three Late O'Neill Plays.* Athens: University of Georgia Press, 1985.

Björk, Lennart A. "The Critical Reception of Eugene O'Neill in Sweden 1923–1963." Diss. Princeton University, 1966.

Black, Stephen A. *Eugene O'Neill: Beyond Mourning and Tragedy.* New Haven: Yale University Press, 1999.

Bogard, Travis. *Contour in Time: The Plays of Eugene O'Neill.* New York: Oxford University Press, 1988.

  "From the Silence of Tao House": Essays about Eugene and Carlotta O'Neill and the Tao House Plays. Danville, CA: Eugene O'Neill Foundation, *ca.* 1993.

  The Later Plays of Eugene O'Neill. New York: Random House, 1967.

  and Jackson R. Bryer. *Selected Letters of Eugene O'Neill.* New Haven: Yale University Press, 1988.

Bowen, Croswell. *Curse of the Misbegotten*. New York: McGraw-Hill, 1959.

Cerf, Bennett. *At Random: The Reminiscences of Bennett Cerf*. New York: Random House, 1977.

Commins, Dorothy. *What Is an Editor? Saxe Commins at Work*. Chicago: University of Chicago Press, 1978.

Coolidge, Olivia. *Eugene O'Neill*. New York: Scribner, 1966.

Cunningham, Frank R. *Sidney Lumet: Film and Literary Vision*. Lexington, KY: University Press of Kentucky, 1991.

Estrin, Mark W. *Conversations with Eugene O'Neill*. Jackson: University Press of Mississippi, 1990.

Floyd, Virginia, ed. *Eugene O'Neill: A World View*. New York: Ungar, 1979.

Frenz, Horst and Susan Tuck, eds. *Eugene O'Neill's Critics: Voices from Abroad*. Carbondale, IL: Southern Illinois University Press, 1984.

Gago, Júlio, Editor. *Dalila Rocha: Homenagem*. Lisbon: Fundação António de Almeida, 1998.

Garvey, Sheila Hickey. " 'Not for Profit': The History of the Circle in the Square." Ph. D Diss., New York University, 1984.

Gelb, Arthur and Barbara Gelb. *O'Neill*. Enlarged Ed. New York: Harper & Row, 1988.

O'Neill: Life with Monte Cristo. New York: Applause, 2000.

Greenberger, Howard. *The Off-Broadway Experience*. Engelwood Cliffs, NJ: Prentice-Hall, 1971.

Hays, David. *Light on the Subject*. New York: Limelight, 1989.

Little, Stuart. *Off-Broadway: The Prophetic Theatre*. New York: Coward, McGann and Geoghehan, 1972.

Lumet, Sidney. *Making Movies*. New York: Vintage, 1995.

Marker, Lise-Lone and Frederick J. Marker. *Ingmar Bergman: A Life in the Theater*. Cambridge: Cambridge University Press, 1992.

McDonough, Edwin J. *Quintero Directs O'Neill*. Pennington, NJ: a capella books, 1991.

Michalski, Yan. *Ziembinski e o Teatro Brasileiro*. São Paulo–Rio de Janeiro: Editora Hucitec, 1995.

Miller, Jordan Y. *Eugene O'Neill and the American Critic: A Bibliographical Checklist*. 2nd ed. New York: Archon, 1973.

Playwright's Progress: O'Neill and the Critics. Chicago: Scott, Foresman, 1965.

Mirlas, León. *O'Neill y el Teatro Contemporáneo*. 2nd. ed. Buenos Aires: Editorial Sudamericana, 1961.

Olivier, Laurence. *On Acting*. New York: Simon and Schuster, 1986.

Olson, Sarah. *Historic Furnishings Report: Eugene O'Neill National Historic Site, California*. [Harper's Ferry, W. Va.]: US Department of the Interior, National Park Service, Harper's Ferry Center, 1983.

O'Neill, Eugene. *Inscriptions: Eugene O'Neill to Carlotta Monterey O'Neill*. New Haven: privately printed, 1960.

    Long Day's Journey Into Night. New Haven: Yale University Press, 1956.

Orlandello, John. *O'Neill on Film*. Rutherford, NJ: Fairleigh Dickinson University Press; London: Associated University Press, 1982.

Quintero, José. *If You Don't Dance They Beat You*. 1974. New York: St. Martin's, 1988.

    Lines in the Palm of God's Hand: Eugene O'Neill and I. Ed. Joseph Arnold and John Brugaletta. [Fullerton, CA]: South Coast Press, *ca* 1989.

Reed, Joseph W. *Literary Revision: The Inexact Science of Getting It Right*. New Haven: Beinecke Rare Book & Manuscript Library, 1990.

Savran, David. *The Wooster Group, 1975–1985: Breaking the Rules*. Ann Arbor: UMI, 1986.

Scheibler, Rolf. *The Late Plays of Eugene O'Neill*. Bern: Francke, 1970.

Sena, Jorge de. *Do Teatro em Portugal*. Lisbon: Edições 70, 1988.

Sena, Mécia de. "Introdução." In Eugene O'Neill. *Jornada para a Noite*. Trans. Jorge de Sena. Lisbon: Cotovia, 1992.

Shaughnessy, Edward L. *Eugene O'Neill in Ireland: The Critical Reception*. New York: Greenwood, 1988.

Sheaffer, Louis. *O'Neill: Son and Artist*. 1973. New York: Paragon House, 1990.

    O'Neill: Son and Playwright. Boston: Little, Brown, 1968.

Steene, Kerstin Birgitta. "The American Drama and the Swedish Theater, 1920–1958." Ph. D Diss., University of Washington, 1960.

Tinsley, Mary Adrian. "Two Biographical Plays by Eugene O'Neill: The Drafts and the Final Versions." Ph.D. Diss., Cornell University, 1969.

Törnqvist, Egil. *A Drama of Souls: Studies in O'Neill's Super-naturalistic Technique*. New Haven: Yale University Press, 1969.

Articles

General

Atkinson, Brooks. "One Man's Truth." *New York Times* 3 Mar. 1957: sec. 2, 1.

"Tragedy Behind a Tragic Masque." *New York Times Book Review* 19 Feb. 1956: sec. 7, 1, 30.

Babb, James T. "Letter to the Editor." *New York Times Book Review* 11 Mar. 1956: 37.

Barlow, Judith E. "*LDJIN*: From Early Notes to Finished Play." *Modern Drama* 22 (Mar. 1979): 19–23.

"Mother, Wife, Mistress, Friend and Collaborator: Carlotta Monterey and *LDJIN*." In *Eugene O'Neill and the Emergence of American Drama.* Ed. Marc Maufort. Amsterdam: Rodopi, 1989: 123–31.

Breit, Harvey. *New York Times Book Review* 19 Feb. 1956: 8.

Chapman, John. "The 7 Haunted O'Neills." *Sunday News* 16 Dec. 1956.

Clurman, Harold. "The O'Neills." *The Nation* 182 (3 Mar. 1956): 182–83.

Crichton, Mamie. "A Call from the Widow in Black Meant Fame." *Scottish Daily Express* 9 Sep. 1958. [José Quintero interview]

Dallat, C. L. "Confession Is Enough." *Times Literary Supplement* 19 July 1996: 20.

Eisen, Kurt. "O'Neill on Screen." *The Cambridge Companion to Eugene O'Neill.* Ed. Michael Manheim. Cambridge: Cambridge University Press, 1998: 116–134.

Eisenberg, Bronwyn. "An Interview with Director Laird Williamson on *Long Day's Journey Into Night.*" In *Words on Plays: Long Day's Journey Into Night.* San Francisco: American Conservatory Theater, 1999: 36–46

Ekerot, Bengt. "Propaganda tragedi i teater-arbete: några funderingar." *Teaterkonst* 1 (1956): 18–19.

Fagin, N. Bryllion. "Remembrance of Things Past." *New Republic* 134 (5 Mar. 1956): 20.

Funke, Lewis "Billy Rose Joins Quest for O'Neill Play." *New York Times* 3 June 1956: sec. 2, 1.

"News and Gossip on the Rialto." *New York Times* 23 July 1956: sec. 2, 1.

"Sponsors for Reading Tour of O'Neill's Play are Set." *New York Times* 17 June 1956: sec. 2, 1.

"Eugene O'Neill's Widow Makes a Statement." *New York Times* 1 July 1956: sec. 2, 1.

Funke, Phyllis. "José Quintero and the Devil of Success." *Wall Street Journal* 15 May 1974: 20.

Garvey, Sheila Hickey. "Desecrating an Idol: *LDJIN* as Directed by José Quintero and Jonathan Miller." *The Recorder* 3.1 (Summer 1989): 73–85.

Gelb, Arthur. "Long Journey Into Light." *New York Times* 25 Nov. 1956: sec. 2, 3 [Jason Robards interview].

Gelb, Barbara. "A Touch of the Tragic." *New York Times Magazine* 11 Dec. 1977: 43–45, 118, 120, 122, 124, 126–28, 131–38 [José Quintero].

"Quintero in the Square." *New York Times* 16 Feb. 1964: sec.2, 3.

"To O'Neill, She Was Wife, Mistress, Mother, Nurse." *New York Times* 21 Oct. 1975: 1, 13.

Gierow, Karl Ragnar. "Eugene O'Neill's Posthumous Plays." *World Theatre* 7 (Spring 1957): 46–53.

"Why O'Neill Opened Here." *Industria International* 9 (1958–1959): 94–95, 117.

Gierow, Karl Ragnar and Pat M. Ryan. "*LDJ* Was the 'Wrong.' Play." *Theatre Survey* 29 (May 1988): 103–12.

Glover, William. "Old Sorrow Written in Tears and Blood." *Baltimore Sun.*

"O'Neill's Plays More Popular Than When He Was Alive." *New Haven Register* 28 Apr. 1957.

Gonzalez, José B. "Homecoming: O'Neill's New London in *LDJIN.*" *New England Quarterly* 66 (1993): 450–57.

Gussow, Mel. "José Quintero's Long Journey Back." *New York Times* 28 Jan. 1974: 34.

Hart, Doris. "Whose Play Is This, Anyway? – Interpreting Mary and James Tyrone." *The Recorder* 3.1 (Summer 1989): 115–22.

Johnson, Kenneth. "Robards: He's Like Hotspur, Noted for Fire and Storm." *Boston Globe Magazine* 5 Apr. 1958: 11–13.

Jones, Edward T. "The Tyrones as TV Family: O'Neill's *LDJIN*, Primetime." *Literature/Film Quarterly* 22.2 (1994): 93–97.

Kerr, Walter. "He Gave It to 'Em, Boy." *New York Herald Tribune* 14 Apr. 1957: 1, 3.

Killen, Tom. "Jason Robards and the O'Neill Connection." *Westport News* 14 Oct. 1981: sec. 2, 19, 22 [interview].

Krutch, Joseph Wood. "Domestic Drama With Some Difference." *Theatre Arts* 40 (Apr. 1956): 25, 89–91.

Lawson, Carol. "Broadway Celebrates Eugene O'Neill's Birthday." *New York Times* 20 Oct. 1981: C9.

Lawson, Steve. "Jose, Jason, and 'Gene.'" *Horizon* (Jan. 1978): 36–42.

Little, Stuart W. "Quintero Back in Theater After Doing Film Abroad." *New York Herald Tribune* 27 June 1961: 16.

Maufort, Marc. "Eugene O'Neill and Poetic Realism: Tragic Form in the Belgian Premiere of *LDJIN*." *Theatre Survey* 29.1 (May 1988): 117–25.

"The Tyrone Family in Bruges: A Belgian *LDJIN*." *The Eugene O'Neill Newsletter* 11.2 (Summer–Fall, 1987): 32–35.

Millstein, Gilbert. "José Quintero." *Theatre Arts* 44 (May 1960): 10–12.

Morton, Frederick. "Quintero the Fortuitous." *New York Times* 6 May 1956: sec. 2, 3.

Norton, Elliot. "Salute to Mrs. O'Neill." *Boston Sunday Advertiser* 25 Nov. 1956.

Olsson, Tom. "O'Neill and the Royal Dramatic." In *Eugene O'Neill: A World View*. Ed. Virginia Floyd. New York: Ungar, 1979: 34–60.

"The O'Neill Tradition at Stockholm's Royal Dramatic Theatre." *The Recorder* 3.1 (Summer 1989): 86–99.

Ooi, Vicki. C. H. "Transcending Culture: A Cantonese Translation and Production of O'Neill's *LDJIN*." In *Languages of Theatre: Problems in the Translation and Transposition of Drama*. Ed. Ortun Zuber. Oxford: Pergamon Press, 1980.

Ormsbee, Helen. "Likes Acting With Husband." *New York Herald Tribune* 1 Sep. 1957 [Florence Eldridge interview].

Peck, Seymour. "Talk with Mrs. O'Neill." *New York Times* 4 Nov. 1956: sec. 2, 1, 3.

Prescott, Orville. "Books of the Times." *New York Times* 20 Feb. 1956: 21.

"Books of the Times." *New York Times* 24 Feb. 1956: 23.

Quintero, José. "Carlotta and the Master." *New York Times* 1 May 1988: sec. 6, 56.

"The Dance: What It Means to Me." *Dance Magazine*, June 1957: 17.

"Quintero Talks to Directors." *The Theatre* (Apr. 1956): 33.

Raphael, Jay E. "On Directing *LDJIN*." *Eugene O'Neill Newsletter* 5.1 (Spring 1981): 7–10.

Ross, Don. "New O'Neill Play About His Family." *New York Herald Tribune* 4 Nov. 1956: 1, 3.

Seldes, Gilbert. "LDJIN." *Saturday Review* 39 (25 Feb. 1956): 15–16.

Shaughnessy, Edward L. "Ella, James, and Jamie O'Neill." *The Eugene O'Neill Review* 15.2 (Fall 1991): 5–92.

Tallmer, Jerry. "José Quintero: On Keeping the Faith." *New York Post* 19 Jan. 1974: 15.

Vadeboncoeur, Joan E. "LDJIN." *Herald-Journal* (Syracuse, NY) 20 Nov. 1988.

Van Itallie, Jean-Claude. "An Interview with José Quintero." *The Transatlantic Review* 11 (Winter 1962): 37–47.

Vena, Gary A. "Eugene O'Neill: World Playwright." *Eugene O'Neill Newsletter* 12.2 (Summer–Fall 1988): 57–62.

Wainscott, Ronald. "Notable American Stage Productions." *The Cambridge Companion to Eugene O'Neill*. Ed. Michael Manheim. Cambridge: Cambridge University Press, 1998. 96–115.

Weatherby, W. J. "Mrs. Eugene O'Neill." *The Guardian* (Manchester): 18 July 1962: 5.

"Yale University Press." *Publisher's Weekly* 17 Mar. 1956.

Zolotow, Sam. "'Littlest Revue' Taking First Step; London Will See O'Neill's 'LDJ.'" *New York Times* 22 May 1956: 29.

"Plans to Return to Ambassador." *New York Times* 13 July 1956: 24.

"Schools May See Drama by O'Neill." *New York Times* 11 May 1956: 24.

Reviews and Criticism of Individual Productions

1956

Stockholm 10 February

Bæckström, Tord. "Lång dags färd mot natt." *Götborgs Handels-och Sjöfartstidning* 11 Feb. 1956.

Belair, Felix, Jr. "Stockholm Hails World Premiere of Autobiographical O'Neill Play." *New York Times* 11 Feb. 1956: 12.

Bergman, A. Gunnar. "Så föddes en diktare!." *Afton-Tidningen* (Stockholm) 11 Feb. 1956.

Beyer, Nils. Världspremiär på O'Neill." *Morgon-Tidningen* (Stockholm) 11 Feb. 1956.

"Dramatens Världspremiär ett mäktigt realistiskt drama." *Svenska Dagbladet* (Stockholm) 11 Feb. 1956.

Engberg, Harald. "Til verdens-première i fire en halv time." *Politiken* 11 Feb. 1956: 7.

Erichsen, Svend. "O'Neills gave til Dramaten." *Social Demokraten* 11 Feb. 1956.

Funke, Lewis. "News of the Rialto: From Sweden." *New York Times* 8 Apr. 1962.

Glover, William. "Posthumous O'Neill Play Is Revealing." (AP release) *Worcester Telegram* 19 Feb. 1956.

Harrie, Ivar. "En förkrossande teaterkväll." *Expressen* (Stockholm) 11 Feb. 1956.

Hewes, Henry. "O'Neill and Falkner via the Abroad Way." *Saturday Review* 39 (20 Oct. 1956): 58.

Heyman, Viveka. "Världspremiär på Dramaten." *Arbetaren* (Stockholm) 11 Feb. 1956.

Heintzen, Harry. "O'Neill's Last Premiere." *New York Herald Tribune This Week* 29 Jan. 1956: 126.

"Last Play of O'Neill Performed." *New York Herald Tribune* 11 Feb. 1956.

Johanson, Sam. "Världspremiär på Dramaten." *Ny Dag* (Stockholm) 11 Feb. 1956.

Jytte. "O'Neill's eget familiedrama." *Information* 11 Feb. 1956.

Kragh-Jacobsen, Svend. "Dette latterlige fortvivlede Liv." *Tidende* 11 Feb. 1956.

"Lång kvälls färd mot klarhet." *Aftonbladet* (Stockholm) 11 Feb. 1956.

"The Last O'Neill Tragedy." *Life* 40 (12 Mar. 1956): 93–94, 96, 99.

Linde, Ebbe. "En ohyggligt skakande kammarsymfoni." *Dagens Nyheter* 11 Feb. 1956.

Loke. "Lysande världspremiär." *Stockholms-Tidningen* 11 Feb. 1956.

"O'Neill Premiere." *Theatre Arts* 40 (May 1956): 65.

"O'Neill Première in Stockholm." *The Times Weekly Review* (London) 213 (23 Feb. 1956): 13.

"O'Neill's Last." *Newsweek* 47 (20 Feb. 1956): 92.

"O'Neill's Last Play." *Time* 67 (20 Feb. 1956): 89–90.

"O'Neill's Wish." *Christian Science Monitor* 28 Apr. 1962.

Ryan, Pat M. "Stockholm Revives Eugene O'Neill." *Scandinavian Review* 65 (Mar. 1977): 18–23.

Selander, Sten. "O'Neill's postuma drama." *Eftertryck Förbjudes* 11 Feb. 1956.

"Stockholm to See Last O'Neill Play." *New York Times* 5 Jan. 1956: 26.

"O'Neill's Journey." *New York Times Magazine* 19 Feb. 1956: sec. 6, 56.

"O'Neill's 'Self-Portrait' Play Hailed at Swedish Premiere." *Boston Daily Globe* 11 Feb. 1956.

"Stockholm to See Last O'Neill Play." *New York Times* 5 Jan. 1956: 26.

"Sweden Hails World Premiere of 1941 Engine [*sic*] O'Neill Drama." *Boston Herald* 11 Feb. 1956.

Whicher, Stephen. "O'Neill's Long Journey." *The Commonweal* 16 Mar. 1956: 614–15.

Williamson, George. "Plaudits for O'Neill." *New York Times* 15 Feb. 1956: sec. 2, 1.

Rome 22 February

De Chiara, Ghigo. " 'Lunga giornata verso la notte'." *Avanti* 23 Feb. 1957.

Contini, Ermanno. "Lunga giornata verso la notte." *Messaggero* 1957.

Prosperi, Giorgio. "Le Prime a Roma." *Il Tempo* 23 Feb. 1957.

Savioli, Aggeo. "Lunga giornata verso la notte." *L'Unita* 23 Feb. 1957.

Berlin 26 September

Burger, Eric. "Kein Licht scheint in dieser Finsternis." *Kurier* (Berlin).

"Eines langen Tages Reise in die Nacht." *Der Abend* (Berlin).

Fehling, Dora. "Die Hölle sind wir selbst." *Telegraf* (Berlin).

Karsch, Walther. "Ein Abend großer Schauspielkunst." *Der Tagesspiegel/ Feuilleton* 27 Sep. 1956.

Luft, Friedrich. "Unerbittlich und wahrhaft wie die klassische Tragödie." *Welt* (Berlin-Hamburg).

Wanderscheck. "Vier verdammte Seelen um einen runden Tisch." *Hamburger Abendblatt.*

Weigel, Hans. "Ein solcher Tag macht auch die Nacht unserer Theater hell." *Bild-Telegraf* (Vienna).

Zivier, Georg. "Berliner Festwochen 1956." *Morgenpost* (Berlin) 27 Sep. 1956.

Boston 14 October; New Haven 29 October

B. C. W. "Have You Seen LDJIN?." *Record* (New Haven) 30 Oct. 1956.

"Boston Hails O'Neill Drama." Associated Press 16 Oct. 1956.

Converse, C. M., Jr. "O'Neill's 'LDJIN' Unveiled at Shubert." *Yale Daily News* 16 Oct. 1956.

Durgin, Cyrus. "*LDJ*' O'Neill's Last, Great Play." *Boston Daily Globe* 16 Oct. 1956.

Guy. "LDJIN." *Variety* 16 Oct. 1956.

Hughes, Elinor. "*LDJ*' an Absorbing Emotional Drama." *Boston Sunday Herald* 21 Oct. 1956: sec. 3, 1.

"'LDJIN'." *Boston Herald* 16 Oct. 1956.

"Young Actors Get Key Roles in Last Eugene O'Neill Play." *Boston Herald* 15 Oct. 1956.

Maloney, Alta. "*LDJ*': O'Neill Drama, Wilbur." *Boston Traveler*, 16 Oct. 1956: 68.

Norton, Elliot. "Did O'Neill Malign His Own Father?" *Boston Daily Record* 7 Nov. 1956.

"O'Neill Play Needs Cut." *Boston Sunday Advertiser* 21 Oct. 1956.

"O'Neill Drama in US Premiere." *Boston Sunday Herald* 14 Oct. 1956: sec. 1: 14.

R. J. L. "Eugene O'Neill's Last Play." *New Haven Register* 30 Oct. 1956.

S. P. "Boston Welcomes Last O'Neill Play." *New York Times* 17 Oct. 1956: 40.

Milan 16 October

E.P. "Lunga giornata verso la notte." *Corriere Della Sera* 17 Oct. 1956.

F. G. "Le Prome del Teatro." *Il Popolo Italiano.*

Ciarletta, Nicola. "Un dramma postumo di O'Neill al Teatro Eliseo." *Il Paese.*

Cimnaghi, M. R. "Autobiografia di Eugene O'Neill." *Il Popolo.*

De Monticelli, Roberto. "Si chiamano Tyrone ma sono gli O'Neill." *Il Giorno* 17 Oct. 1956.

M. R. C. "'Lunga giornata verso la notte' al Teatro Valle." *Il Popolo.*

"Most of Milan Crix Liked O'Neill's Night." *Variety* 31 Oct. 1956.

O. V. "'Lunga giornata verso la notte, di O'Neill al Piccolo Teatro." *Corriere d'informazione* 17–18 Oct. 1956

New York 7 November

Atkinson, Brooks. "The Old Soaks at Home." *New York Times Book Review* 6 Oct. 1996: 80.

"O'Neill's 'Journey'." *New York Times* 18 Nov. 1956: sec. 10, 2.

"Autobiographical Play." *New York Herald Tribune* 17 July 1956: sec. 2, 1.

Calta, Louis. "Circle in Square to Do O'Neill Play." *New York Times* 14 July 1956: 12.

Chapman, John. "Did O'Neill Have the Right to Write It?." *Sunday News* (New York) 30 Dec. 1956.

   "A Masterpiece by O'Neill." *Sunday News* (New York) 18 Nov. 1956: sec. 2, 1.

   "The 7 Haunted O'Neills." *Sunday News* (New York) 16 Dec. 1956.

Clurman, Harold. "Theatre." *The Nation* 183 (24 Nov. 1956): 466.

Eldridge, Florence. "Reflections on LDJIN." In *Eugene O'Neill: A World View.* Ed. Virginia Floyd. New York: Ungar, 1971: 286–87.

"Fredric Marches to Play Top Roles in O'Neill Play." *New York Herald Tribune* 23 July 1956.

Funke, Lewis. "News and Gossip Gathered on the Rialto." *New York Times* 22 July 1956: sec. 2, 1.

Gelb, Arthur. "Space-Ship Play to Be Launched." *New York Times* 16 July 1956: 16.

Gibbs, Wolcott. "Doom." *New Yorker* 32 (24 Nov. 1956): 120–21.

Harris, Leonard. "Quintero Given Blessing by Mrs. Eugene O'Neill." *New York World-Telegram and Sun* 19 Feb. 1964.

Hewes, Henry. "O'Neill: 100 Proof – Not a Blend." *Saturday Review* 39 (24 Nov. 1956): 30–31.

Kerr, Walter. "He Gave It to 'Em, Boy." *New York Herald Tribune* 14 Apr. 1957.

   "'LDJ' Actor and Playgoer Share Impact of O'Neill Drama." *New York Herald Tribune* 18 Nov. 1956: 1, 3.

   "Season's Outstanding Performances." *New York Herald Tribune* 2 June 1957.

Lerner, Max. "To Face My Dead at Last." *New York Post* 7 Jan. 1957: 26.

Lewis, Emory. "Journey Uptown with O'Neill." *Cue* 3 Nov. 1956: 13 [José Quintero interview].

"Long and Short of It." *The Christian Century* 74 (20 Feb. 1957): 235.

"'LDJIN'." *Vogue* 128 (15 Nov. 1956): 105.

"LDJIN." *Theatre Arts* 41 (Jan. 1957): 25–26.

Land. "LDJIN." *Variety* 6 Feb. 1957.

McDermott, William F. "Audiences Still Flock to O'Neill Play, Financial

Whiz and Likely Prize Winner." *Cleveland Plain Dealer* 20 Jan. 1957: sec. G, 1, 4.

Morehouse, Ward. "Broadway After Dark." *Star Ledger* (Newark) 23 Oct. 1956 [José Quintero interview].

"Mrs. Eugene O'Neill Ups Eyebrows." *Variety* 25 July 1956.

"New Play in Manhattan." *Time* 68 (19 Nov. 1956): 57.

New York Theatre Critics' Reviews 17.20 (1956): 217–20:

Atkinson, Brooks. "Theatre: Tragic Journey." *New York Times* 9 Nov. 1956.

Chapman, John. " 'LDJIN' A Drama of Sheer Magnificence." *Daily News* 8 Nov. 1956.

Colman, Robert. "O'Neill's Last Drama Emotional Dynamite." *Daily Mirror* 8 Nov. 1956.

Donnelly, Tom. "A Long Journey Worth Taking." *New York World-Telegram and Sun* 8 Nov. 1956.

Kerr, Walter. " 'LDJIN.' " *New York Herald Tribune* 8 Nov. 1956.

McClain, John. "Superb Cast Supplements O'Neill Genius." *Journal American* 8 Nov. 1956.

Watts, Richard. "A Superb Drama by Eugene O'Neill." *New York Post* 8 Nov. 1956.

"O'Neill's Youth on US Stage." *Life* 41 (19 Nov. 1956): 123–24.

Quintero, José. "Postscript to a Journey." *Theatre Arts* 41 (Apr. 1957): 27–29, 88.

"Onstage." *Playbill* Aug. 1975: 23, 26.

Ranald, Margaret. "When They Weren't Playing O'Neill: The Antithetical Career of Carlotta Monterey." *Theatre History Studies* 11 (1991): 81–100.

Rubenstein, Annette. "The Dark Journey of Eugene O'Neill." *Mainstream* 10 (Apr. 1957): 29–33.

Savery, Ranald. "The American Stage." *Stage* (London) 20 Dec. 1958.

"Triumph from the Past." *Newsweek* 48 (19 Nov. 1956): 117.

Tynan, Kenneth. "Message from Manhattan." *The Observer* (London) 26 May 1957.

Wilson, Earl. "A Responsible Position." *New York Post Magazine* 30 Apr. 1961: 3.

Zolotow, Sam. "March and Wife Pick O'Neill Play." *New York Times* 20 July 1956: 9.

[Zunser, Jesse]. "O'Neill's 'Journey' Takes a High, Exciting Road." *Cue* 17 Nov. 1956.

Turin 7 December

Brogaglia, A. G. "O'Neill na Itália." *Anhembi* (São Paulo) 31 (June 1958): 195–96.

F. B. "Lunga giornata verso la notte di Eugenio O'Neill al 'Carignano.' " *La Nuova Stampa* 8 Dec. 1956

L. G. " 'Lunga giornata verso la notte' di O'Neill applaudita a Torino." *Il Popolo Nuovo* 8 Dec. 1956.

Q. "Il dramma di O'Neill al Teatro Carignano." 9 Dec. 1956.

Quadrone, Ernesto. "Ha scritto con le lacrime e col sangue la tragedia della propria famiglia." *Stampa Sera* 7–8 Dec. 1956.

Trevisani, Giulio. "Eugene O'Neill ha narrato in un dramma la sua 'vecchia pena.' " *L'Unita* (Edizione piemontese) 8 Dec. 1956.

1957
Copenhagen 5 January

Budtz-Jørgensen, Jørgen. "Lan rejse til haabløsheden." *Dagens Nyheder* 6 Jan. 1957.

Engberg, Harald. "Lang aftens rejse mod O'Neills onde ungdom." *Politiken* 6 Jan. 1957.

Erichsen, Svend. "Helveden – det er os selv." *Social-Demokraten* 6 Jan. 1957.

"Kgl. kammerspil af O'Neills kœmpepartitur." *Berlingske Tidende* 6 Jan. 1957.

Buenos Aires 27 March

Adip, Amado. "El Drama Póstumo de E. O'Neill, un Genial Testamento Autobiográfico." *El Pueblo* 28 Mar. 1957: 13.

"Amarga y Cruel es la Obra Póstuma de Eugene O'Neill." *La Prensa* 28 Mar. 1957: 9.

"Esta Noche se Estrena la Obra Póstuma de O'Neill." *La Nacion* 27 Mar. 1957: 8.

"Intenso Drama Autobiográfico en el T. Odeón." *La Nacion* 29 Mar. 1957: 9.

Mexico City 14 June

Canton, Wilberto. "Viaje de un largo dia hacia la noche." *Excelsior* 30 June 1957, *Diorama de la Cultura*: 3.

Churchill, Allen. "Holgazan y . . . Premio Nobel." *Excelsior* 16 June 1957, *Diorama de la Cultura*: 1, 3.

"Gran Exito de la Obra de Eugene O'Neill." *Excelsior* 27 June 1957: B3.

Magaña Esquivel, Antonio. "Estrenos en Junio." *Suplemento Semanario de El Nacional* 14 July 1957: 13.

Paris 2 July

Curtiss, Thomas Quinn. "'LDJ' a Hit." *New York Herald Tribune*, Paris Edition 4 July 1957.

"Designer in Paris for O'Neill Play." *New York Times* 1 July 1957: 19.

"French Critic Finds O'Neill Play Boring." *New York Times* 6 July 1957: 9.

Gautier, Jean-Jacques. "'Le long voyage dans la nuit.'" *Le Figaro* 4 July 1957.

Joly, G. "Long voyage vers la nuit." *L'Aurore* 4 July 1957.

"Journey Is Staged in Paris." *New York Times* 3 July 1957: 14.

"'Journey' Wins Paris Sans Air-Conditioning." *New Haven Register* (AP Release) 3 July 1957.

"'Journey' a Long Night's Paris Hit." *Variety* 10 July 1957.

Kemp, Robert. "La grand pièce d'O'Neil [*sic*]." *Le Monde* 5 July 1957: 13.

Norton, Elliot. "O'Neill's 'Long Day' Goes to Paris." *Boston Record* 22 Feb. 1957.

Quintero, José. "Note From Abroad." *New York Times* 11 Aug. 1957: sec. 2, 1.

1958
Porto 4 January; Lisbon 11 April

"'Jornada para a Noite' do dramaturgo Americano Eugene O'Neill." *Diário de Notícias* 10 Apr. 1958: 9.

Jacobbi, Ruggero. "O ultimo O'Neill." *Estado de São Paulo* 22 Feb. 1958: Supl. Lit.

K., "Primeras Representações." *O Primeiro de Janeiro* 5 Jan. 1958: 7.

Leite, Cândida Teresa Teixeira. "Jornada de um longo dia para dentro da noite." *Anhembi* (São Paulo) 34 (Mar. 1959): 282–83.

"Teatro Experimental do Porto." *O Comércio do Porto*, 5 Jan. 1958: 4.

R[odrigues], U[rbano] T[avares]. "'Jornada para a Noite'." *Diário de Lisbôa*
12 Apr. 1958: 4, 13.

National Touring Company
Bloomfield, Arthur. "O'Neill Play Long But Good." *San Francisco Call-Bulletin* 9 Apr. 1958.
Bradley, Van Allen. "Eugene O'Neill Is Real Star of LDJ." *Chicago Daily News* 7 Jan. 1958: 16.
Cassidy, Claudia "Eugene O'Neill's Last Testament is Powerful, Pitiful, and Magnificent." *Chicago Daily Tribune* 7 Jan. 1958: sec. 2, 13.
    "Business Picks Up, O'Neill 'LDJ' Cancels Erlanger Closing." *Chicago Daily Tribune* 14 Jan. 1958: sec.2, 5.
"Chi Bally Keeps 'Journey' on Road." *Variety* 22 Jan. 1958.
Coe, Richard L. "Great Drama: A Week Only." *Washington Post* 18 Mar. 1958: A23.
Dettmer, Roger. "Bainter Superb in 'Journey'." *Chicago American* 7 Jan. 1958: 11.
Knickerbocker, Paine. "O'Neill Drama at Geary is Somber, Searching." *San Francisco Chronicle* 10 Apr. 1958.
Kogan, Herman. "Force of O'Neill's Drama 'Of Old Sorrow' Overrides Defects." *Chicago Sun-Times* 7 Jan. 1958: 34.
Morton, Hortense. "'LDJ' An Effort Worth Waiting For." *San Francisco Examiner* 10 Apr. 1958.
Murdock, Henry T. "O'Neill's Stature Hits Peak." *Philadelphia Inquirer* 4 Mar. 1958.
Steif, William. "Love and Hate." *San Francisco News* 9 Apr. 1958.

Edinburgh 8 September
A. C. D. S. "A Long Night of Tragedy." *Evening Dispatch* 9 Sep. 1958: 13.
"Bold Experiment on the Edinburgh Stage." *The Times Weekly Review* (London) 346 (11 Sep. 1958): 13.
Darlington, W. A. "Drama by O'Neill Opens at Festival." *New York Times* 9 Sep. 1958: 40.
    "Obsessions in a Family." *Daily Telegraph* 9 Sep. 1958.
Hope-Wallace, Philip. "LDJIN." *Manchester Guardian* 10 Sep. 1958.
J. McK. "Far-from-nice Family." *Glasgow Evening Times* 16 Sep. 1958.

L. V. B. "O'Neill Exposure Is Poetic Experience." *Glasgow Herald* 16 Sep. 1958.

Mavor, Ronald. "Quality of Truth Bars Criticism." *The Scotsman* (Glasgow) 9 Sep. 1958.

Millar, Robin. "O'Neill's 'Long Day' Brings a Torrent of Grief." *Scottish Daily Express* 9 Sep. 1958.

"O'Neill's Bold Experiment in Stage Autobiography." *The Times* (London) 9 Sep. 1958: 5.

"O'Neill's 'Long Day' Is a Grim Portrayal of Sorrow." *Edinburgh Evening News* 9 Sep. 1958.

"A Theatrical Curiosity: Piercing Play by O'Neill." *The Scotsman* (Glasgow) 16 Sep. 1958: 11.

Wilson, Cecil. "Long Night's Peep at a Keyhole." *Scottish Daily Mail* 9 Sep. 1958: 7.

London 24 September

Barabar, John. "Now – The Year's Finest Drama." *Daily Express* (London) 25 September 1958.

Barker, Felix. "A Play for Everyone Who Thinks." *Evening News* 25 Sep. 1958.

Conway, Harold. "Gwen the Dope Addict – She's Magnificent!" *Daily Sketch* (London) 25 Sep. 1958.

Cookman, Anthony. "A Playwright's Personal Drama." *The Tatler* 8 Oct. 1958: 82.

Darlington, W. A. "O'Neill Play Tautened." *Daily Telegraph* 25 Sep. 1958.

Dent, Alan. "Almost High Tragedy." *News Chronicle* 25 Sep. 1958.

Hobson, Harold. "Excitement in the Theatre." *Sunday Observer* (London) 28 Sep. 1958.

R. B. M. "O'Neill Takes Us on His 'LDJIN.'" *Stage* (London) 2 Oct. 1958.

Shulman, Milton. "O'Neill's Genius Makes a Tragic Story Succeed." *Evening Standard* 26 Sep. 1958.

Shrapnel, Norman. "O'Neill's Stature: 'LDJ'." *Manchester Guardian* 26 Sep. 1958.

Tynan, Kenneth. "Massive Masterpeice." *The Observer* (London) 28 Sep. 1958.

Wilson, Cecil. "This Grim Game of Unhappy Families." *Daily Mail* 25 Sep. 1958.

Wraight, Robert. "Big Hangover." *The Star* 25 Sep. 1958.

1959
Oldenburg 11 February; Kassel 20 February
Hampel, Norbert. "'Eines langen Tages Reise in die Nacht'." *Nordwest-Zeitung* 12 Feb. 1959.
Westecker, Dieter. "Die Liebe in der Schuld." *Kasseler Post* 21 Feb. 1959.
Fehse, Willi. "O'Neill aus dem Nebel des Rausches." *Die Abendpost* (Frankfurt) 28 Feb. 1959.

Montreal 9 March
Caplan, Rupert. "Montreal's Link with O'Neill." *Montreal Star* 7 Mar. 1959: sec. 2, 1.
"O'Neill Play is Important Event." *The Gazette* 28 Feb. 1959: 24.
"Veteran Performer in 'LDJ'." *The Gazette* 21 Feb. 1959: 18.
Sabbath, Lawrence. "Stage Director O'Neill Expert." *The Gazette* 7 Mar. 1959.
Saucier, Pierre. "Caplan donne un version envoûtante de la tragédie célèbre d'Eugene O'Neill." *La Patrie du Dimanche* 15 Mar. 1959: 126.
Whitehead, Harold. "O'Neill Play a Great Work." *The Gazette* 10 Mar. 1959: 12.

Dublin 28 April
A. R. "Eugene O'Neill at the Abbey." *The Irish Times* 29 Apr. 1959.
J. J. F. "A Long Day with the Tyrone Family." *Evening Herald* 29 April 1959.
M. G. "'LDJ' Excellent Acting by Abbey Players." *Irish Independent* 29 Apr. 1959.
R. M. F. "Eugene O'Neill's Sombre Drama of Conflict." *Dublin Evening Mail* 29 Apr. 1959.
"'Long Day' a Fine Night at the Abbey." *The Irish Press* 29 Apr. 1959.
Letters to the Editor, 'LDJ' *Evening Press* (Dublin) 1 May 1959.

Paris 26 November
"Gaby Morlay: un drame de la drogue pour sa rentrée chez Hébertot." *L'Aurore* 27 Nov. 1959: 4.
Gautier, Jean-Jacques. "Long Voyage vers la nuit." *Le Figaro* 28–29 Nov. 1959: 18.

Joly, G. "Long Voyage vers la nuit." *L'Aurore* 30 Nov. 1959: 4.

Poirot-Deipech, Bertrand. "Long Voyage vers la Nuit." *Le Monde* 28 Nov. 1959: 13.

S. R. "Le Long Voyage vers la nuit." *Le Monde* 26 Nov. 1959: 12.

1960
Toronto 5 October 1960

Whitaker, Herbert "O'Neill's Work Dimmed, but Cast Puts It Over." *Globe and Mail* (Toronto) 6 Oct. 1960: 16.

1962
Embassy Pictures reviews

"A Serpent that Eats Its Tail." *Time* 80 (12 Oct. 1962): 102.

"LDJIN." *Variety* 31 May 1962: 3.

"One Day in One House." *Newsweek* 60 (15 Oct. 1962): 109.

Beckley, Paul V. "'LDJIN'." *New York Herald Tribune* 10 Oct. 1962: 20.

Bentley, Byron. "LDJ Into Film." *Theatre Arts* 46 (Oct. 1962): 16–18, 70–71.

Cameron, Kate. "O'Neill's Family Life Drama on Film." *Daily News* (New York).

Cook, Alton. "'LDJ' at Loew's Tower East." *New York World-Telegram and Sun* 10 Oct. 1962.

Crowther, Bosley. "Screen: 'LDJ' Opens." *New York Times* 10 Oct. 1962: 57
"Vintage O'Neill." *New York Times* 14 Oct. 1962: sec. 2, 1.

Gilbert, Justin. "O'Neill's 'Journey' – Classic Film." *New York Mirror* 10 Oct. 1962.

Gow, Gordon. "LDJIN." *Films and Filming* 10 (July 1964): 20.

Hatch, Robert. "Films." *The Nation* 195 (13 Oct. 1962): 227–28.

Kauffmann, Stanley. "Fate *Accompli*." *Show* (Nov. 1962): 33–34.

Knight, Arthur. "Total Recall." *Saturday Review* 45 (6 Oct. 1962): 30.

Murdock, Henry T. "'LDJ' Is Gripping." *Philadelphia Inquirer* 14 Mar. 1963.

Pelswick, Rose. "It's All O'Neill, All Eloquent, Exactly as It Ran on Stage." *New York Journal-American* 10 Oct. 1962: 28.

Sragow, Michael. "LDJIN." *American Film* 11 (Nov. 1985): 68.

Winsten, Archer. "'Journey' Arrives at Tower East." *New York Post* 10 Oct. 1962: 71.

Embassy Pictures – Other Pieces

Archer, Eugene. "Long Day of 'Night' in the Bronx." *New York Times* 22 Oct. 1961: sec. 2, 7.

"O'Neill Movie Set as Cannes Entry." *New York Times* 11 Apr. 1962: 48.

Bean, Robin. "The Insider: Sidney Lumet Talks to Robin Bean about His Work in Films." *Films and Filming* 11.9 (June 1965): 9–13.

Costello, Donald P. "Sidney Lumet's 'LDJIN.'" *Literature-Film Quarterly* 22.2 (Apr. 1994): 78–92.

Crosby, John. "Katherine [*sic*] Hepburn Thrilled with Making O'Neill Movie." *Boston Sunday Globe* 26 Nov. 1961.

Curtiss, Thomas Quinn. "US Shows Film of O'Neill's Play 'LDJ.'" *New York Herald Tribune*, Paris 22 May 1962.

"Eugene O'Neill Properties to Be Filmed." *Provincetown Advocate* 10 Aug. 1961: 9.

Finkelstein, Sidney. "O'Neill's 'LDJ.'" *Mainstream* 16.6 (1963): 47–51.

Luciano, Dale. "LDJIN: An Interview with Sidney Lumet." *Film Quarterly* 25.1 (Fall 1971): 20–33.

Lumet, Sidney. "On a Film 'Journey.'" *New York Times* 7 Oct. 1962: sec. 2, 7.

Morgenstern, Joseph. "Filming O'Neill's House of Anguish." *New York Herald Tribune* 22 Oct. 1961.

Myers, Harold. "Distribution Takes Too Much – Lumet." *Variety* 30 May 1962: 20.

Petrie, Graham. "The Films of Sidney Lumet: Adaptation as Art." *Film Quarterly* 21.2 (Winter 1967–68): 9–18.

Ross, Don. "A Moral Obligation to Leave O'Neill Alone." Oct. 1962, clippings file, NYPL.

Sipple, William L. "From Stage to Screen: *The Long Voyage Home* and *LDJIN*." *The Eugene O'Neill Newsletter* 7.1 (Spring 1983): 10–14.

Thompson, Howard. "George Justin: Local Movie Man on Our Town." *New York Times* 26 Nov. 1961: sec. 2, 7.

"Passing Picture Scene." *New York Times* 30 July 1961: sec. 2, 5.

Swedish World's Fair Production, Seattle and New York

Bolton, Whitney. "Our Actors Can Take Cue from Swedish." *Morning Telegraph* (New York) 21 May 1962.

Fleisher, Frederic. "Sweden's Royal Theater in Seattle." *Christian Science Monitor* 28 Apr. 1962.

Gelb, Arthur. "Theatre: O'Neill Tragedy." *New York Times* 16 May 1962: 35.

Hewes, Henry. "Food for Thought." *Saturday Review* 45 (2 June 1962): 24.

Hughes, Elinor. "Theater of Sweden Coming to America." *Boston Sunday Herald* 15 Apr. 1962.

J. T. "Theatre Uptown." *Village Voice* 24 May 1962: 13–14.

Link, Ruth. "The Royal Dramatic: Where O'Neill's Genius Found a Home." *American Swedish Monthly* (May 1962): 40–50.

Lundberg, Holger. "A Unique Theatrical Academy." *American Swedish Monthly* (May 1962): 31.

Maddocks, Melvin. "Swedes in New York." *Christian Science Monitor* 19 May 1962.

New York Theatre Critics' Reviews 23.13 (1962): 285–87:

    Chapman, John. "O'Neill Packs Punch in Swedish." *Daily News* 16 May 1962.

    Gelb, Arthur. "Theatre: O'Neill Tragedy." *New York Times* 16 May 1962.

    Kerr, Walter. "Royal Swedish Theater 'LDJ . . .'" *New York Herald Tribune* 16 May 1962.

    Nadel, Norman. "'Long Day's Journey' Played by Swedish Company at Cort." *New York World-Telegram and Sun* 16 May 1962.

    Watts, Richard, Jr. "'LDJ' in Swedish." *New York Post* 16 May 1962.

Sheaffer, Louis. "Swedish Specialty: O'Neill Journey." *New York Herald Tribune* 13 May 1962.

1965

Tokyo

Clurman, Harold. *Long Day's Journey* Notebook. Harold Clurman Collection. Billy Rose Theatre Collection. New York Public Library for the Performing Arts.

    "Notes from Afar: Part I." *The Nation* 201 (16 Aug. 1965): 84–86.

M. E. "Kumo's O'Neill Production Well Learned from Clurman." *The Japan Times* 8 Sep. 1965: 12.

Trumbull, Robert. "US Shows Japan How to Do O'Neill." *New York Times* 24 June 1965.

1971

New York 21 April

Burke, Tom. "Geraldine's Long Journey." *New York Times* 13 June 1971: sec. 2, 1, 7.

Clurman, Harold. "Theatre." *The Nation* 212 (10 May 1971): 605–06.

Fitzgerald, Geraldine. "Another Neurotic Electra: A New Look at Mary Tyrone." In *Eugene O'Neill: A World View.* Ed. Viriginia Floyd. New York: Ungar, 1979: 290–92.

Gent, George. "Ryan Sees Something of Himself in O'Neill's People." *New York Times* 5 Apr. 1971: 45.

"Geraldine Fitzgerald Talks of O'Neill and Morphine." *The Day* (New London) 5 Aug. 1978.

Hahn, Marshall. "Anytime is Ripe for an O'Neill." *New Haven Register* 21 Mar. 1971: sec. 2, 1, 7.

Kauffmann, Stanley. "LDJIN." *New Republic* 164 (12 June 1971): 26, 35–36.

Kalem, T. E. "Doom Music." *Time* 97 (3 May 1971): 62.

Kerr, Clark. "Do the Tyrones Live Here?." *New York Times* 2 May 1971: 3.

Kroll, Jack. "American Classic." *Newsweek* 77 (10 May 1971): 122.

New York Theatre Critics' Reviews 32.13 (1971): 266–70.

Davis, James. "Eugene O'Neill Revival Grand Night in Theater." *Daily News* 22 Apr. 1971.

Gottfried, Martin. "LDJIN." *Women's Wear Daily* 23 Apr. 1971.

Harris, Leonard. "LDJIN." WCBS TV 21 Apr. 1971.

Popkin, Henry. "O'Neill's 'Old Sorrow' Returns." *Wall Street Journal* 23 Apr. 1971.

Probst, Leonard. NBC TV "LDJIN." 21 Apr. 1971.

Schubeck, John. "LDJIN." WABC TV 21 Apr. 1971.

Watts, Richard. "An O'Neill Masterpeice." *New York Post* 22 Apr. 1971.

Oliver, Edith. "Off Broadway." *The New Yorker* 47 (1 May 1971): 94, 96.

Oppenheimer, George. "On Stage." *Newsday* 22 May 1971.

Scholem, Richard J. "LDJIN." WGSM Radio 23 Apr. 1971.

Sheaffer, Louis. "Morphine Took Its Toll on O'Neill's Mother." *The Day* (New London) 17 Aug. 1978.

Washburn, Martin. "Out of the Depths Back onto Olympus." *Village Voice* 29 Apr. 1971: 63.

London 21 December; ITC/ABC TV 1973

Barber, John. "O'Neill's Masterpiece from Tears and Blood." *Daily Telegraph* 23 Dec. 1971: 5.

Barnes, Clive. "The Theater: 'LDJ.'" *New York Times* 7 Sep. 1972: 53.

Bok. "LDJIN." *Variety* 14 Mar. 1973: 46.

Brustein, Robert. "Britain Discovers America – And Finds?." *New York Times* 10 Dec. 1972: D3, 15.

   "LDJIN." *The Observer* (London) 10 Dec. 1972: 36.

   "Countersigns." *Harper's Magazine* 246 (May 1973): 47.

Dawson, Helen. "O'Neill's Show Shop." *The Observer* (London) 2 Jan. 1972: 24.

   "Drama Mailbag." *New York Times* 31 Dec. 1972: D5, 12.

Hewes, Henry. "The London Scene." *Saturday Review* 55 (8 April 1972): 8.

Hobson, Harold. "Olivier's Triumph." *Sunday Times* (London) 2 Jan. 1972, Arts: 14.

   "Olivier's Triumphant London Stage Return." *Christian Science Monitor* 3 Jan. 1973: 6.

Kalem, T. E. "LDJIN." *Time* 100 (18 Sep. 1972): 76–77.

Kingston, Jeremy. "Theatre." *Punch* 262 (5 Jan. 1972): 27–28.

Krebs, Albin. "A. B. C., in a Shift, Plans Series of Serious Dramatic Specials." *New York Times* 28 June 1972: 91.

Leonard, Hugh. "LDJIN." *Plays and Players* 19.5 (Feb. 1972): 46–50, 67.

Marriott, R. B. "National Company Are Masterly in O'Neill Masterpiece." *The Stage & Television Today* 30 Dec. 1971: 13.

Pit. "LDJIN." *Variety* 29 Dec. 1971: 37.

Wardle, Irving. "Olivier Fascinating in London 'LDJ.'" *New York Times* 23 Dec. 1971: 16.

1973

Melbourne

Hutton, Geoffrey. "A Great Writer's Last Testament." *The Age* (Melbourne) 15 Nov. 1973.

"Long Night's Journey." *Listener* (Melbourne) 24–30 Nov. 1973.

Mayhead, Gerald. "One of the Year's Best." *The Herald* (Melbourne) 15 Nov. 1973: 31.

Palmer, Howard. "A Horrifying Family Brew." *The Sun* (Melbourne) 15 Nov. 1973.

1975

Washington D. C.; Brooklyn

Barnes, Clive. "'LDJ' Into Greatness." *New York Times* 29 Jan. 1976: 26.

Feingold, Michael. "Robards Returns to O'Neill's 'Journey.'" *New York Times* 25 Jan. 1976: sec. 2, 5.

Gardner, R. H. "This 'LDJIN' Turns Out to Be a Bad Trip." *Baltimore Sun* 26 Dec. 1975.

Gussow, Mel. "Robards and a Long Career's Journey." *New York Times* 22 Dec. 1975: 44.

Kroll, Jack. "The Haunted Tyrones." *Newsweek* 87 (9 Feb. 1976): 52–53.

New York Theatre Critics' Reviews 37.5 (1976): 343–47:

Gottfried, Martin. "An Endless 'Night' in Brooklyn." *New York Post* 29 Jan. 1976.

Kissel, Howard. "LDJIN." *Women's Wear Daily* 29 Jan. 1976.

Probst, Leonard. "LDJIN." NBC Radio 29 Jan. 1976.

Sterritt, David. "Jason Robards: Back to O'Neill." *Christian Science Monitor* 5 Feb. 1976.

Watt, Douglas, "A Divided Homefront." *Daily News* 29 Jan. 1976.

Oliver, Edith. "Off Broadway." *The New Yorker* 51 (9 Feb. 1976): 78, 80–81.

Tucker, Carll. "O'Neill Explores the Wilderness of Despair." *Village Voice* 9 Feb. 1976: 99.

White, Jean M. "Robards–O'Neill: A Long Journey." *Washington Post* 19 Dec. 1975.

1977

Los Angeles

Murray, William. "A Long Night's Journey to the Bar." *New West* 14 Mar. 1977: 19–20.

Pennington, Ron. "LDJIN." *Hollywood Reporter* 22 Feb. 1977: 3, 16.

1980

Stratford, Ontario

Czarnecki, Mark. "LDJIN." *Maclean's Magazine* 93 (20 Oct. 1980): 69.

Point Judith *New York*

Coe, Robert. "Everybody's Autobiography." *Soho Weekly News* 27 Dec. 1979: 47.

Dace, Tish. "Pointing Out Private Lives." *Other Stages* (10 Jan. 1980): 6.

Gussow, Mel. "Stage: Spalding Gray's 'Point Judith.'" *New York Times* 30 Dec. 1980: C4.

Hart, Steven. "'Point Judith': A Dark Awakening." *Villager* 3 Jan. 1980: 11.

Leverett, James. "Point Counterpoint." *Soho Weekly News* 10 Jan. 1980: 46.

Munk, Erika. "Cross Left." *Village Voice* 21 Jan. 1980: 83.

"Time Out of Mind." *Village Voice* 14 Jan. 1980: 81–82.

Stasio, Marilyn. "On Way to Rhode Island 'Judith' Misses Point." *New York Post* 3 Jan. 1980: 31.

Sterritt, David. "The Free-Wheeling Spalding Gray Style: Monologue and Spectacular." *Christian Science Monitor* 30 Dec. 1980: 18.

"Pioneering a New Kind of Language." *Christian Science Monitor* 14 Dec. 1981: 14.

"Probing, Inventive Theater – Way Off Broadway." *Christian Science Monitor* 30 Jan. 1980: 19.

1981
New York

Blau, Eleanor. "Papp Provides a Stage for 'LDJ.'" *New York Times* 11 Mar. 1981: C19.

Fagin, Steve. "First All-Black Cast Finds Mood for 'LDJ' in Trip Here." *The Day* (New London), clippings file, SHEAFFER.

Gussow, Mel. "Theater: Black Cast Stages O'Neill." *New York Times* 3 Mar. 1981: C10.

Kroll, Jack. "LDJIN." *Newsweek* 97 (20 Apr. 1981): 104.

Lawson, Carol. "McCowen Returning in May with 'St. Mark's Gospel.'" *New York Times* 27 Mar. 1981: C2.

New York Theatre Critics' Reviews 42.8 (1981): 270–73:

Barnes, Clive. "'Long Day's' Worth the Journey." *New York Post* 4 Mar. 1981.

Sharp, Christopher. "LDJIN." *Women's Wear Daily* 3 Mar. 1981.

Sterritt, David. "Splendid Black Version of O'Neill Drama." *Christian Science Monitor* 23 Apr. 1981.

Watt, Douglas. "'Journey' with Black Cast Retains Strength." *Daily News* 3 Mar. 1981.

Oliver, Edith. "At Home Again with the Tyrones." *The New Yorker* 57 (16 Mar. 1981): 62, 65.

Simon, John. "LDJIN." *New York* 14 (20 Apr. 1981): 56.

1983
Lisbon 3 June
"Longa viagem para a noite." *Diário de Lisbôa* 17 June 1983: 111.

"Longa viagem para a noite." *Diário de Notícias* 18 June 1983: 15.

Melo, Guilherme de. "Teatro – ou Cinema?." *Diário de Notícias* 22 June 1983: 6.

"O'Neill no Teatro Nacional." *Diário de Notícias* 7 June 1983: 37.

"Viagem ao fim da noite." *Diário de Lisbôa* 20 June 1983: 19.

1984
London
London Theatre Record Mar. 26–Apr. 8 1984: 259–60:
   Chaillet, Ned. *Wall Street Journal* 19 Apr. 1984.
   de Jongh, Nicholas. *The Guardian* 7 Apr. 1984.
   Denselow, Anthony. BBC Radio London 8 Apr. 1984.
   Fox, Sheila. *City Limits* 13 Apr. 1984.
   Hoyle, Martin. *Financial Times* 9 Apr. 1984.
   Moore, Oscar. *Time Out* 12 Apr. 1984.
   Ratcliffe, Michael. *The Observer* 8 Apr. 1984.
   Shorter, Eric. *Daily Telegraph* 9 Apr. 1984.
   Shulman, Milton. *London Standard* 6 Apr. 1984.
London Theatre Record Apr. 9–22 1984: 323:
   de Jongh, Nicholas. "LDJIN." *The Guardian* 14 Apr. 1984.
Hoyle, Martin. "LDJIN." *Plays and Players* 369 (June 1984): 32–33.

1985
Manchester
London Theatre Record Mar. 13–26 1985: 272–73:
   Asquith, Ros. *The Observer* 24 Mar. 1985.
   Flint, Stella. *Daily Telegraph* 16 Mar. 1985.
   Thornber, Robin. *The Guardian* 15 Mar. 1985.
   Young, B. A. *Financial Times* 19 Mar. 1985.
McManus, Irene. "LDJIN." *Plays and Players* May 1985: 31.

1986

New York 21 April; London 4 August

Billington, Michael. "Why See A Short Day's Journey? The Answer Is a Lemmon." *Manchester Guardian Weekly* 27 Apr. 1986: 21.

Bloom, Steven F. "*LDJIN.*" *The Eugene O'Neill Newsletter* 10.2 (Summer–Fall 1986): 33–39.

"Conned Again." *Jerusalem Post Magazine* 31 Oct. 1986: B:1.

Cropper, Martin. "A Fretful Ghost of O'Neill." *The Times* (London) 6 Aug. 1986: 15.

Freedman, Samuel G. "Lemmon Relives the Past in O'Neill's 'Journey.'" *New York Times* 27 Apr. 1986: sec. 2, 1.

Garvey, Sheila Hickey. "Rethinking O'Neill." *Eugene O'Neill Newsletter* 10 (Winter 1986): 13–20.

Gill, Brendan. "LDJIN." *The New Yorker* 135 (12 May 1986): 93–94.

Hornby, Richard. "Role Playing, Self Reference, and Openness." *Hudson Review* 39 (Autumn 1986): 472–74.

Hummler, Richard. "Stars to Brighten B'Way Season." *Variety* 30 Oct. 1985: 1, 108.

"'Journey' Notice Up; Fourth Straight Flop for O'Neill." *Variety* 18 June 1986: 93–94.

Lee, Brian. "Accelerating the Decline." *Times Literary Supplement* 15 Aug. 1986: 891.

Leech, Michael. "Miller's Journey." *Plays and Players* 1 Sep. 1986: 11–13.

"Lemmon Sees British As Receptive Public for 'Journey' Revamp." *Variety* 30 July 1986: 79.

London Theatre Record 30 July–12 Aug. 1986: 824–30:

Billington, Michael. *The Guardian* 5 Aug. 1986.

Couling, Della. *Tablet* 16 Aug. 1986.

Coveney, Michael. *Financial Times* 5 Aug. 1986.

Edwardes, Jane. *Time Out* 13 Aug. 1986.

Edwards, Christopher. *Spectator* 16 Aug. 1986.

Freedman, Peter. *Sunday Today* 10 Aug. 1986.

Hiley, Jim. *Listener* 14 Aug. 1986.

Hirschhorn, Clive. *Sunday Express* 10 Aug. 1986.

Hurren, Kenneth. *Mail on Sunday* 10 Aug. 1986.

Jameson, Sue. *London Broadcasting* 5 Aug. 1986.

King, Francis. *Sunday Telegraph* 10 Aug. 1986.

Morrison, Blake. *The Observer* 10 Aug. 1986.

Nathan, David. *Daily Mirror* 6 Aug. 1986.

Jewish Chronicle 8 Aug. 1986.

Pascal, Julia. *City Limits* 14 Aug. 1986.

Shannon, David. *Today* 5 Aug. 1986.

Shorter, Eric. *Daily Telegraph* 6 Aug. 1986.

Shulman, Milton. *London Standard* 5 Aug. 1986.

Tinker, Jack. *Daily Mail* 5 Aug. 1986.

"LDJIN." *Variety* 2 Apr. 1986: 88.

McCarren, Paul J. "LDJIN." *America* 155 (2 Aug. 1986): 52–53.

Melly, George. "It's Miller Time." *Vanity Fair* (May 1986): 106, 108, 128–29.

Miller, Jonathan. "Jonathan Miller Defends His 'Journey.'" *New York Times* 15 June 1986.

New York Theatre Critics' Reviews 47.6 (1986): 302–08:

Barnes, Clive. "'Day's Journey' to Glory: B'way at Its Greatest." *New York Post* 29 Apr. 1986.

Beaufort, John. "O'Neill – With Accent on Pace, Humor." *Christian Science Monitor* 1 May 1986.

Cohen, Ron. "LDJIN." *Women's Wear Daily* 29 Apr. 1986.

Henry, William A., III. "Not Revival, But Rediscovery." *Time* 127 (12 May 1986): 97.

Kroll, Jack. "Jack's Journey." *Newsweek* 5 May 1986.

Rich, Frank. "Stage: A New 'LDJ.'" *New York Times* 29 Apr. 1986.

Siefel, Joel. WABC-TV "LDJIN." 28 Apr. 1986.

Watt, Douglas. "Here Comes the Son." *Daily News* 29 Apr. 1986.

Wilson, Edwin. "LDJIN." *Wall Street Journal* 30 Apr. 1986.

Winer, Linda. "Condensed 'Journey' Retains Its Power." *USA Today* 29 Apr. 1986.

"Rave Notices, Good Biz for 'Journey' in Tel Aviv." *Variety* 5 Nov. 1986: 95.

Richards, David. "The 'Journey,' Shortchanged." *Washington Post* 28 Mar. 1986: D1, 8.

Rieff, David. "A Shorter 'Day's Journey.'" *Vanity Fair* May 1986: 108–09.

Sauvage, Leo. "LDJIN." *The New Leader* 69 (5 May 1986): 21–22.

"Sets Duke U. Tryout." *Variety* 9 Oct. 1985: 127, 130.

Simon, John. "Speeded-Up O'Neill, Tarted-Up Fellini." *New York* 12 May 1986: 138.

Sweeney, Louise. "Director Miller Demands Fresh Approach to Classics." *Christian Science Monitor* 1 May 1986: 33, 36–37.

Valdes, Lesley. "Long Day's Journey Onto Broadway." *Wall Street Journal* 11 Apr. 1986: 25.

1987
Showtime/American Playhouse

Bianculi, David. "Well Worth the Trip." *New York Post* 4 May 1988: 73.

Christon, Lawrence. "'LDJIN' Journeys to TV." *Los Angeles Times* 11 Dec. 1986: sec. 6, 5.

Feldberg, Robert. "A Tedious 'Journey' on Screen." *Record* (Bergen, NJ) 12 Apr. 1987: E1.

"High-Minded TV Drama Excites Lemmon." *Denver Post* 14 Apr. 1987: D2.

Jarvis, Jeff. "LDJIN." *People Weekly* 27 (13 Apr. 1987): 11.

Kuchwara, Michael. "A 'LDJ' That Plays Better on Television." Associated Press file 4 May 1988.

Leonard, John. "LDJIN." *New York* 21 (9 May 1988): 75.

"LDJ with Jack Lemmon to Be Taped in Metro." *Toronto Star* 16 Oct. 1986: C1.

O'Connor, John J. "Lemmon in O'Neill Drama." *New York Times* 13 Apr. 1987: C18.

1988
New Haven; New York

"Dewhurst, Robards and O'Neill." *New York Times* 31 July 1987: C2.

Hill, Holly. "O'Neill's Journey Doesn't Make It." *The Advocate* (Stamford, CT) 15 June 1988: C10, 14.

Hodgson, Moira. "LDJIN." *The Nation* 247 (27 Aug. 1988): 178.

Hummler, Richard. "Public Says No, No O'Neill Again; Fifth Straight B. O. Flop on B'way." *Variety* 27 July 1988: 63, 66.

New York Theatre Critics' Reviews 49.10 (13 June 1988): 223–34:

Barnes, Clive. "Through the Past, Darkly." *New York Post* 15 June 1988.

Beaufort, John. "Robards's Long Journey With O'Neill." *Christian Science Monitor* 16 June 1988.

Henry, William A., III. "The Theater." *Time* 27 June 1988.

Kissel, Howard. "A Worthwhile 'Journey.'" *Daily News* 15 June 1988.

Stearns, David Patrick. "O'Neill Centennial Hits a Winning Double Play." *USA Today* 24 June 1988.

Watt, Doug. "'Journey' of a Lifetime." 24 June 1988.

Wilson, Edwin. "O'Neill's Redeeming Values." *Wall Street Journal* 8 July 1988.

Winer, Linda. "A 'LDJ' Revisited." *New York Newsday* 15 June 1988.

Rich, Frank. "The Stars Align for 'LDJ.'" *New York Times* 15 June 1988: C21.

Robertson, Nan. "Broadway." *New York Times* 31 July 1987: C2.

"Rotating Repertory Returning to B'way With Two By O'Neill." *Variety* 16 Mar. 1988: 99.

Nightingale, Benedict. "Why O'Neill's Ghosts Haunt Us Still." *New York Times* 12 June 1988: sec. 2, 1, 14.

Oliver, Edith. "LDJIN." *The New Yorker* 64 (4 July 1988): 59–60.

Seibert, Gary. "LDJIN." *America* 159 (23 July 1988): 64.

Simon, John. "LDJIN." *New York* 21 (11 July 1988): 48.

Stockholm

Marker, Lise-Lone and Frederick J. Marker. "Bergman and the Actors: An Interview." *Theater* 21 (Winter/Spring 1990): 74–80.

Palatsky, Gene. "Repertory Companies – Old and New." *Newark Sunday News* 4 Aug. 1963: sec. 6, 1.

Törnqvist, Egil. "Ingmar Bergman and *LDJIN*." In *Eugene O'Neill in China: An International Celebration*. Westport, CT: Greenwood, 1992: 241–48.

  "Ingmar Bergman Directs 'LDJIN.'" *New Theatre Quarterly* 5 (Nov. 1989): 374–83.

Moscow

"American Plays on Soviet Stage." TASS 1 Feb. 1988.

Barringer, Felicity. "But Will It Play in Podolia? Nowadays, Yes." *New York Times* 13 Mar. 1988: sec. 2, 5.

1991
Bristol/London

Campbell, James. "LDJIN." *Times Literary Supplement* 31 May 1991: 18.

Coveney, Michael. "Guilt-Edged Agony Slumbers." *The Observer* 24 Feb. 1991: 61.

Gussow, Mel. "A Recognizable O'Neill and a Strange Chekhov." *New York Times* 17 June 1991: C11.

Nightingale, Benedict. "Bleak House of Tyrone Power." *The Times* (London) 12 Feb. 1991: Features: 15.

"LDJ in Bristol Old Vic." *The Times* (London) 21 Feb. 1991: 22.

Peter, John. "Look Back In Anguish." *Sunday Times* (London) 24 Feb. 1991: sec. 5, 8.

Pit. "LDJIN." *Variety* 3 June 1991: 60–61.

Theatre Record 21 May–3 June 1991: 632–34:

   Bayley, Clare. *What's On* 29 May 1991.

   Dodd, Ian. *Tribune* 7 June 1991.

   Grant, Steve. *Time Out* 29 May 1991.

   Hirschhorn, Clive. *Sunday Express* 15 May 1991.

   Kingsley, Louise. *The Independent* 28 May 1991.

   Kingston, Jeremy. *The Times* 23 May 1991.

   Koenig, Rhoda. *Punch* 19 May 1991.

   Morley, Sheridan. *Herald Tribune* 29 May 1991.

   Nathan, David. *Jewish Chronicle* 24 May 1991.

   Peter, John. *Sunday Times* 2 June 1991.

   Shulman, Milton. *Evening Standard* 22 May 1991.

   Tinker, Jack. *Daily Mail* 22 May 1991.

   Wolf, Matt. *City Limits* 30 May 1991.

Brooklyn

Brustein, Robert. "LDJIN." *New Republic* 205 (29 July 1991): 30–31.

Marker, Lise-Lone and Frederick J. Marker. "Three Plays, One Vision – Bergman's." *New York Times* 9 June 1991: sec. 6, 5, 36.

Oliver, Roger W. "Bergman's Trilogy: Tradition and Innovation." *Performing Arts Journal* 14 (Jan. 1992): 74–86.

Paulsson, Kristin. "'LDJ' Repeats the Rave Reviews." *Nordst Jernan-Svea* 20 June 1991.

Sheaffer, Louis. "Bibi Andersson's Performance Convincing in 'LDJIN.'" *Brooklyn Heights Press* 20 June 1991: 3.

Wetzeon, Ross. "Long Day's Journey Home." *New York Newsday* 19 June 1991: 15–16.

1994

Stratford, Ontario

Bemrose, John. "A Great Actor Comes Home." *Maclean's Magazine* 107 (27 June 1994): 50–51.

"The Masks of a Great Pretender." *Maclean's Magazine* 108 (19 June 1995): 58.

Chapman, Geoff. "Martha Henry Returns Gloriously Triumphant." *Toronto Star* 1 June 1994: D2.

Garebian, Keith. "Revisionism (Part II): The 1995 Stratford Festival." *Journal of Canadian Studies* 31.2 (Summer 1996): 166–73.

Johnson, Reed. "The Search for Self Obsesses Canada's Stratford Festival." *American Theatre* 11.8 (Oct. 1994): 96–100.

Richards, David. "Casting a Fearless Eye on a Sacred Text." *New York Times* 9 June 1994: C15–16.

Simon, John. "LDJIN." *New York* 27 (5 Sep. 1994): 52.

"Of Dogs, their Masters, and Others." *New York* 27 (5 Sep. 1994): 51–52.

Wagner, Vit. "Brilliant Cast Makes Long Day a Delight to Remember." *Toronto Star* 25 June 1995: C2.

"Shadows of Their Former Play." *Toronto Star* 6 Aug. 1995: B4.

1996

Cineplex-Odeon Film

Bemrose, John. "Long Day's Film Journey: A Revered Stage Production Gets Adapted to the Big Screen." *Maclean's Magazine* 109 (15 Jan. 1996): 60.

Johnson, Brian D. "LDJIN." *Maclean's Magazine* 109 (16 Sep. 1996): 64.

Leonard, John. "That Giant Buzzing Sound." *New York* 32 (20 Sep. 1999): 70–72.

Thompson, Howard. "O'Neill's Family Affair." *New York Times* 22 Sep. 1996: sec. 12, 36.

1999

Hartford

Ascheim, Skip. "Subtle Staging Enhances O'Neill Classic." *Sunday Boston Globe* 10 Mar. 1999: F7.

Highet, Alistair. "Long But Wonderful Journey." *Hartford Advocate* 11 Mar. 1999: 21.

Johnson, Malcolm. "Moving Voyage Into Lost Dreams." *Hartford Courant* 5
    Mar. 1999: F1, 8.
Klein, Alvin. "Of Shards of History, Love, Hate and Family." *New York Times*
    28 Mar. 1999: sec. 14 (Connecticut Edition), 4.
Marks, Peter. "A Girlish Domestic Terrorist." *New York Times* 30 Mar. 1999:
    E9.

2000
Tokyo
Rudd, Jerry. "'LDJ' a Harrowing Trip." *The Daily Yomiuri* 18 May 2000: 13.
    "Theatrical Baton to be Passed from Watanabe to Kuriyama at NNTT."
    Mainichi Daily News 8 May 2000: 6.

INDEX